THE CONDENSED WORLD
OF THE READER'S DIGEST

Samuel A. Schreiner, Jr. is also the author of

**THINE IS THE GLORY
PLEASANT PLACES**

THE CONDENSED WORLD
of the
Reader's Digest

Samuel A. Schreiner, Jr.

STEIN and DAY/*PUBLISHERS*/NEW YORK

First published in 1977
Copyright © 1977 by Schreiner Associates, Inc.
All rights reserved
Designed by Giorgetta Bell McRee
Printed in the United States of America
Stein and Day/*Publishers*/Scarborough House
Briarcliff Manor, N.Y. 10510

Library of Congress Cataloging in Publication Data

Schreiner, Samuel Agnew.
The condensed world of the Reader's digest.
Includes Index.

1. The Reader's digest. I. Title.
PN4900.R3S5   051   76-44425

ISBN 0-8128-2162-9

CONTENTS

To those unsung and unpaid heroines of American corporate life—my own Dorrie and all the wives who defuse their husbands' frustrations, cook for their office friends, chauffeur their children, clean their homes, balance their check books, wash their clothes—and lie awake in the night wondering if it's all worth while.

THE CONDENSED WORLD
OF THE READER'S DIGEST

I

A Priest for the Digest

Some five years after I had gone to work as an editor for the Reader's Digest, I committed what was an indiscretion, if not a sin. I asked for a raise. (It would be much later, when I was researching this book, in fact, that I would learn that almost nobody ever asks for a raise at Reader's Digest.) There followed a series of events that even now seem incredible.

I was first asked to take a test doing the very job for which I was being paid some $15,000 a year, including bonuses—editing an article. The condition of the test was that Kenneth W. Payne, then executive editor of the magazine and second only to DeWitt Wallace, the founder and owner, in legendary editorial prowess (for which Payne was paid in six figures), would edit the same article. Our work would be compared to see whether I was worth a raise.

Obviously, the odds were long against me, and some days after the test was concluded when I was summoned into the presence of Mr. Wallace himself, I was literally trembling with anxiety. Then in his sixties, Wallace was tall, thin, sharp-eyed, white-haired and somewhat imposingly stiff—a posture I've come since to think had more to do with a World War I wound than any personal attitude about the world. Though soft of voice and somewhat hesitant of speech, Wallace radiated the power of a man who had invented and operated since the time of my birth a business singularly unmarked by catastrophe from without or disagreement from within. In short, I knew by then that whatever Wallace said went.

While he didn't actually tell me that I had flunked the test, Wally, as we all were encouraged to call him, made it clear that I had a long way to go and that there were lots of other magazines out there—I think he specifically mentioned *Harper's*—where I might find myself happier exercising such meager talents as I had. There ensued a very worrisome week until my paycheck arrived, proving not only that I was still employed but that, after suffering the stick, I had been deemed worthy of munching on the carrot of a very small raise.

That should have been that, but it wasn't. I was transferred out of the department where I was working, evidently because I had embarrassed my straw boss by going over his head and seeking a raise, and was simultaneously moved into an office half the size I was then occupying, making it obvious to anyone who cared that something had gone awry in my Digest career. One such, an older man with long Digest experience, felt moved to have a heart-to-heart talk with me. I'll never forget his final words of advice, "If you want to get anywhere around here, you have to become a priest for the Digest." Amen.

I never did become a priest, but I guess that I did get as far as altar boy. I conclude this from the fact that although I never again asked for a raise, I found myself on a slowly rising escalator of salary and other benefits that reached a point so high that it was almost frightening to jump off. By the time I left to take up the challenge of writing my first novel, my sin had evidently been forgotten, and the magazine was treating me very well indeed. I hope that I was serving it well in return.

Aside from giving a glimpse of life at the Digest, this bit of personal experience belongs here at the beginning of the book as a way of showing where this writer stands in relation to his subject. I left the Digest with such feelings of mutual goodwill that

I have since written a number of articles for the magazine and served it in other ways. I still have many friends and professional colleagues on the staff and hope that I always shall. On the other hand, having never been fully ordained, I do feel free at this distance in time and space to view the organization with some degree of objectivity.

Like the church itself, the Reader's Digest is a very human institution, but again like the church, it doesn't like to admit it. Over the years, DeWitt Wallace has maintained a reticence, not to say secrecy, peculiar to a man whose business is spreading the word to more people around the world than have been reached by any other means of communication except the Bible. As a result, only two books have yet been written about what has to be the publishing phenomenon of this century. The first, a volume the size of its title, *Little Wonder, or The Reader's Digest and How It Grew,* suffered from being such an outside job that the author made many errors of fact and assumption in an obvious effort to make the magazine look bad; the second, *Of Lasting Interest,* suffered from being such an inside job— indeed, the Digest's "authorized" book—that it is as dull as its title. Still, I sympathize with both writers. Doing a book about the Reader's Digest isn't easy, and I would not have attempted this task had I not stood by the altar.

The fact that I was an insider does, however, raise some questions about the ethics of this enterprise. The first, of course, is whether I have a right to make public what I can about an organization which I served willingly, knowing its preference for secrecy. It isn't an easy question to answer. Before I undertook this project, the publisher made clear to me his intention of having a book about the Reader's Digest written by *somebody.* I agreed with him. While, in fact, the Reader's Digest is a private company, there is no company more actively seeking public approval. The magazine reaches into every fourth American home; a hundred million people around the world read it. My own feeling is that they have a right to know as much as possible about how the words they are asked to accept, and pay for, are brought into being. Beyond that, the Digest has made itself into such a wonder of the world, like the Pyramids or the Great Wall of China, that it cannot forever escape paying the price of curiosity that such wonders provoke. As to my own authorship, I accepted the job on the grounds that being now a writer, I had a right if not a duty to tackle a subject for which I was peculiarly equipped.

Not everyone has agreed with me. Imbued with the Wallace sense of secrecy, a number of old Digesters have either evaded me or bluntly refused to talk. One man declined on the basis of his "confidential relationship" with Wallace. When I wired saying that I was coming to see him anyway, he responded with an invitation but added that he would "not talk about Reader's Digest"; he didn't. The man who told me I ought to be a priest for the Digest warned me off with a letter saying, "I hate to sound like 'an old lady in tennis sneakers' but it seems to me that if you produce as you suggest a gossipy type of job about R.D. like Brendan Gill did on the New Yorker you are bound to infuriate a lot of people." I have purposely not interviewed Wallace to relieve him of embarrassment either way over the things said about him. Nevertheless, Wallace himself and the present management of the Digest have cooperated with the release of official documents and much more, besides. So have hundreds of other Digesters, active or retired, who evidently feel as I do that the world ought to know more about this amazing institution. Without such cooperation, the job would have been much harder, if not impossible.

The second question in the matter of ethics is: Having been an insider, what is my bias? Aware of this, I decided that it would be futile, if not dishonest, to try to write a heavy and so-called objective report on the Reader's Digest. This, therefore, is a very personal look at a very complex institution. The opinions and a lot of the reporting are my own; the effort is to, in a phrase now hopefully going out of style, "tell it like it is"— or was.

If I have to own up to a general point of view, it would be that of a member of the Fourth Estate. Although it has no Hippocratic oath or licensing procedures, a profession of journalism, of seeking to uncover the truth within the limits of human perception and reporting it in many forms, does exist. I've been a part of it all my working life and known hundreds of its practitioners. They're no better than anybody else, maybe worse, but most of them in my experience do share a sense of calling to their profession that can often transcend loyalty to whatever particular publication they serve. While they do not take vows of poverty, most editorial workers find themselves on the economic level of ministers, teachers, civil servants, social workers and others whose callings do not demonstrably make money; hence, there is a tendency among them to at least sympathize with the dispossessed of the earth. As a newspaper reporter, editor, free-lance writer, novelist, I consider myself to be a dues-paying member of this profession. For me, then, the Reader's Digest was a way station on a long road, the end of which is not yet in sight.

Someday, perhaps, a scholar or historian will write the definitive story of the Reader's Digest. Meanwhile, I'll be content with cracking open a door that in my opinion has been too long closed. If, as a result, the thousands of people, who come every year to the Digest's headquarters to gaze about in wonder like pilgrims at a shrine, can see beyond the paintings and the flowers and the gently purring computers into the human hearts at work there, I'll have done my job better than I have any right to hope.

II

Giant With a Soul

The Reader's Digest is without peer. It stands astride the world of publishing like Gulliver in Lilliput, and the sensation of riding the back of a gentle giant eventually gets to most people who work there. I experienced it early on when I was telling a seasoned Digest editor about a friend who sold an article to the *Saturday Evening Post,* then still America's leading weekly magazine. "Well, I guess it's all right," said the editor, puffing away at his pipe, "if he's happy with publishing secretly."

Arrogant perhaps, but true. With a circulation of nearly 30 million copies monthly in 170 countries and 13 languages, the Digest's worldwide readership is conservatively estimated at 100 million people. No publication in all history has ever spread the word to so many people in so many places. Even the great stand in awe of it, as I discovered one day when I went to visit the late John Steinbeck.

As a Nobel Prize winner, Steinbeck was then America's leading man of letters. I wanted to persuade him to write a Digest travelogue on the U.S. Virgin Islands where I knew he had spent many vacations. Although I was empowered to offer him a heftier fee than usual—I think it was $5,000—I was afraid that the great writer would share the contempt for the Reader's

Digest that seemed so prevalent in literary circles. So I knocked rather timidly at the door of Steinbeck's New York town house.

A big, bearded, bear of a man with a rumbling voice to match, Steinbeck received me as warmly as he would an old friend. After introducing me to his poodle, Charlie, whom he was soon to make famous in a book, he said, "You know, I'd really like to do this, and I'll tell you why. A while back I was in a little French village. When I introduced myself to one of the local citizens as John Steinbeck, he said, 'Say, you must be the fellow who wrote about ospreys in the Reader's Digest!' "

Although Steinbeck's travels with Charlie kept him too busy to write the piece, I went away from that interview with a new appreciation of the power of the little magazine I served. I've since had equally revealing experiences. Once, for example, I was talking to a Thai psychiatrist at his office in the little town of Chieng Mai, almost exactly halfway around the world from the Digest's offices in Pleasantville, New York. When he found out that I worked for the Reader's Digest, he jumped up excitedly and took me to a book shelf where he proudly displayed a complete file of the magazine, dating back to 1928. Another time, sailing in the Caribbean, I fetched up on tiny Levango Key. Before long, the black fisherman, who with his wife constituted the islet's entire population, was showing me his collection of Digests from which, he said, he had educated himself over a period of thirty years.

Indeed, far more impressive than the large circulation figures, with which the Digest baits its hooks for advertisers, are the testimonials to the magazine's effect on individuals to whom few things are more crucially important than life itself. The number of times the Digest has been credited specifically with the saving of a life are beyond count. One article alone, "How to Recognize—and Survive—a Heart Attack," in the magazine's November 1973 issue evoked two dozen such testimonials. A sampling: ". . . due to the article which he had read, my husband recognized the symptoms and got to the hospital in time. Had he been a few minutes later it would have been too late"; "I believe I am alive today because of the article . . . the shortness of breath, nausea and heavy sweating fit my case perfectly. I realized I may be having a heart attack"; "Last week a woman came to the emergency room because she . . . felt she may be having a heart attack. . . . If she had not read the article she would not have known of the warning signs."

Repeated Digest articles updating the techniques of first aid and emergency treatment have had similarly dramatic results over the years, as a story in the *Holyoke* (Massachusetts) *Daily* in the summer of 1968 attests. The paper reported that a playground director, Roberta Kelly, saved the life of a two-and-a-half-year-old girl who had sunk to the bottom of a wading pool, by using mouth-to-mouth resuscitation, a technique she had learned from reading a Digest article.

Next to staying alive, feeling fit while you're doing it may be the average person's most vital concern. Readers by the hundreds and thousands have thanked the Digest for tips on diet, exercise, physical and mental checkups and the like. One unusual case was that of a Missouri man who over a period of three years had lost fifty pounds when a decreasing sense of taste and smell had made it hard for him to eat. Doctors he consulted told him the trouble was "in my head." Then, in June 1971, he read a Digest article, "Accounting for Taste," which described the new discoveries of Dr. Robert Henken of the National Institute of Health in the area of taste. The man contacted Dr. Henken, was admitted to the NIH Clinic as a research patient and within three weeks had gained ten pounds and gone back to work.

There are times, however, when Digest advice on health has gone awry. One letter in the Digest files from a Plainfield, New Jersey reader reported: "A South American friend was visiting during the holidays. During a conversation about dieting he said dog biscuits have helped him control his weight. A discussion followed on the human consumption of dog biscuits. In support of his argument, our friend whipped out a clipping from Reader's Digest ('How to Lose Weight and Stay Thin,' September 1966) saying, 'A few animal crackers between meals will curb the appetite.' "

People presumably already fit are continually crediting the Digest with improving their means of livelihood. Two recent acknowledgments show the geographic and commercial range of these effects. Cabin Creek Quilts of Eskdale, West Virginia, informed Pleasantville that they got 225 inquiries as a result of a single mention in an article on the ancient art of quilting. From Dietlikon, a suburban area near Zurich, Switzerland, came the thanks of businessman Rudolf Stahel. Wishing to build a large supermarket, Stahel was frustrated by a Swiss government limit on the amount that could be spent for such a project. In the Swiss edition of the Digest for October 1971, he read an article, "Bubbles—Newest Thing in Building," investigated the possibilities with a German construction firm and put up the first supermarket in a bubble, well under the government ceiling.

The Digest has also acknowledged involvement in affairs of the heart. After an article appeared on the possibility of determining the sex of your baby by following certain procedures in its conception, a worker in the magazine's index was somewhat surprised to pick up the phone and hear a sweet young female voice say, "My husband and I are going away for the weekend. Can you tell me how I can get a copy of your article about choosing a baby's sex?" Another woman, a schoolteacher who had written a testimonial essay that was published in Reader's Digest, wrote in to report: ". . . the happiest development is discovering that romance is 'black and white and read all over.' A man I used to know on the West Coast was scanning worn magazines in the doctor's office last summer when he ran across my article. He phoned me that day. We met—and met again, often. And now we are married."

The personal uses to which people put the Reader's Digest are often astonishing. A man in Silver Spring, Maryland, was inspired by a Digest article to take on the Internal Revenue Service in small claims tax court. A convict doing life for murder in Tulsa, Oklahoma, nearly won parole with an impressive letter—until a member of the Parole Board recognized it as straight plagiarism from a Digest article. A member of a skydiving club in Oregon began collecting old Digests because, he said, ten pages of the magazine made a perfect wind direction indicator. A Vietcong messenger killed in combat was found to be using tear sheets from the Overseas Military Edition of the Digest as envelopes for his dispatches. The evidently Americanized daughter of a Chinese cooking instructor used a Digest feature as an excuse for breaking away from the family as the father's plaintive letter of complaint recounts:

"I always consider that Reader's Digest is a very good reading material for every one, therefore, soon as I came to the states in 1969, I subscribed it for my daughter—Linda. I could never forget that one of your selection, 'What's Your Maturity Quotient?' gave a very high score to my daughter. You know what happened now?

"Linda patiently waited for her birth-day of 21, several months ago, and run away from us, went to Reno and married with a Chinese young man who came from South America as student. They are now in South America, and what made me upsetted is the young man who is nothing good. To name just one example, before he left from the States, he used his credit cards, bought many things, amount thousand dollars childish toys to my point of view, and of course he is not preparing to pay them! Before all these happened, I tried all of my effort to reason with my daughter, but she thought that she is Matured according to the article from your magazine!

"I wish you should never publish such kind of silly and nonsense article anymore in your magazine which I respect very much."

This variety and reach of Digest influence, for good or ill, evidently drives many observers of the phenomenon to the dictionary in search of superlatives. In his book, *The 100 Most Important People in the World Today,* Donald Robinson wrote, "In the history of the printed word, no one editor has ever had so much influence on so many people in so many different countries as DeWitt Wallace, the creator of Reader's Digest. . . . The underlying reason for Wallace's far-flung influence isn't only to be found in his vast readership. It stems even more from the unique hold which his magazine has on its readers. They trust it implicitly." Syndicated radio commentator Barry Farber waxed even more eloquent: "When we're talking influence, there is no competitor to the Reader's Digest. The Digest makes all the others look like a rose petal being dropped down a canyon, waiting for an echo. The Reader's Digest is thunder around the world."

It's hard not to use such language when you take a look at some of the figures. Not only is the Digest's circulation immense, but it is remarkably steady. The key figure in circulation is something called the renewal rate, that is, the percentage of people who, having sampled the magazine's contents, come willingly back for more. The Digest renewal rate in the United States is some 70 percent. But other figures dazzle, too: Not long ago, a Digest promoter discovered that the number of people who buy the magazine in the United States exceeds the combined total population of New York, Los Angeles, Philadelphia, Chicago and San Antonio; in sharper focus, more people in New York buy the Digest than the *New York Times*, more people in Boston buy the Digest than the *Boston Globe*, more people in San Francisco buy the Digest than the *San Francisco Chronicle*. And this is only a little more than half the magazine's total circulation—the rest is scattered the world around—which is why the giant can still look comfortably down upon its only American rivals in the numbers game: the very specialized *TV Guide*, and *Parade*, a Sunday supplement with spotty circulation dependent upon the newspapers in which it is folded.

David Reed, the Digest's farthest-flung roving editor, is fond of saying, "The three great international institutions are the Catholic Church, the Communist Party and the Reader's Digest." It's a self-serving statement, to be sure, but nearly true. In a great many countries where it appears the Digest is the largest magazine, and in some, such as Australia, its sales per capita are even greater than they are in the United States. Moreover, in the countries where the Digest has published longest, such as Great Britain, an increasing number of readers regard it fondly as a native product. One of the more than a million British subscribers making his first visit to the United States is said to have spotted the magazine on an airport newsstand and commented to his American host, "Isn't it amazing, you have that over here, too!"

While appreciation of a publication often called "as American as apple pie" in Western, and particularly Anglo-Saxon, communities might be understandable, the ease with which the Digest has vaulted the highest linguistic and cultural barriers is greater proof of its pulling power. In a recent poll in Taiwan, where more than 100,000 copies of the magazine circulate in Chinese, the Digest ranked fourth in recognition among American products, following Coca-Cola, Hilton Hotels and Ford Motors. And, shortly after he left his post, former United States Ambassador to India, Daniel P. Moynihan, informed the Digest: "I came away from India persuaded that incomparably the most important American institutions in South Asia are Rotary and the Reader's Digest. (I don't know if you like being an institution, but there you are.) Your readership is incomparable in size and quality." Among the self-confessed avid readers of the Digest in that area are, for example, the king and queen of Thailand who, because of their exalted position, could not be ordinary subscribers—it would be inappropriate for their majesties' names to appear on a mailing list—and they had to borrow copies from members of the palace staff until a recent confidential arrangement was made with Pleasantville.

As can be imagined, the logistics of getting a magazine to so many people in so many places every month are formidable. Some years ago the enterprising editor of the Digest's house organ, *Courier*, took a pop-eyed look at the most important raw material, aside from ideas, that goes into the product—paper. He discovered that the 10 presses printing the Digest in the United States alone were consuming 25,000 miles of paper every month which, in one year, would produce a five-and-one-half-foot-wide ribbon of paper 372,000 miles long, enough to girdle the earth 15 times. The amount of paper used in all editions for a year would, if rolled into one huge sheet, cover an area of 608 square miles—almost twice the combined area of New York

City's five boroughs, or just half the area of the whole state of Rhode Island.

Spreading all this paper around produces figures calculated to give the sturdiest postman back-aching nightmares if he thought about them. Going in and out of Pleasantville every year are something like 666 million pieces of mail. The volume abroad is literally staggering, too, and the Digest estimates that its total worldwide mailing bill amounts to $100 million a year.

But big as it is, the familiar pocket-sized magazine is in some ways only "The Little Engine That Could" in the Reader's Digest roundhouse. It pulls a lengthening train of corporate cars, some loaded with pure gold. With its Condensed Books, Special Books, and Reader's Digest Press, the Digest is one of the world's largest hardcover book publishers. The Digest also sells specially produced record albums around the world. Although products like globes, and investment shares have been tried and found wanting, a curious combination of service and goodies called QSP (Quality School Products), through which school classes, scout troops, Babe Ruth League teams are enlisted to peddle magazine subscriptions, records, candy, placemats to neighbors to raise money for uniforms and such, is proving lucrative in the United States and moving gradually abroad. The Digest is stepping more tentatively into the travel business with a subsidiary called Foreign Study League and into the production of television shows and motion pictures, the most notable so far being the musical version of "Tom Sawyer." When the whole train pulls into the Pleasantville station every year, it delivers to the Reader's Digest Association, its owner, a gross cargo of some $700 million.

This fifty-five-year-old giant that straddles the globe—telling a man when he's having a heart attack, putting strange ideas into a Chinese girl's head, dropping magazines on the coffee tables of an Oriental palace, selling candy to Mexican children, chewing up miles of paper, scooping up millions of dollars—had the smallest of beginnings. Its anxious father was DeWitt Wallace who, entering his thirties, had so far managed to drop out of college after trying the first two years twice, got himself wounded as a sergeant in World War I and been fired as a promotion writer for Westinghouse in Pittsburgh. Its midwife was Lila Bell Acheson, a social worker who had recklessly become engaged to the unpromising Wallace. Almost totally without funds, the couple borrowed some $1,800, mostly from Wallace's father and brother, for a test mailing that brought back enough returns while they were honeymooning to put them in business and pay off the debt. The Wallaces, now in their late eighties and still sole owners of the giant (except for some non-voting stock distributed to favored employees), have never owed a cent since.

Freed thus from the restraint, advice and prying eyes of stockholders, lenders and government regulators, Wallace has been able to breathe into the growing giant a single soul—his own. To an extent perhaps unparalleled today in a business of such size and scope, the Reader's Digest was—and is—in all of its detail the extension of the enigmatic personality of one human being. It may, therefore, be an anachronism in the modern corporate world, but if so, a study of the reasons for its growth and survival becomes all the more fascinating, as would be the case of some rare beast that defies extinction in an alien environment.

The beginning, and perhaps the end, of an understanding of the Reader's Digest is an understanding of DeWitt Wallace whose long shadow will necessarily fall across nearly every page of this book as it does across the lives of every Digester from Pleasantville to Paris, from Helsinki to Sydney. When I first went to the Digest, a number of us reasonably young and reasonably new editors formed a small group, the purpose of which was to invite our superiors to lunch in an effort to find out how the magazine worked. One of our more helpful guests was Paul Palmer, then co-executive editor with Kenneth Payne. Years before, he told us, he had fought a losing battle against Wallace over the publication of a certain article which Palmer was sure would needlessly offend some powerful interests. When a delegation of the offended arrived in Pleasantville in a rage after the piece appeared, Wallace sent Palmer out to them with instructions to uphold the magazine's position. "The moral of that story," Palmer explained to us neophytes, "is that you must never forget that it is *his* magazine."

It was the soundest sort of advice and proved, over the years, the clue to solving many mysteries. The giant whose back we all were riding was a very human being, and the way to begin to understand a human being is to listen to what he says. For this, you don't even have to know DeWitt Wallace. Though personally reticent, he has been speaking out to half the world every month for half a century. His singular voice is the Reader's Digest, and in its evidently beguiling tone lies the secret of the whole company's astonishing success.

III

A Voice Crying in the Wilderness

For more than fifty years now, the voice of the gentle giant of Pleasantville has been saying things that an astonishing number of people, not only in America but all over the world, want to hear. The evidence that this is so is irrefutable. Not only do more people buy the little magazine than any other publication on earth, but their loyalty in terms of renewal rate is held to be remarkable for the industry. Thus, any understanding of the phenomenon that is the Reader's Digest must begin with an understanding of what there is in that voice that so many find irresistible.

To begin with, in a changing world, it is unchanging. Going through half a century of Reader's Digests induces a kind of vertigo. The time machine seems to go out of whack. Consider these titles from two issues for the same month in the year: "How To Keep Young Mentally," "The Philippines Inside and Out," "Henry Ford, Dreamer and Worker," "What Kind of a Husband Are You?" "Advice From a President's Physician"; then "How to Cope With Boredom," "Superman of the New Iran," "Houdini, the Man No Lock Could Hold," "The Marriage

Game," "Formulas for Fitness." The first titles come from the very first issue of the Reader's Digest in February 1922; the last come from the cover of the Digest for February 1976. If nothing else, they prove that DeWitt Wallace, a minister's son and founder, owner, and until recently editor of the Reader's Digest, must have taken to heart one lesson from the Bible: that there's nothing new under the sun.

Not only is the voice unchanging, but it speaks directly to you, the reader. Examine any table of contents of the Reader's Digest for any month of any year in any country, and the titles that speak to what are probably your most pressing personal problems cry out at you: "They Hire YOU," October 1936; "The Repair Man Will Gyp You . . ." October 1941; "Divorce Granted!" October 1954; "Is There Room at the Top for a Woman?" October 1968; "Facts and Fallacies About Exercise and Losing Weight," October 1974. Or abroad: *"Pour vaincre le cancer,"* France, October 1976; "A Diet to Save Your Life," Australia, October 1976; "First Aid for Failing Marriages," Britain, October 1976.

The voice is also clear. An immeasurable help to anyone making a study of what the Reader's Digest has been saying is the fact that its editors, taught by DeWitt Wallace, write titles so simple and direct that, with few exceptions, you know from a glance at them exactly what's in any article. If you read the blurb—the selling line above or below the title—you probably also know the whole argument of the piece. The brief, fast-moving body of the text will be packed with quotes, anecdotes, facts to support the title and blurb. Even when the Digest raises a question in the headline, it has a knack of telling you the probable answer in the blurb. In what may be the neatest trick of all, the Digest can do this with *two* questions, as in this sample from November 1971: title—"Which Way the World Council of Churches?" and blurb—"Has this 'ecclesiastical United Nations' become just another platform from which communism seeks to flay the free world?"

But even a voice that's consistent, direct and clear can pall if it has nothing to say of special value to the listener. It's here that in my opinion the Digest's voice is unique, and its message can almost be summed up in a word—optimism. Through wars and rumors of war, through depression and inflation, through fire and pestilence, it keeps telling people that the world is not only a pretty good place but can be made better, that life is what you make of it, that laughter is the best medicine, that there's no sting in death. According to an old joke, the ultimate Digest title would be "New Hope for the Dead." It's not really much of a joke. In its October 1974 issue, the Digest ran a first-person story entitled "I Died at 10:52 A.M." by one Victor D. Solow who related how his heart stopped for twenty-three minutes, adding, "Words only vaguely approximate the experience . . . The new 'I' was not the I which I know . . . This 'I' had no connection to ego. It was final, unchangeable, indivisible, indestructible, pure spirit. . . ." In its January issue, the Digest saluted 1977 with a half book section along the same lines entitled "Life after Life" which leaves even the most jaded reader with the feeling that if he hasn't died yet he's missed something.

Since there aren't all that many people able to report on conditions in the great beyond, the Digest generally contents itself with how things can be made better for the living. Over the years, its reports on new cures for everything from athlete's foot to syphilis have often surprised doctors—who haven't had time to keep up with the medical journals—as much as laymen and are so notorious that they need no documentation. But other publications are pretty good at keeping up with medical news, too, so it's in that grayer area of emotional malaise that the Digest seems to stand almost alone in bringing instant help to its readers. Dip in almost anywhere, and you'll get a shot in the spirit. I have picked Octobers, largely because the issue for that month is designed for a vital time of the year when everybody's back at work, when schools are in full swing, when elections are in the offing, when winter's sure to come. You need something cheery then. In October 1936, when depression-poor people couldn't go anywhere anyway, the Digest made a virtue of it with an article called "The Art of Staying Home." Another piece in the same issue, "Happiness as Deep as Tears," turned tragedy into a kind of triumph; Gail Carey, describing life as mother of a Mongoloid child, asserted, "After all—agony can be made to count for something. We have learned that the small annoyances of life can be so easily disregarded; that they are as nothing beside the greater sorrow we have had to meet." If you didn't have any specific worry, just that terrible fall in spirit at the end of another year, you'd probably get more lift out of "That Vital Spark—Hope," a kind of cure-all by Ardis Whitman, condensed from *Christian Herald,* in the November 1974 Digest: "Hope is against odds . . . all life is a contest of light against darkness, joy against despair. Yet, most of us *do* hope, most of the time. . . . We hope again as naturally as the seeds sprout and the sun rises, and perhaps for the same reason. Hope's signature seems to be written on earth and sky and sea and on all that lives. . . ."

This sort of thing is so endlessly repeated in different variations in what now amount to more than 660 issues of the Reader's Digest that your mind would reel along with mine if I were to go on with the exercise. Another way, however, of catching the Digest's unique tone is to compare it with a different voice. You could probably make a scientific study of this, but I'm not sure it would make sense: Tone is what young people would call "vibes," a kind of immediate sensation you get on contact with something. My feeling about the Digest tone was sharpened suddenly, almost casually one day when I came back from the local news store with a copy of the then current Reader's Digest in one hand and the day's *New York Times* in the other. Obviously, the *Times* with its policy of running "all the news that's fit to print" every day is a great, discordant symphony, while the Digest is a neat little chamber ensemble; nevertheless, listen to these solo voices within them, voices I picked out just browsing for my own interest.

On the Op Ed page of the *Times* was a piece by Pat Watters entitled "Fed Up" and beginning, "They are supposed to be among the most powerful elements in the society, but they discover themselves virtually powerless. They have done all the things they were told would make them happy and secure, and after half a lifetime of bedeviled striving, they are neither. They are angry middle-aged men . . . I am convinced they are the majority of my generation." It went down from there. In a piece excerpted from Gilbert Highet's "The Immortal Profession," and entitled "The Pleasures of Learning," the Digest that day told me, among other things, "During our earthly life, the body gradually dies; even the emotions become duller. But the mind in most of us continues to live, and even grows more lively and active, enjoys itself more, works and plays with more expansion and delight . . . The chief danger confronting us is not age. It is laziness, sloth, routine, stupidity . . . You can live longest and best and most rewardingly by attaining and preserving the happiness of learning." It can hardly go up from there.

Let's try a laugh. In that day's *Times* humorist Russell Baker in "The Joys of Summer" told of an island vacation which consisted mostly of a round of social events with dreadful people and wound up, "It was quite hopeless. Nothing worked, and summer was ending, and so one day, after cocktails at the Cardozos' we all went to the beach and lay down and dozed, and a car ran over us." In the Digest humorist Will Stanton had a go at "Little Things Bother You?" and said that the worst for him was a garrulous baby sitter who talked to him all the way home. Stanton ended up: "'Tune her out,' Maggie (his wife) said. I asked her what she meant. 'Don't you know how to tune somebody out?' she asked. 'You just think about something else.' 'That's not easy when you have Mrs. Nivvins right beside you,' I said, 'telling you about Byron, and the hole in Elm Street, over and over, all the way to her house. How are you going to tune *that* out?' Maggie looked over at me. 'Tune what out?' she asked."

Nothing is hopeless in the Digest, even in humor which in other hands is so often a kind of gallant shrug of despair. Humor, in fact, is viewed so positively by the Digest that its main joke department is called "Laughter, the Best Medicine." In addition to what's collected under this heading, anecdotes and ticklers of one kind or another are scattered throughout most of the 300 or so pages of each issue. In this, the Digest voice has changed a bit through the years. Perhaps because of having more space and more staff to fill it, there are many more jokes and other departments nowadays than there were forty years ago. They're a lot more sophisticated, too. From April 1936: "The modern girl has a bleaches and cream complexion." From February 1974: "An airline commercial: 'Our coach flights now have four hostesses instead of two, and with wider seats, too.' ('Line o'Type' in Chicago *Tribune*.)"

A kind of gentle double entendre has become almost a staple of Digest humor; I counted six in one recent issue. Two samples: "One San Franciscan saw a truly patriotic couple in Golden Gate Park: 'They were going 50 miles an hour and the car was parked.' (Chase Webb, quoted by Herb Caen in San Francisco *Chronicle*.)" Or: "The pill: a gadget to be used in any conceivable circumstances. (L. H.)" For the most part, though, Digest jokes are wholly wholesome, tending often toward the groaner type of puns. A few: "Did you hear about the religious moth who gave up woolen for lint? (Jane Wheat, quoted by Alex Thein in Milwaukee *Sentinel*)" Or: "Shrimp and lobster now cost so much that they are known in marine circles as the Upper Crustaceans (Edward Stevenson in *The Wall Street Journal*)."

As in the last pun, Digest humor, along with the little anecdotes in departments like "Life in These United States," sometimes seems to make pithier comments on the way things really are out there than the carefully crafted, optimistic articles. I found many scattered through some summer issues for 1974, a time we can still remember. An example: "*Doctor's Dilemma.* Two doctors decided to play golf and one said, 'I'll have to call my office and cancel my afternoon appointments.' Ten minutes later he hung up in frustration: 'It's no use. All I get is my own voice telling me I'm not in.' (Robert Brault in *National Enquirer*.)"

It's pretty hard not to flip through any issue of the Reader's Digest looking for this sort of thing, and it's almost equally difficult not to pause in the process and get caught up in headlines that promise to tell you how to give a woman an orgasm, or sell your old house for more money, or know whether you are having a heart attack. And no matter how cynical you are, you'll probably have a hard time not plowing through one of those dramas in real life like "Two Seconds to Live" by Joseph P. Blank in July 1976 which had a blurb beginning, "Suddenly, young Ron Gillis was being pulled, inexorably, toward the whirling blades of the sawmill's chipper. . . ." In the end, the most beguiling feature of the little giant's voice may be variety; out of some thirty articles it's almost impossible not to see *something* you'd like to read. I have to confess that before I went to work there, I was a regular Digest reader only in the sense that I almost invariably found myself picking it off a newsstand on my way to a plane or a train, because its cover was the only one that guaranteed me several items of interest; a whole issue of *Life*, say, or even *Saturday Evening Post* might be preempted by articles on subjects I didn't care about.

To get the real pitch of the Digest voice, it is instructive to compare it with the cacophony arising from ongoing life. In an effort to do this I went through the whole magazine for a year that most of us will remember as being particularly disharmonious—1968. Let's look at a few things that were happening around us that year. In his overview of forty years of American life, *The Glory and the Dream*, William Manchester called 1968 "The Year Everything Went Wrong." It began with the United States' being humiliated by the North Korean capture of the U.S.S. *Pueblo* and then the Tet offensive in Vietnam. Things, in fact, were so bad in Vietnam that a President effectively resigned. Later that year Martin Luther King, Jr., and Robert Kennedy were assassinated. Riots at Columbia climaxed five years of such student turbulence that one college president described campuses as "fox holes." Even nice kids were into drugs—47 percent of college students had smoked marijuana, according to *Playboy;* and sex—a national survey reported that 65 percent of all girls had premarital sex. You could see just about anything on the stage, *Oh, Calcutta*, or at the movies, *Deep Throat*. Blacks who had already won some bloody and tragic battles were unusually quiet that year, perhaps because of King's death, but women weren't; under militant leadership they were moving toward an organized drive for rights significantly called NOW. In the face of all this, Richard M. Nixon was winning his campaign for the presidency.

From placid Pleasantville, the Digest viewed this chaotic scene with distaste and alarm, tempered of course by optimism. Taking somewhat of an overall view of troubles behind and struggles ahead, the Digest "Press Section" in February 1968 led off with this item: "Beloit (Wis.) *News*—'I'm For the Upperdog'—I've about reached the end of my tolerance for our society in one-sided sympathy for the misfit, the ne'er-do-well, the drug addict, the chronic criminal, the loner—in general, the underdog. I feel it's time for someone to stand up and say: 'I'm for the upperdog!' (From an address by Miller Upton, President of Beloit College.)"

Among the upperdogs the Digest favored were the South Vietnamese and their American allies. About the time the enemy had shown its strength at Tet and President Johnson was dropping out of the race, in March 1968, the Digest carried a lead article, "Report from Vietnam," by Hanson W. Baldwin, condensed from the *New York Times*, in which he concluded: ". . . the allies are winning, and the enemy is being hurt. But the road ahead could be long and slow, with no clear end in sight. 'The real issue now,' as one officer put it, 'is whether or not the American people will have the patience and fortitude to stay the course.'" A press item in the same issue quotes former Secretary of State Dean Acheson as saying in *National Review* that there is "no possibility of negotiating our way out of Vietnam." Then to make it all worthwhile comes a piece from candidate Nixon, condensed from *Foreign Affairs*, which proclaims, according to one of those revealing blurbs, "The American presence in Vietnam has had a powerful influence in strengthening the rest of Asia against communism . . . the former Vice President looks beyond the war to the emergence of a dynamic community of nations which will hold Asia on the course toward freedom."

By the next month, April, the Digest's voice was crying alarm about events at home. A major piece by ex-President

Eisenhower, "Let's Close Ranks on the Home Front," was blurbed "Former President Eisenhower speaks out against those critics of the war in Vietnam who, in defiance of both common sense and their country's best interests, preach discord and rebellion." Another article, an interview from *U.S. News & World Report* with one Richard H. Sanger, a former foreign service officer, gave a positive answer to the title question, "Is Insurrection Brewing in the United States?" But the real heavy was a piece by the Digest's own William Schulz, "Martin Luther King's March on Washington," timed for that very month by the still-living King, thus making the article a sharp departure for the Digest which usually reports on events both past and of lasting interest. Said Schulz: "One thing is certain; whether or not all of the protestors' plans materialize, the nation faces international humiliation as a result of the Washington campaign. Communism's worldwide propaganda apparatus is set for a field day. . . . By publicly condoning the tactics of disruption, the Nobel Prize-winning King has given them a legitimacy and a respectability they do not deserve. . . ."

As to rebellious youth, the Digest seemed almost as baffled as most parents. But in a reprint in March from *Time*, "The Difficult Art of Being a Parent," it held out some hope: "There's no reason to view the generation gap as insurmountable . . ." Nor was there any reason to let down standards. An April piece, "Why Students Turn to Drugs," by Anonymous was a "warning" from "a recent college graduate who has 'been there.'" Contemplating young sex, the Digest published a condensation from *Family Weekly*, "The Pill and the Teen-Age Girl," by Pearl Buck who didn't say *no* exactly but added: "What is the sex act when it is nothing but release or sport? It is nothing— it is less than nothing. It becomes tiresome and even disgusting." In November, another one of those anonymous authors, a father, gave a mostly negative answer to the title question, "Teen-Age Marriage—Yes or No?" in a supposed letter plucked out of *Seventeen*, to his daughter.

Despite banners in the streets, as it were, the Digest maintained such a calm consistency in its view of the role of women

—young girls should be virgins, older women warm wives—that it's worth a digression here. In November 1968, the Digest noted that women might want something more by reprinting a cautious piece from *Saturday Evening Post* by Marilyn Mercer, asking "Is There Room at the Top for Woman?" and blurbed "Because of discrimination, habit and the facts of life, the gentler sex still takes a back seat in the working world. But prospects for the future are encouraging." In the body of the text, Ms. Mercer opined: "Full integration of women into business would mean, ultimately, changing some of our most deep-rooted ideas about sexual roles. And this is something that has never happened before in the civilized—or uncivilized—world." Through most of the year, though, the Digest was more concerned, as usual, with woman's relationship to man, preferably her husband: to quote from a piece in August, "What Every Husband Needs," condensed from Hannah Lees' "Help Your Husband Stay Alive"—"Marriage is for motherlings all right, and this is one of the kinds of love that wives must learn to provide. . . . He may even need to be wooed, as a man woos a woman, to break down his anxieties. A wife who is willing to do this may change her husband's whole life."

The Digest approach to woman's role is almost caricatured in its first issue of February 1922 by an article called "Whatever Is New for Women Is Wrong." The piece, a reprint from *Ladies' Home Journal* by Edna Kenton, is in fact a tongue-in-cheek account of how the world has managed to stagger on despite the shocking things women started doing like becoming physicians and acrobats and going to conventions, but it ends curiously, "And so most of the old bogies, tested out, disappear, and new ones take their place. But, today, as in 1700, the home and marriage and the child and female delicacy are still in imminent danger, and, as in every decade, 'are endangered as never before.'" This could pass for wry humor to anyone who hadn't jumped forward in that curious Digest non-time machine to discover an original article in May 1972 by Elsieliese Thrope called "But Women *Are* the Favored Sex" and blurbed "If Women's Libbers win their war, they will certainly lose the peace." In between have come such gems as one from *Vogue* in June 1964, "The Power Men Have Over Women," by Marya Mannes which got off to this start: "They (men) are not necessarily brighter, but they usually have us where they want us. Like a man with a dog." This provoked such reader response that in November that year, the Digest ran a collection of letters, "The Power Women Have Over Men," one of which set forth in a sentence another consistent Digest theme, "The power of women over men is 'No!' "

Next to stopping inflation, getting young ladies to say no may well be the Digest's longest losing battle. Notable articles almost a generation apart proclaimed "The Case for Chastity" and then "The *New* Case for Chastity." Despite this, while the virginity count continued to go down, the Digest did not give up. As late as September 1974, they found a piece in *Seventeen*, "A Girl's Right to Say No," by Alice Lake who asserted: "Despite tremendous pressures to go along with the 'new' social behavior, a lot of teen-agers are resisting. The assumption that 'everybody's doing it' is far from valid."

At considerable risk of misunderstanding, it must be said that an overview of half a century of Digests leads one to the conclusion that the main subject other than women about which the Digest voice has been almost boringly consistent is animals. It began in the first issue where Albert Payson Terhune told readers that "if Solomon could seriously commend the Ant to his people as a tutor, then no one need be ashamed to take a course of instruction from the dog." Throughout the years, and in almost every month of them, the Digest has discovered anew that God's dumb creatures have something to teach us; what's more, except for the kind of insects that threaten economic progress by eating crops, there isn't a villain among them. Consider, in May 1936, a piece by Henry Morton Robinson threateningly entitled "Rats" but hastily softened by a blurb that said "Man's enemy is also his teacher." In February 1941, a piece called "Mothers of the Wild" by Archibald Rutledge and condensed from *Field & Stream* established the Digest's broader view, as noted in this blurb: "Eyewitness tales of maternal acts

of courage and devotion among birds and animals." Dip in anywhere, and you're likely to encounter a friendly beast. Just a
few: "The Witless, Wonderful Turkey," November 1974; "That
Remarkable Creature, the Snail," February 1968; "The Mole:
Mighty Midget Tunneler," April 1968. This thing about animals
reached a kind of climax in August 1974 with a piece entitled
"Who *Really* Needs Alligators?" by Robert Bendiner which
went on to prove out the case made in the blurb: "Or tigers,
whales and wolves? We *all* do—because every time a species
disappears our future on earth is jeopardized in ways we can't
conceive."

People are another matter, perhaps because they ought to
know better. It would be tedious beyond endurance even to list
the titles of Digest articles asserting that the world would be
better off without Washington bureaucrats, Communists of
every kind but particularly Russians and Chinese, economists
who think inflation might be more tolerable than unemploy-
ment, most union leaders who have been depicted as Communists and/or gangsters depending on the times, federal revenue
agents, environmentalists who even in the interests of saving
animals might inhibit the growth of industry, young people who
don't take the Digest to heart or even read it, and Democrats.
Since more than half its readers may well fall into that last category, the voice of the Digest has been more sly than direct in
making it evident that the country, and probably the world,
would be better off under Republican domination. One reason
for looking closely at October issues was to see how the Digest,
supposedly a reprint magazine without an editorial policy as
such, has handled the desire of its owner and editor, a heavy
Republican contributor, to see that his party prevailed. On
balance, until the issue of October 1976, containing a rigidly
even Ford-Carter debate, it was to pretend that Democrats don't
exist. The October issue for that turbulent year of 1968 is illustrative. While Hubert Humphrey, who almost won, was not
mentioned, there was a leading article by Richard M. Nixon,
"Let a New Day Dawn for the U.S.A.!" which was "condensed
from Mr. Nixon's acceptance address at the Republican

National Convention on August 8, 1968." Further along in the book, there's a throw-the-rascals-out piece by the Digest's own John Barron called "Tell Us the Truth, Uncle Sam" and blurbed "Federal agencies and bureaucrats are increasingly engaged in a self-serving policy of official deceit—a shabby practice that debases the quality and character of our democratic process."

At that, Humphrey may have been lucky. In the October 1972 issue of the Digest, Senator George McGovern's name appeared a number of times. The last sentence of the lead item in the press section, taken from London's *The Economist*, said, "As they see it, the South Vietnamese have less to fear from Hanoi than from the election of Sen. George McGovern." That was the only mention that there might be a presidential candidate named McGovern, but his name popped up twice again in a piece taken from *Newsweek* contending that the Soviets might take over Europe if McGovern and his colleague, Senate Majority Leader Mike Mansfield, prevailed in their proposal for United States troop withdrawals from the continent. The Digest didn't think it necessary to mention that President Nixon was also running, but its lead article was "A Time for Toughness in America" by Nixon stalwart John B. Connally. In a supporting role, as in 1968, a Digest Washington writer, Eugene H. Methvin, weighed in with "The Supreme Court Changes Course," pointing out how Nixon appointees were bringing the court around to right thinking, and blurbed: "Today the Supreme Court appears almost exactly poised between opposing Constitutional philosophies. Your vote this November may well tip the balance."

As everybody knows, Nixon didn't need the Digest to win big although the stink of Watergate was beginning to seep out even before the election. By 1974, the United States was in another year rivalling 1968 for bad news, especially from the Digest point of view. The magazine's communist-fighting hero for twenty-odd years, Richard M. Nixon, became the first president in United States history to resign the office under a cloud; the war the Digest had pushed until the very end was lost. Yet you'd hardly know it from a look through Digests of that year. An acknowledgement of Watergate in February 1974 appeared in a press section quote from John Connally, again, in the New York *Daily News:* "When there's a loss of confidence, do we want a President to resign? . . . Shouldn't we be patient enough to let the system work its will through the judicial processes of the country?" Rather than dwell on gloomy tidings, the Digest seemed more determinedly optimistic than ever that year. It even found something good to say about the gas shortage, quoting James Reston from the *New York Times* as saying, "What America really needs is more shortages. It is not our shortages but our surpluses that are hurting us. Too much gas, too much booze, too much money, talk, noise, and newsprint are our problem. . . . The Arab nations have done us a favor by cutting off our oil. . . ." And louder than ever that year, in a kind of desperate crescendo to drown out the disharmony of a decade or more, the Digest's April 1974 lead article, "Optimism—the Creative Attitude," by René Dubos and condensed from the *American Scholar,* boomed out in its blurb: "To those despairing of the times, a distinguished scientist offers this reminder: mankind has time and again successfully handled far more drastic changes than those we face today."

Surrounding this grand chord of optimism are a number of grace notes that must be counted as part of the Digest's tone. These are the many articles, again too numerous to catalogue, pointing out specific ills that an informed and aroused citizenry can correct such as bad schools, corrupt local officials, drab streets, hazards to health. As in the case of personal advice on sex, diet, religion and the like, these pieces have demonstrably resulted in the kind of action that might sometimes be called a miracle. In any case, their overall effect on the regular Digest reader might be to leave him with the ebullient feeling that he not only should, but can, fight City Hall. Such articles probably had a lot to do with the fact that DeWitt Wallace once told an interviewer somewhat wistfully that the world would be a lot better place if people practiced what they read in the Reader's Digest.

Whether the world would be a better place or not, it would

certainly be a different place if people really listened to the giant's voice. Lord knows, enough of them hear it to make a very large dent in human affairs. That so much going on out there in the world doesn't seem to correspond with the way Pleasantville sees it leads to at least one conclusion: human beings, no matter how much they want to hear otherwise, are by nature as obdurately unchangeable as the Digest itself. But such a conclusion never seems to have crossed the mind of DeWitt Wallace who, as undaunted as the prophets of old, goes on trumpeting the good news that seems to have been part of his heritage.

IV

The Rise of the
Preachers' Kids

Speaking of his former employer, DeWitt Wallace, Eugene
Lyons, author and longtime senior editor at the Reader's Digest,
says, "I like to tell people he's a perfect Digest character." So he
is. It would be hard to imagine a life that more amply fulfills in
the flesh all those optimistic, individualistic, patriotic, philanthropic and practical ideas expressed within the pages of the
little magazine Wallace invented. As a result, efforts to recount
the Wallace life almost inevitably take on the somewhat unreal
and almost childish quality of manufactured myth. The man's
too good to be true. Not only did he rise from genteel poverty
to incredible wealth in the Horatio Alger tradition, but he
managed to keep it from going to his head. Unlike those other
publishing giants of his time, Henry Luce and William
Randolph Hearst, Wallace never confused circulation with
potential votes and thus eliminated from his life the colorful
drama of struggling for political power. By staying married to
the same woman for more than half a century, he deprived
biographers of the juicier kind of scandal that often enlivens the
lives of the rich. Once a compulsive cigarette smoker, he followed his magazine's advice years ago and gave up the weed; a
social drinker, he has never been reported drunk, or even tipsy,

in the wildest Wallace tales. About the only fleshly flaw that emerges when people discuss Wallace is his tendency to scare the Beejesus out of passengers when he gets behind the wheel of a car—a not too surprising trait in a man who had gone so far so fast.

DeWitt Wallace had the good fortune to be born into a very special social class; he was a p.k., or preacher's kid. Perhaps owing to the thought in some Christian circles that there is something Godly about poverty, ministers have generally been kept in that state by their understanding followers. This usually provides their children with a strong incentive to live otherwise in the future. Fortunately and in contrast to most of the impoverished in this land, p.k.s generally find the means to improve their lot readily at hand. Whatever their financial status, most ministers are educated far above the common level, and their homes are filled with books and talk of learning, a taste for which often rubs off on their children. Out of respect and sympathy for the pastor's plight, people go out of their way to give the children a boost in the form of jobs, scholarships and the like; it is presumed that p.k.s have absorbed with their pablum a good part of the moral injunctions their fathers hurl from the pulpit, and quite often it is true.

DeWitt Wallace was a p.k. in depth. His father, Dr. James Wallace, was a kind of preacher's preacher, a devout Presbyterian who served first as professor of Greek and Modern Languages at the College of Wooster in Ohio and then came to St. Paul, Minnesota as president of the struggling church-related Macalester College some six years before the birth of his fifth child and third son on November 12, 1889. DeWitt Wallace's mother was Janet Davis Wallace, daughter of Rev. T. K. Davis, librarian at Wooster. With the college always in the red, Dr. Wallace and his family were liberally lashed by the chastening rod of poverty. In his authorized version of the Digest story, *Of Lasting Interest,* James Playsted Wood describes it this way:

"As a daughter put it years later, there was 'too much cold house and irregular salary.' 'Cold House' was not a figure of speech. Tall, scholarly James Wallace was a vibrant and forceful

presence, a man possessed of a devouring idea. He was willing
to endure hardships, privations, and rebuffs, anything if he could
make his vision of Macalester College come true . . . he knew
about lesser things, but they seemed unimportant. In the middle
of one particularly severe Minnesota winter, when he had
neglected to pay an overdue bill, the company repossessed the
coal it had delivered to the Wallace household."

Though he doesn't recall feeling especially deprived—living
on campus in the president's house, however cold, obviously
had status—DeWitt showed signs of rebellious ambition at the
earliest possible age. Left to mind DeWitt while Janet visited
her family in Wooster, Dr. Wallace wrote his wife: "The baby
is a rogue, a rascal, a bandit, a thief, a vandal, without character
or reputation—utterly lawless, wandering where he will and in
all kinds of mischief." Not much later, DeWitt is said to have
announced: "I want to live in a house that my papa owns and
nobody else so I can dig a hole in the yard." If young DeWitt's
ambition was to have a house of his own, he certainly went
about it the hard way.

Although he was good enough in the early grades of school to
skip two years, he ran into trouble in Macalester Academy
when, two years younger than his classmates and still in embarrassing knickerbockers, he took to sports instead of books to
salvage his self-respect. This led to declining grades, and it was
decided that he should try evangelist Dwight L. Moody's Mt.
Hermon School for boys in Northfield, Massachusetts. In what
may be the first of the selling letters that were to make his
fortune, young DeWitt wrote to Mt. Hermon on June 29, 1906:
". . . I can say this, whatever my occupation may be, I intend to
do as much good in the world as possible." The letter was
enough to get him in, but not to keep him there. Disciplined for
a dormitory rumpus in which he took part, DeWitt took off with
a classmate for Boston, New York, and ultimately California
where they earned their way by doing construction jobs in
earthquake shattered San Francisco. Entering Macalester College in the fall of 1907, he majored in baseball, handball and
hockey for two years, went to Colorado to work in an uncle's

bank for a year, enrolled again as a freshman at the University of California where he concentrated, by his own admission, on becoming "The Playboy of the Western World." At the end of another sophomore year, the son of Dr. James Wallace, M.A., Ph.D., D.D., LL.D., and brother of Benjamin Wallace, Macalester's first Rhodes scholar, became a college dropout, fifty years before it was the thing to do.

Not long ago, DeWitt Wallace, commenting on the long and fabulous success of the Reader's Digest, told John W. Garberson, a former Digest promotion director who turned to teaching journalism, "It goes to show what can happen if you have a good idea." But the recorded events of Wallace's life show equally well that good ideas are often long in the maturing. The year of 1909-10 when Wallace worked in his uncle's bank in Monte Vista, Colorado, he spent a lot of time alone in his room reading magazines. Some articles seemed better to him than others, and he began keeping a card file of the salient points of the good ones. This notion was still simmering in 1912 when he went back to St. Paul and got a job writing promotion letters for Webb Publishing Company, one of whose products was a magazine, *The Farmer*. Looking over the pamphlets on farming produced by state and federal agencies, Wallace felt that a lot of good advice wasn't getting into the hands of farmers who needed it, because there was no one place they could learn about what was being published. After four years with Webb, he put together a booklet called *Getting the Most Out of Farming*, listing available publications and summarizing their contents. He got a line of credit from Webb for printing it, bought a Model T Ford and set out to sell the booklet to banks for free distribution to their customers. He sold an encouraging 100,000 copies, enough to clear expenses, and while lying awake in a Montana bunkhouse one night, began to ponder the enormous potential of doing somewhat the same thing for a general audience.

In addition to being born into the right social class, Wallace was also born into the right time and place for the nurture of his idea. The years of his maturing, from 1889 through World War

I—the war to end all wars—were years of a rising tide of American optimism; there wasn't anything a man, or the country, couldn't do. The areas Wallace frequented throughout his youth—Minnesota, Wisconsin, Ohio, Colorado, Montana, California—were the open plains of America's rural and small-town West. They were largely peopled by middle-class entrepreneurs and sturdy pioneers, mostly of white, Anglo-Saxon, Christian stock. Often isolated from centers of any kind of culture, these self-improving people were avid for information, as the success in those years of the Chautauqua Literary and Scientific Circle, the nation's first correspondence school, as well as the tent Chautauquas so amply demonstrated. Wallace, talking to these people, being in fact one of them, must have developed an instinctive understanding of this yearning for knowledge, as well as a feel for exactly what they wanted to learn.

Still, 1916 was an uncertain year for any new venture, and Wallace went back to work as mail order correspondence manager for Brown & Bigelow, a greeting card and calendar company in St. Paul. When America declared war in April 1917, Wallace enlisted. "This impatient patriotism he ascribes entirely to his enthusiasm for escaping the insupportable dullness of his job," writes James Playsted Wood. Whatever the reason for the patriotism, the price Wallace paid for it was high. In the Meuse-Argonne offensive in October 1918, Sergeant Wallace was hit with shrapnel which penetrated his neck, nose, abdomen and lungs. Recovering from this took several months in the general hospital at Aix-les-Bains where he whiled away the time going through American magazines and actually trying out his theory that many of their better articles could be reduced in length without losing the point and flavor.

By the time he was discharged in 1919, Wallace had perfected the technique. Back in St. Paul, instead of looking for a job, he spent the next six months in the Minneapolis Public Library, where his aunt Miriam was librarian, and put together a sample copy of what he already was calling The Reader's Digest. Virtually every element of the magazine of today was in it—"31 articles each month from leading magazines, each article of

enduring value and interest, in condensed and permanent form."
Even the titles have a current ring: "The Shortest Route to the
Top," "The Art of Opening a Conversation," "Taking the Water
Out of the Cost of Living." He had several hundred copies
printed and began circulating them among publishers in the
hope that they would fund the venture and hire him as editor.
The negative reaction was universal. William Randolph Hearst,
for example, wrote that such a magazine might sell 300,000
copies, a venture too limited for his interest.

At this low point, a discouraged Wallace realized perhaps the
most significant benefit of his rather unorthodox education. In
his years at Macalester College, he had been friends with
Barclay Acheson, a fellow student and also a p.k. While he was
in California, Wallace was invited to visit the Acheson home in
Tacoma where he met Barclay's sister, Lila. They had a lot in
common, for the Achesons were as preacherly poor as the
Wallaces. As Lila recalled for Felicia Warburg Roosevelt,
author of "Doers and Dowagers," her minister father had,
among other privations, to do without a much needed Sunday
suit to get her clothes for school, and she "cried for hours." But
the other p.k. advantages along with the right omens—when
she was born in Virden, Manitoba, Canada, on Christmas 1889
a bright blue ball fell off the Christmas tree—and natural
beauty had produced a vivacious, confident young woman by
the time Wallace met Lila. Unfortunately, she was engaged to
somebody else, and he was obliged to forget her.

In 1921, having failed to sell his publishing idea and slogging
along as a salesman for a wholesale grocer, Wallace ran into
Barclay Acheson, now a minister himself, in St. Paul. Catching
up on the Acheson family, Wallace found that Lila was not
married or engaged but, a graduate of the University of Oregon,
was doing social work with women in Bridgeport, Connecticut.
Immediately, Wallace wired her: "Conditions among women
workers in Saint Paul ghastly. Urge immediate investigation."
By one of those coincidences—or divine blessings—that make
a perfect Digest story, Lila was transferred temporarily to nearby Minneapolis to establish an industrial YWCA. Within a day

after their meeting, Wallace proposed; within two days, she accepted. Wallace shyly showed her a copy of The Reader's Digest, still his dream. "I knew right away," she said later, "that it was a gorgeous idea."

Fundless, they were forced to go their separate ways—she to New York and he to Pittsburgh where his brother Ben had got him a job in the international publicity department of Westinghouse. They nevertheless planned marriage as soon as he could get settled, and Lila was thinking about decorating a Pittsburgh apartment when Westinghouse began dismantling Wallace's department in the postwar recession. Wallace learned the truth of the old adage: last hired, first fired. Jobless, and driven by desperation, Wallace decided the time had come to try his magazine on his own. From Pittsburgh he sent out his first circular appealing for subscribers, and the results were good enough that he went on to New York to enlist Lila in the cause.

After that, things moved with almost bewildering speed. On October 15, 1921, they went up to the sleepy little village of Pleasantville in Westchester County to be married by Rev. Barclay Acheson. Meanwhile, Lila found an apartment at MacDougal and Bleeker Streets in Greenwich Village and a basement room for an office under a speakeasy at 1 Minetta Lane, chosen largely for the euphonious name. With the funds borrowed from the Wallace family, they got another circular into the mail and went off for a two-week honeymoon in the Poconos. Coming back, they found enough provisional subscriptions, together with the Pittsburgh returns, to bring a promise of nearly $5,000 if the first issue pleased their readers. Borrowing another $1,300, they ordered from a Pittsburgh printer 5,000 copies of Volume 1, Number 1 of The Reader's Digest, to appear in February 1922.

That first year the Wallaces spent in Greenwich Village had all the essential elements of the manufactured myth. To get the early issues into the mails, they hired customers from the speakeasy upstairs and girls from a community club down the street to wrap and address; they then trundled the magazines off to the post office in a taxi. To keep the wolf from the door, they sublet one room of their apartment to a New York University instructor and his wife, awkwardly sharing bath and kitchen. To save on magazine subscriptions and perhaps gain room for thought, Wallace did most of his editing in the periodical room of the New York Public Library, a favorite spot of warmth for derelicts in those days of the 1922 depression. Among them, he stood out as something of a "library freak" as day after day he sat there, ordering magazines and painfully copying off his condensations in long hand on yellow sheets of paper.

Circulation, followed by subscription payments (25 cents a copy; $2.97 a year) rose as relentlessly as the tide. The money came in so regularly that only once in the first half year did Wallace fall behind in paying his printing bill; for reasons of convenience in delivery, printing was soon shifted from Pittsburgh to Long Island. Who were all those people out there so eager to get rid of three dollars in a time of economic uncertainty? Wallace got his first lists from nurses' registries, teachers' associations, church groups, college catalogues, professional societies. The first takers spread the word by mouth. My own father, significantly a Pittsburgh lawyer, was spending a rare week or so sick in bed that historic Digest year of 1922 when my uncle, significantly a United Presbyterian minister, brought a copy of this new little magazine to entertain him; Dad became almost a charter subscriber. And so it went. By fall of 1922 with subscriptions up to 7,000, the Wallaces were ready literally to seek greener pastures.

Perhaps for sentimental reasons, the Wallaces were fond of Pleasantville—another euphonious name. When they saw a notice on the bulletin board of their Greenwich Village apartment for a garage apartment in the Westchester community, they acted with characteristic speed. They hopped a train at Grand Central and caught the owner of the estate on which the garage was located, a prominent New York public relations man named Pendleton Dudley who was just fiinishing a round of golf at the Nannahagen course. Intrigued by the young couple, Dudley, who was to become almost a Godfather to the little magazine in time, let them set their own rent—twenty-five dollars a month. The one room, bath and kitchen apartment soon proved too small for the enterprise, and the Wallaces added another ten dollars a month for use of a pony shed attached to the garage into which they crowded Wallace's desk and facilities for a couple of female clerical helpers.

In this rustic retreat, surrounded by hollyhocks and gold-turning maples and far from the madding crowd, began a life so concentrated upon one purpose—the production of the Reader's Digest—that it remains almost bare of any intriguing personal detail to this day. Both Wallaces worked virtually around the clock; for variety, they would sometimes escape for a few days or a week to a country inn, taking their work with them. Even Wallace's passion for sport was sublimated into work. He got what exercise he could from quickie activities like pitching horseshoes or playing catch with a guest behind the garage. Wallace developed a lifelong interest, as amply reflected in his magazine, in the kind of exercise that barely interrupts work such as isometrics or knee jerks at the desk; in his eighties, he is still taking steps at a run, working on the roadways and paths of his estate and chopping wood in such abundance that he would often call some Digester and offer to have the excess delivered to his home. Speaking of sports, he once told an associate, "I play every sport. But I do it all vicariously through my reading. I play baseball with the Yankees, I'm on the Olympic team, I follow golf. I get as much thrill out of that as if I took the time out to play." In later years when several thousand people were helping him put out the magazine he and Lila published alone from the pony shed, Wallace began taking time to go to sporting events, particularly baseball games as befit a former semi-pro second baseman. He often took Digesters along as company, and George Lawrence, a former Digest printing buyer, recalls one such event:

"One day I got a note from Mr. Wallace which said, 'George, would you like to go to a ball game with me?' I don't care much about baseball, but of course I turned it over and wrote on the back, 'Glad to. What arrangements should I make?' He replied by note, 'Contact Paul and Harry (two top executives),' and added, 'P.S. I'll bring the sandwiches.' Well, Paul and Harry and I went to the game in style—in a limousine with a chauffeur. We parked across the street from the stadium where it said no parking, went to the club and had a drink. When we got into our seats, here comes Mr. Wallace with beer and a bucket of sandwiches big enough to feed the whole crowd. I never did get to see much of that game, because I was too fascinated watching Wally drinking beer, eating a sandwich and keeping score all at the same time."

Besides sports, there was no time for children in the strict Wallace regimen. It seems a pity in retrospect since the editors of the world's most widely read family magazine denied themselves the humanizing experience thrust upon all parents everywhere—a daily confrontation with the imponderable and uncontrollable. In any case, the Digest has been called repeatedly and publicly their "baby," and many of Mrs. Wallace's flourishes have been put down to a matronly concern for Digesters as "the children she didn't have." The Wallace attitude toward Digester's children has been somewhat ambivalent. A number of babies, not always of Scottish descent, have turned up with Wallace in their names with no noticeable improving effect upon their parents' careers. After the early years when a few family dynasties seemed to be establishing themselves in the halls of Pleasantville, an official anti-nepotism policy was established, at least to the extent of avoiding having two generations on the premises at the same time. Once at a meeting where the subject under discussion was a paid leave of absence and expenses to allow younger editors and their wives to travel around and familiarize themselves with the United States, the father of several young children asked whether the company would pay for baby sitters. Wallace sighed, "Children can be a nuisance, can't they?" On the other hand, the Wallaces have been generous in providing scholarships abroad for Digesters' children, helping foot the bill for small-fry excursions to movies, parks and the like, and of course the Wallace charitable contributions to the general education of the young in America have been massive.

For some three years, DeWitt and Lila alone were the Reader's Digest Association—he with 52 percent of the stock and she with 48. By 1925, with circulation in the 16,000 range and paper overstuffing the pony shed, they bought land next to the Dudley estate and built a Normandy style house to serve as both home and office; they also hired their first full-time employee. Tall and sandy-haired, Ralph Ernest Henderson had been raised in the Burmese jungles where his parents were missionaries. He graduated from Harvard and returned to Burma to teach for four years before he showed up in Pleasantville looking for a job. So little known was the Digest then that people at the Pleasantville station couldn't tell Henderson where to find it. Once he did, though, the Wallaces took him on as business manager, an all-inclusive job that involved such things as carting some 16,000 wrappers, addressed in Pleasantville, over to the Long Island printer's in the Wallace roadster every month.

But even with Henderson's help, they couldn't long cope with the mounting circulation or house their enterprise under their own roof. The Wallaces began renting space in Pleasantville, first in the post office, then over one bank, then over another, and hiring local workers to take care of subscriptions. Their next significant employee was Rev. Harold A. Lynch, assistant rector of St. Mark's-in-the-Bouwerie in Manhattan, who decided that the life of the cloth was not for him and came aboard as business manager, thus freeing Henderson to begin the editorial career that culminated in his creating and running the company's most spectacular offshoot, Condensed Books. And still the circulation climbed. By 1929, it had reached more than 200,000 with gross revenues of $600,000. Not only did the people of Pleasantville now know where the Digest was—it was creeping like crab grass through all of the town's open office space—but the publishing world was finding out about it, too. The Wallaces were being dragged, kicking and screaming, out from their rural retreat and into the marketplace.

DeWitt Wallace has been described publicly by his wife as a worrier and a brooder, despite the determinedly cheerful tone of the articles he publishes. It's a well-known Scottish trait, perhaps intensified in his case by the vicissitudes of his early life and the rebuffs he faced in realizing his dream. At any rate, like the poker player he is, Wallace held his cards very close to his chest in those early years—and has tried to do so ever since. He had two consuming concerns: that other magazines, fearing competition, would suddenly deny him the material upon which the Digest fed; and that other publishers, having more money, would put him out of business with richly funded competition when they saw how good his idea was. Since the Digest took no advertising, the Wallaces were under no obligation to reveal their swelling circulation, and for quite some time editors whom Wallace approached for permission to reprint articles granted it freely, sensing no competition and feeling that an additional appearance would promote their own publication. To keep his profile even lower, Wallace declined to let his magazine be sold on newsstands. Then, along about 1929, the nightmares that occasionally interrupted the smooth flow of his dream threatened to come true.

Imitators began popping up on the newsstands. Knowing that this would at least confuse the public, Wallace finally entered an arrangement with S-M News, a distributing organization, to sell single copies of the magazine. Like the rest of the Digest story, this move was a matter of incredible serendipity. The vice president of S-M News was the publisher of *Popular Science Monthly,* a man named A. L. Cole, who in 1932 became business adviser to Wallace and in 1939 general manager of Reader's Digest—the veritable rock upon which the organization's vast business was ultimately built. To insure his source of material, Wallace began calling upon editors and offering to pay for the right to reprint their articles. This very nearly backfired. The fact that Wallace had that kind of money to throw around alerted editors to the Digest's success and, led by *Scribner's,* they began to rebel against granting reprint rights. Here again came one of those ever upward twists of the Wallace fate. Kenneth W. Payne of *North American Review,* a staunch believer in the Digest, argued his fellow editors back into line on the grounds that the magazine was stimulating mass reader interest in their quality material. In 1930, Payne became perhaps the first true editorial professional to start working in Pleasantville.

I have been credited rather gratifyingly by some of my colleagues with coining the phrase that "the Digest is put out by gifted amateurs." If that was true in my day, it was even truer in those early years. By 1936 when a reported circulation of 1,450,000 and a gross of $2,178,000 caused *Fortune* to take a lengthy look at the Digest, their reporter was open-mouthed: "Beyond doubt it is the most curious staff that ever put out a first rate magazine." In addition to Wallace, Henderson, Lynch (who had moved to editorial when another "business manager" could be found) and Payne, *Fortune* listed Charles W. (Fergie) Ferguson among the top editors. His background included a stint of circuit-riding preaching in Texas and Oklahoma after graduation from Southern Methodist University, authorship of a religious book, *The Confusion of Tongues,* and operation of something called Round Table Press, a religious book publishing firm. Only Managing Editor Payne, a third generation newspaperman who had studied at the Sorbonne and Wisconsin, worked for news syndicates and magazines, got high professional marks from *Fortune.* He got even higher marks from Wallace who, *Fortune* reported, was paying him $102,467 a year against $32,567 for Henderson and $20,750 for Lynch. Wallace paid himself $30,000 and his wife $12,000, but their dividends amounted to $145,000. Not bad in the midst of history's worst depression.

The *Fortune* piece was the first penetration of fortress Pleasantville. A caption on a picture of Wallace, taken from the doorway of his office, reads: "THIS CLOSE AND NO CLOSER MAY A CAMERA APPROACH . . . the person of DeWitt Wallace who for fourteen years has edited his Reader's Digest in a vacuum of 'no publicity.'" Undoubtedly by publishing such items as salary figures—still one of the Digest's most highly guarded secrets—*Fortune* only firmed up Wallace's determination to avoid the limelight. But the picture *Fortune* gave of the organization then rings true, and is astonishingly like one that might be given today, for by then DeWitt Wallace had stirred the final ingredient into the editorial stew that is still being served. Shaken by the abortive revolt of other editors, he had begun creating articles himself to make certain that the magazine would never run out of meat to digest.

Like Topsy—and nearly everything else at Reader's Digest—original material "just growed." It began inconspicuously in April 1930 with an unsigned item called "Music and Work" that was billed as "A special compilation for Reader's Digest." There followed a number of other anonymous articles, most of which seemed to be an editorial regurgitation of indigestible material from various sources. Finally, in February 1933, the Digest ran its first signed original, "Insanity—The Modern Menace" by Henry Morton Robinson who was later to turn his talents to writing best-selling novels. But the article that really put the Digest into the business of editorial creation was Wallace's own idea. After talking one day to a Pleasantville garageman about the horrors of traffic accidents, he commissioned J. C. Furnas to write "—And Sudden Death" in August 1935. The piece was a sensation: it was reprinted in newspapers around the country; within three months Pleasantville sent out 4 million additional copies to individuals and organizations clamoring for them; circulation took another upward leap. If there had ever been any doubt that the amateurs of Pleasantville could compete with the best in the business, "—And Sudden Death" put an end to it.

By 1938, the Digest had its first foreign edition going in Britain; by 1939, it had its own $1.5 million Georgian headquarters. The Wallaces themselves could look out over the world from their hilltop palace in Mt. Kisco, a few lateral miles but a nearly incredible vertical ascent from their Pleasantville pony shed. Though the giant they had spawned was just beginning its growth, all the essential parts were in place and recognizable today in larger outline—strong right arm of editorial technique, developing left arm of business expertise, arteries pumping cash, breathing lungs of dedicated personnel. If the Wallaces themselves, now entering their fifties, were firmly fixed as Digest characters, they in turn had implanted their little giant with a character of its own. Although we've heard the giant's voice, the only way to form a picture of what it's really like is, as in the case of the blind man "looking at" an elephant, to feel out the function of each of its parts.

V

Along Murderer's Row

Next to the words it speaks, the way in which it speaks them may be the most important element in the Digest's ascendancy. Norman Cousins, editor of *Saturday Review* and an astute observer of the American magazine scene, told me flatly: "The secret of the Reader's Digest is editing. I tell my audiences, often to their surprise especially in academic circles, that the Reader's Digest is the best edited magazine in America. Wally himself is the best pencil man, and the result of his technique is clarity—the words lift right off the page into your mind."

Whether the editing process of the Digest can be called a "secret" is questionable. It has been described publicly countless times, most recently by the Digest's new editor-in-chief, Edward T. Thompson, at an Overseas Press Club meeting. If there's any single point that seemed to emerge from Thompson's account of the Digest editorial methods, it was that the Digest must certainly be the most edited magazine in the world, whether it is the best or not.

As in every other aspect of the Digest story, the figures tend to amaze. To begin with, there's the amount of man (and woman) power—"more than ninety editors, researchers, art

editors, copy editors, etcetera," according to Thompson. As long
ago as 1955, another famous magazine editor, A. C. Spectorsky,
mused upon this unusual feature of the Digest in his book, *The
Exurbanites:* "From twice as many editors as the magazine contains articles in a given month, it is now approaching thrice as
many, and there seems no reason to believe that the end is in
sight." His prediction is steadily coming true, and with salaries
for these ninety ranging from, say, $10,000 to $50,000 and
above, the Digest is obviously making an enormous investment
in editorial people power that few, if any, competitors would
even think of matching.

In this connection an interesting contrast to my talk with
Norman Cousins was my last conversation with Arthur H.
(Red) Motley, the publishing genius who brought *Parade* from
third and last place in the Sunday supplement race to a position
so far in front that the others all dropped out. When I resigned
as assistant managing editor of *Parade* to go to the Digest in the
same year that Spectorsky noticed the swelling of the Pleasantville staff, Red Motley invited me to lunch, during the course of
which he told me that he would do the same thing in my place
since *Parade* wasn't about to pay that kind of money for an
editor and then added, "If I ever got hold of the Digest, the first
thing I'd do is cut down the editorial staff." Motley, listed in his
time as one of America's twelve top salesmen, was totally
business-oriented; Wallace, an even better businessman than
Motley, knew that his business thrived upon providing the
public with the editorial expertise they had come to expect.

In my job interview with Wallace, a week or so before the
Motley lunch, he threw me one of the usual Wallace curves.
"Tell me, what did you do in the office yesterday?" he asked. I
can't recall my answer specifically, but it would have been something like this: attended two editorial meetings, wrote at least
one story for the week's issue, read copy and wrote headlines on
a number of other stories, caught, if I was lucky, the 7 p.m. train
to my Connecticut home. "Well, I hope you won't be bored up
here," said Wallace with uncanny perception. For months, even
years, I *was* bored in Pleasantville. Dropping from the front

lines of journalism—I'd been with a daily newspaper before going to the weekly *Parade*—into the support troops at the Reader's Digest (at a much higher salary, remember) was something that really had to be experienced to be believed. Thompson estimates that each Digest article receives the benefit of a total of twenty to thirty man hours of attention, divided among some five different editors; by contrast, I had cut a whole book for *Parade* on the fifty-five-minute train ride from New York to Darien to meet a deadline. When I took my guilt feelings over being allowed, even pressed, to use so much time on a single job to my straw boss at the Digest, he soothed me with these words: "Here we take time to polish the diamond."

While time to dwell upon the choice of every word and punctuation point is one part of the Digest editorial "secret," another is the old idea that five or six heads are better than one. The editorial structure that adapts this notion to the polishing of articles is rigidly hierarchical, thus allowing for the input of many minds but preserving the right of the highest, and presumably most competent, mind to exercise intuitive, individual judgment. An article scheduled for publication in the Digest, whether it is an original or a reprint from another publication, rises from the hands of a first cutter to a more experienced or skilled check cutter to an issue editor to a managing editor for the issue to the editor-in-chief and/or DeWitt Wallace. Each of these editors is charged with putting the article into what he personally feels is the best length and shape for final publication in the Digest. In the process, anything from whole pages to phrases to single words are taken out or restored, according to the preference of the last—and highest—editor working on the piece. While, in general, the top two or three editors limit their blue pencilling to fairly subtle refinements, I once saw an article, whittled down by half a dozen editors from eight or ten large-sized magazine pages to four Digest pages, come back from the desk of DeWitt Wallace cut once more in half; he had simply dropped off the first two pages in which the author was indulging in some dazzling "writing" and started with the point the piece was trying to make. Since the offices in which these operations go forward tend to be lined up along one corridor for the sake of convenience, that part of the Pleasantville headquarters is understandably referred to, mostly by bleeding authors, as murderer's row.

Rather than a slaughter house, the area seems more like a distillery to me, an operation in which the verbal water is boiled off over a series of editorial flames until there's nothing left but stuff of the highest proof. If it all tastes much alike, as liquor ranging over the 100 mark does, it certainly delivers a kick. There are those who would argue that today's distillation isn't clearly five times stronger than the brew DeWitt Wallace cooked up alone in his pony shed, but any practiced palate can detect that the stuff is smoother. Incidentally, headlines, subheads and blurbs go through the same process, each editor writing his own and the editor above him accepting, revising or rejecting it.

Describing just how to turn the rough stone of an original article or a reprint into a Digest gem is so difficult that nobody's really tried to do it. There are no manuals on the art of digesting; newcomers to the Digest staff are not even given verbal instructions or told, for example, what to take out of an article or how to reorder its sequence to make it move more swiftly and logically or what other things might be done to improve it. You learn by observing what seasoned editors do, by your own trial and error. In the cutting phase of the Digest process, previous experience in writing or editing can often be more of a handicap than an asset. It's said, for instance that the late Thomas Heggen, author of *Mister Roberts,* could never get over the desire during his brief Digest sojourn to roll a sheet of paper into the typewriter and rewrite the story his way instead of pushing the author's own words around with a pencil. In doing so, he was flying in the face of the closest thing to an editorial dictum on cutting ever issued, a single sentence from the lips of former Executive Editor Payne: "When it is not necessary to change, it is necessary not to change." Perhaps because it has some of the density of holy writ, that sentence has been passed along for a generation. It does, however, describe the Digest intent, which was taken more seriously in the days when most of the magazine came from other sources against which it could easily be checked, to deliver to the readers as many of the actual words of the original as seem relevant.

Fortunately, the Digest cutting process is a perfectly logical operation that any literate person should be able to learn. The basis of it is deciding what point the article to be cut is trying to make and eliminating anything extraneous to this point. If, for example, an author uses three anecdotes to show that his subject is a generous man, it's obvious that the best of them is enough to get that point across (what isn't obvious is which is the best—a matter of personal preference, often of the last and highest editor working on the piece). Or take any one of a number of *Time* cover stories which may feature, say, the secretary of state with an interweaving of exposition about his policies and details of his personal life, such as what he eats for breakfast. If the Digest's intent in reprinting the piece is to inform its readers about policy, the cutter may drop the personal details entirely—or vice versa. Along the way, of course, the cutter straightens out awkward phrases, writes "bridges" for gaps he may leave in the story, expunges unnecessary adjectives, and so on. Where cutting departs from logic is in the finesse the editor brings to the job—harder to acquire than the basic skill but again mostly a matter of developing an eye and ear, by continuous exposure, for what has proved popular with the Digest's vast audience.

Curiously, the Digest has made no effort to have its original articles—now 70 to 80 percent of the magazine's content—written to length or even style. The theory seems to be that the author is so close to his subject that he can't take a properly detached view, can't "see the woods for the trees," to coin a phrase. So the idea is to let him write it all out and let the objective editor, laboring in the service of the reader, bring it into proper focus. Although perhaps raised to a higher power in Pleasantville than elsewhere, this is not an uncommon journalistic or literary practice, as witness Maxwell Perkins' editorial salvage job on the sprawling novels of Thomas Wolfe. An indication of its merit is the fact that even the first Digest cutter, often the same editor who recommended purchase or reprint of a piece he liked in the original, generally finds it hard to eliminate favorite passages and phrases. Hence, the need for check cutters, issue editors and others ever farther removed from the passion of creation and closer to the practical demands of the magazine.

The Digest's many-hands method of editing is more of a natural growth than an invention. When DeWitt Wallace first got help, he still went on looking over the articles and freely making changes in them; when his helpers got help, they followed suit. Until about 1960, no copy went out to the press without the initials "DW" on the covering work sheet (he still reads proofs); the initials of whoever was executive editor and managing editor were there, too. Since then, the mandatory DW has been replaced, first by HL, Hobart Lewis, and now, ETT, Ed Thompson, Wallace's successors in the top editorial chair. This practice has given rise to a curious situation. While a young editor at the Digest may work on only three or four articles for an issue, everybody from issue editor on up works on *all* articles; there are thus no clean desk editorial executives at the Digest. As one editor aptly put it, "Life at the Digest is a pie-eating contest in which the prize is more pie to eat." (And digest, I might add.)

The people who eat this pie seem to have been picked over the years in the same haphazard fashion that brought a missionary, an Episcopalian rector and a Texas circuit rider into the fold as Wallace's first assistants. Until very recently at least, the one common denominator was that they, and usually their wives, had to pass inspection from Wallace who used the same sort of gut judgment on people as he did on articles. ("I've never met a representative of Wallace who wasn't a credit to him," Cousins told me.) In the 30's when Wallace needed instant help to cope with his rapidly growing enterprise, he turned to the editors whom he had come to know through negotiating for their material. From *North American Review* came Kenneth W. Payne; from *American* came Merle Crowell; from *Scribner's* came Alfred S. (Fritz) Dashiell; from *American Mercury* came Paul Palmer and later Eugene Lyons; from *Liberty* came Fulton Oursler. Though Wallace continued this practice in later years, picking up people like George Eggleston from the old *Life*, Ben Hibbs from *Saturday Evening Post*, William A. H. Birnie from *Women's Home Companion*, he was meanwhile filling in the lower ranks from secretaries and researchers who had somehow persuaded him to let them try their hands at editing, from promising college graduates who were looking for something to do, from younger professionals like myself who were lured to Pleasantville by tales of editorial prestige and pay. Thus the second generation of editors over whom Wallace presided were largely home grown. Hobart Lewis, who was to become editor-in-chief, president and chairman, came as a young man from a Philadelphia advertising agency; Executive Editors Harry H. Harper, Jr., and Walter B. Mahony, Jr., arrived right out of Yale and Amherst respectively. And so it goes even unto the third generation. Two of the three managing editors, as this is written, Roy A. Herbert and Fulton Oursler, Jr., are second generation Digesters; Peter C. Canning, one of the assistant managing editors, hopped aboard from Harvard; Mary Louise Allin, another assistant managing editor and so far the highest-reaching female in Digest history, sprang from research out of Wellesley; Thompson himself was one of the young professionals, coming from *Fortune* and trailing an impressive journalistic legacy from his father, Edward K. Thompson, once editor of *Life* and now of *The Smithsonian*.

Under Lewis, Harper and Mahony, who knew no other method of operation, Digest editing took on some of the aspects of a priestly rite. Woe unto him who profaned it by making it look easy! One friend of mine, a fast and facile young man, couldn't for the life of him sweat more than two hours over the first cutting job that Thompson rates at ten hours. When our then straw boss, Audrey Dade, another home-grown product now retired, gave him an assignment, he'd proudly take it back the same morning, expecting a pat on the head. Instead, he'd get a reprimand for what obviously must be sloppy work. My friend

solved the problem easily; when Audrey gave him an article to
cut, he'd toss it on his desk and let it sit for twenty-four to
thirty-six hours, then cut it in two hours. His work improved so
miraculously in Audrey's eyes that she rated him one of the best
on the staff. Another young man who tumbled more quickly
than most to the awe in which meticulous copy editing was held
took to xeroxing every article he was given; on one copy he'd
work away messily and happily with pencil, eraser, shears, glue
and then he'd transfer his final editing to the clean copy in the
neat, bold strokes of a pen. Like a man who does crossword
puzzles with a pen, he was held to be a whizz, and his rise has
been truly spectacular. The rewards for skill, or at least effort,
in this endeavor are so tangible that they induce a kind of palsy
in the hand that holds the pencil—what in the world can a
person be doing for those ten or twelve alloted hours if he
doesn't make a lot of marks? (Payne might have understood,
but he's long gone.) This sort of mandatory editing above the
level of removing the obviously excess verbiage can be puzzling
to the altar boys studying the priests to learn their secrets, if any.
One frustrated and earnest junior finally worked up the nerve
to approach a very senior editor noted for trampling all over
copy that had already gone through three or four buffings by
experienced and highly paid people and ask why he did it. The
answer was ridiculously simple. "That's the way I get my kicks,"
he said. But even though it's as humanly imperfect as nearly
everything else in life, the Digest system is likely to go on being
held sacred for one very good reason: it works. Indeed, nearly
everything at the Digest has taken on the sacred aura bestowed
by success—you just don't fool around with your game when
you're ahead.

However highly prized, cutting and shaping articles may be
the smallest part, both in time consumed and talent demanded,
of the Digest editorial "secret." More important in the long run
is finding the right material in the first place. Here again, figures
astound. According to Thompson, Digest editors cover some 550
periodicals, newspapers, weeklies, magazines and supplements,
including thirty from foreign countries. The book department

reviews 1,500 U.S. books and 600 to 800 from abroad to find the baker's dozen of supplements it needs every year. The excerpt editors receive and read 600,000 pieces of mail a year, and the editor in charge of first-person articles gets 30,000 manuscripts in the same period. On top of that, the magazine commissions and buys 300 original articles annually for the United States edition, even more for its editions abroad. (At all times, there is an inventory of some 250 articles deemed usable but not yet published—at a conservative estimate of $4,000 per article for purchase and expenses, this amounts to a million dollars worth of fat waiting to be trimmed.) Winnowing through all this to come up with the thirty or so best articles for any given month requires another skill difficult to define precisely—editorial judgment.

Selection of material is submitted to somewhat the same distilling process as cutting. Editors are assigned to cover a certain number of magazines and/or books, to work with writers in developing original material. Recommendations are screened through a check reader or a very senior editor assigned to make assignments and purchase articles. Material that filters through this screen lands on the desk of the issue editor—a responsibility rotated among some five top editors so that each produces about two issues a year. The issue editor is obviously faced with an embarrassment of riches, a great many more usable articles than he can squeeze into 160 or so editorial pages. This, however, allows him a wide option up to the last minute of deadline in choosing material he thinks will make the liveliest possible magazine. While obviously providing the magazine with great flexibility, this system tends to baffle and frustrate authors, agents, and other publications from whom the Digest acquires materials, not to mention some editors on the staff as well. Rotated mostly among off-duty issue editors, the posts of assignment editor and purchasing editor for original articles are usually held by different persons with the result that the man who had faith in an assignment may not be on deck to exhibit the same kind of faith in the article when it comes up for purchase. And even if an article is bought or arrangements have been made to reprint it from another source, no issue editor may choose to run it, thus dashing a great many high expectations.

Once again, there is no manual defining the ingredients of a good Digest article. As in cutting, you learn by a process of absorption, of osmosis; through reading hundreds of Digest articles a month, the right characteristics just seep into your head. The old journalistic saws about looking for what appeals to the "Kansas City milkman" or "the little old lady in Dubuque" are not heard in the halls of Pleasantville. Efforts to articulate what makes a good Digest article have been vague at best. Wallace himself gave it a try in the early days when he announced that the magazine should contain "articles of lasting interest which will appeal to a large audience, articles that come within the range of interests, experience, and conversation of the average person." Yes—but what are they? Smart Digesters have learned to answer that question for themselves more by Wallace watching than Wallace listening.

Stories of Wallace in action as an editor abound, and they are far more instructive than any amount of theorizing. Paul Palmer, coming from a background of newspapering and the *American Mercury*, got one of his early lessons in Digest editing when he tried to persuade Wallace to run a piece rather specifically detailing techniques by which a person could become a better salesman. "Just think," he argued, "there are three million salesman in the United States." Turning it down, Wallace responded drily, "That's not enough." Wallace simply doesn't believe in firing at specific targets. When the Digest began taking advertising in the mid-50's and was forced to release details of its circulation, the sharpies on Madison Avenue claimed that the magazine was reaching an "older" audience. This news worried the Digest business people since it could be used effectively by rival salesmen in the scramble for ads. During this period, a number of us young editors were having lunch with Wallace, and I asked him, "What are your plans for making the magazine appeal more to a younger audience?" He simply pointed around the table at each of us and said, "You."

Indeed, the only specific instruction given a beginning Digest editor about picking material is, "Recommend what you like." That's the Wallace way. "I simply hunt for things that interest me, and if they do, I print them," he told *Time*. But then Wallace is almost universally hailed as an editorial genius. There is also a fair amount of agreement as to the nature of his genius. The late novelist Louis Bromfield put it somewhat unkindly, considering the fact that he was eating a lot of Wallace bread in those days, when he told *Time* that Wallace's "strictly average" mind "completely reflects the mentality of his readers." A veteran Digest editor with wide experience in other publications agrees in gentler terms. "Most publications have a formula," he says, "but the Digest has no formula. The only formula is Wallace; he is the average American par excellence." In a rather snide *New Yorker* profile that became a book, "Little Wonder, or The Reader's Digest and How it Grew," John Bainbridge played around with a refinement on this theme:

"He (Wallace) has no delusions of grandeur. He has, if anything, delusions of smallness. To Wallace, most things, including himself, seem smaller than they actually are. . . . Wallace's small-scale view of life is a priceless asset. It has made him a multi-millionaire and gained him recognition as a genius. 'He's a genius all right, and a greater genius than Hearst,' an old and worldly friend of his once said. 'He has a more perfect understanding of the herd mind. Wallace looks at the universe constantly through the wrong end of the telescope, and so does the herd. He sees everything neat and tidy, and so do they. He knows what they want, and he lets them have it.' "

A couple of vivid glimpses of Wallace in action tend to confirm this insight. One comes from *The Middle Man; the Adventures of a Literary Agent* by Paul R. Reynolds. Reynolds, representing a writer and lecturer, Peter W. Rainier, who served as a major in the British Eighth Army during the battle of El Alamein, introduced his client to Wallace in the Ritz Bar one late afternoon shortly after the battle had been fought. Wallace asked the major if anything unexpected had happened to contribute to the British victory. Here's how it went after that in Reynolds' own words:

"As a major in charge of water supply he was accustomed to lay his water pipes from the Mediterranean Sea inland a mile or more. As the pipes always had leaky joints, he would pump salt water into the pipes, fix up the leaky joints, and then drain out the salt water and pump in fresh water. Just before the battle of El Alamein the Nazis overran the line of Rainier's pipes. The next day some two hundred German soldiers surrendered. Rainier interviewed some of the prisoners and found that they were hysterical with thirst; they had been shooting holes in his pipe and drinking salt water.

"Wallace said, 'A drink that made history. Paul, could I speak to you for a minute outside?'

"We left Rainier and went into the corridor, I wondering what was to come next. Wallace started right off. 'Paul, how much do you want for a drink that made history,'

" 'What about two thousand dollars?' I said.

" 'Now, Paul,' said Wallace, 'the Digest does not want to bargain, the Digest wants to be more generous than any other magazine, but don't you think eighteen hundred dollars would be fair?'

"I agreed to $1800.

"The Digest published Rainier's piece as their lead article in their January 1944 issue under Wallace's title, 'A Drink That Made History.' The title was magnificent journalism; according to Rainier the title was barely 2 per cent true.

"Prior to the meeting with Wallace I had talked with Rainier at length trying to get good ideas for articles. I had also taken him to editors of other magazines to see if they could draw Rainier out and find suitable subjects. Neither I nor any other editor had gotten this story out of Rainier. It was Wallace's simplicity and directness of thought, his willingness to ask what would seem to most people an impossible question that drew this superb article from Rainier."

Another fascinating look at this Wallace attribute comes from the pages of an uncompleted autobiography, "Just Lucky, I Guess," by Digest Senior Editor Dennis McEvoy. Among other chores for the magazine, McEvoy, equipped with long experience as a student and correspondent in prewar Japan, established the Digest's Japanese edition during the occupation. He writes:

"He (Wallace) had invited me to sit in at a small private luncheon in a little room just off the main Reader's Digest cafeteria, where writers and editors often got together over a meal to talk out ideas for possible articles. It was a most impressive gathering: besides several of our top editors, there was at least one general with wide experience in Asia, several high ranking U.S. government officials, and a professor who was a world famous expert on Japanese and Chinese affairs. The talk was on an extremely high level: geopolitics, estimates of decisions which chiefs of state might or might not make, suggestions on American political and military global strategy, and the like.

"Mr. Wallace, who is normally very quiet anyway, was quieter than usual this day, and I, being the most junior guest present by a good many years, kept my mouth shut during the entire conversation. I confess I was dazzled by the earth-shaking concepts which were being so freely and authoritatively tossed about by the eminent specialists. Suddenly, Mr. Wallace spoke up. The entire table fell silent. To my surprise, it was a question addressed to me:

" 'Dennis, tell me, is it true that the babies in Japan don't cry?'

"I was stunned, and so was the assembled gathering. The look on their faces was memorable. 'Well, come to think of it,' I stammered, 'I don't remember hearing them cry very often, if at all.'

" 'Why?'

" 'Possibly because they are breast fed for longer than Western babies. Or because when they are carried, they are strapped to the backs of their mothers or older sisters. I've seen teenage girls playing softball, and running bases, their younger sisters or brothers tied to them inside their kimonos. It may give babies an additional sense of security. Also, every time a Japanese child opens its mouth to cry, something is pushed into it—a pacifier, a bosom, or a chocolate. But, Wally, these are quick, inadequate answers. If I could study the matter more, I could give you a fuller report.'

" 'I wish you would,' he said. 'I think it might make a good article.'

"The talk of geopolitics and global strategies gradually resumed, but it simply limped along. The participants had not quite fully recovered from their shock. Mr. Wallace listened to them attentively, as usual, and spoke up again after coffee, to remind our guests that there was just time to catch the 1:25 train to New York. No one needed to be told where geopolitics stood on Mr. Wallace's list of priorities—or that an article on the subject was not likely to appear in an early issue."

Genius like Wallace's is unfortunately wholly individual. By observing its results, other intelligent people can approximate it, but they can't possess it. With Wallace able to put things in and out of the magazine at will, the selection of material and assignment of articles has inevitably been a guessing game for even the most seasoned Digest hands. Dorio Mutti, a brilliant young Italian who came to the United States to go to college and stayed on to work at the Digest for a number of years, had an unusual, outsider's look at the operation. "Everybody tries to guess what Wally will like or won't, but he's such a big puzzle nobody can figure it out," Dorio told me. "Younger editors think of a typical Digest story and if it isn't 'a typical Digest story' it shouldn't run. Wally, despite his age, is more with the times than they are." In illustration, Dorio reminded me of an article with which we were both involved in the late 60's.

At that time I was in charge of the editorial material being developed for our foreign editions. Dorio recommended that an article in *Look* entitled "The Contraceptive Society"—a report on the widespread use of contraception in Sweden—be used in the United States edition and, if not, certainly in our foreign editions. It was quickly rejected for domestic use, and I could see why. The author stated in no uncertain terms and without any moral tongue-clucking that one result of this development was that Swedish girls were far freer with their favors than their sisters elsewhere. Because we were in such desperate need of material with local appeal to readers abroad, I passed it along to Editor-in-Chief Hobart Lewis with a rather weak seconding vote. Back it came with a stern admonition to the effect that such a point of view had no place in the Reader's Digest. Meanwhile, DeWitt Wallace, then nearing eighty, came across the article quite independently of all of us, and sent it down from his tower in High Winds with instructions to print it. I will say that Lewis had the graciousness to phone me and remark, "Just shows you how wrong you can be."

If, as Cousins says, "the secret of the Reader's Digest's success is editing," it is as safe as if it were written in code and locked away in the vaults of Fort Knox. Even those who have spent a lifetime trying to understand it end up confessing that they're still guessing. If you can figure out what 100 million people want to read and how much of it they'll tolerate, you win; if you can't, you lose.

VI

The Bland Leading
the Bland

Not everybody loves the Reader's Digest. With some 360 articles
going out every year to so many millions of people around the
world, the magazine is bound to offend someone, somewhere,
virtually all the time. A while back five readers who refuse
to concede the possibility that man evolved from the lower
primates cancelled their subscriptions when the Digest ran a
condensation of *The Naked Ape*. More recently, a hundred or
so citizens of Orfordville, Wisconsin, who apparently still tell
children about the stork, raised hell with their school board
because a biology teacher was using some of the famous Joe
articles in class, namely, "I Am Joe's Prostate," "I Am Jane's
Breast," and "I Am Joe's Man Gland." Reaction might have been
worse if the magazine had not resisted one editor's whimsical
suggestion that the last of these be titled "Gland of Hope and
Glory." But these are, indeed, teapot-sized tempests. Over the
years, the real critical storms have blown up over articles inspired by the magazine's unabashed conservatism about nearly
everything except medicine, exercise and sex.

Perhaps the loudest recent clap of critical thunder followed
the publication in October and November 1971 of two articles

by Roving Editor Clarence W. Hall that attacked the World Council of Churches. How provocative these articles were can be guessed from the titles and blurbs alone: in October, "Must Our Churches Finance Revolution?"—"Preaching the gospel of racial justice, the World Council of Churches is using church power and church funds to back insurrection in the United States and Africa. Is this what Christ taught?" and in November, "Which Way the World Council of Churches?"—"Has this 'ecclesiastical United Nations' become just another platform from which communism seeks to flay the free world?" In the first article, Hall chided the WCC for verbal encouragement and financial support of African groups which he said were engaged in violent guerilla activities and, in some cases, "avowedly communist," and he also took exception to a WCC drive to raise funds "in support of American draft-dodgers and deserters in Canada and Sweden." In the second article, Hall viewed with alarm the admission of the "Soviet-approved Russian, Rumanian, Bulgarian and Polish Orthodox churches" into WCC membership, claiming their presence dampened WCC criticism of life behind the iron curtain while provoking diatribes against social and economic systems in the free world.

Among those aroused by Hall's articles was Donald R. Campion, editor-in-chief of *America,* the Jesuit magazine, whose editorial said in part: "Dr. Eugene L. Smith, executive secretary of the New York office of the WCC and the most Christian and most gentle of Christian gentlemen, made it clear—in responding to the broadsides in the Digest—that honorable men and women can be found on both sides of debate on actions taken by the WCC. What is regrettable, Dr. Smith went on to say, is not that the Digest should oppose WCC action, 'but that its disagreement is expressed with unsubstantiated charges, misstatements of fact, distorted reporting, quotation of statements out of context. . . .' After reading the Digest's articles, my own guess would be—even if I didn't know so from other sources—that the WCC must indeed be doing something right."

More upset with apparent good reason was the *Christian*

Century, a nondenominational Protestant journal. Hall had quoted two of its contributors, Martin E. Marty and Harold E. Fey, in support of his thesis. In his own column, Marty said, "When the Reader's Digest lifts material from other journals it has been—so far as I know—expensively meticulous in checking the accuracy of the most trivial quotations. However, it evidently trusts its own roving editors—a misplaced trust, I am beginning to believe—so the Digest not only forgoes checking on the accuracy of its editorial efforts, but permits distortion and quotation out of context as well. In a November 1971 article aimed at the Digest's 19 jillion readers, an eight line quotation from me contains two patent mistakes—to say nothing of nontrivial misuse of materials." In two subsequent editorials, the *Christian Century* charged that the Digest not only "garbled" Fey's comments, too, but misidentified Roving Editor Hall as a former executive editor of *Christian Century* itself when, in fact, "Hall *was* executive editor of the then right wing *Christian Herald* in the 1950's." In one of its editorials, the *Christian Century* said:

"Over the years the Reader's Digest—that delightful mishmash of family corn, cultural mediocrity and political reaction which so many of us have ceased to read— has lent its pages to some pretty raw know-nothing attacks on religious leaders. In particular, the Digest has lit into persons and movements directed toward religious involvement in social change. Such involvement has been portrayed as heretical Christianity and pink politics. (Stanley High's 'pink fringe of Methodism' article of two decades ago was a notably mean and McCarthyist example of this genre.)

"It is no easy matter to undo the mischief done by such attacks. The Reader's Digest, with over 17 million subscribers, has the largest circulation of any magazine in America—nearly 500 times the circulation of this mighty (mitey?) journal. Moreover, the Digest can indulge in reckless barrages from a redoubtable format which admits no letters-to-the-editor or reader's responses: apparently, readers can send in jokes and heartwarming anecdotes, but not criticism."

The *Christian Century* was right about undoing the mischief, if mischief it was. In the wake of the WCC affair, the *Texas Methodist*, a weekly published in Dallas, polled readers on this question: when there's disagreement over the facts of a given situation, whom do you trust—church leaders or a secular magazine such as the Reader's Digest? Forty-five percent of those replying said they would trust the Reader's Digest more than their church leaders; 32 percent voted for church leadership; 23 percent were undecided. So, although the Digest did bow to criticism to the extent of printing an article in reply, "Should Churches Play it Safe?" by J. Irwin Miller in April 1972, this particular storm did little more than reassure the people of Pleasantville once more that their own slogan, "people have faith in Reader's Digest," is true.

There was a similar and, to Pleasantville, equally heartening response when controversy broke out over the magazine's "Fly This Flag Proudly" campaign, launched in the February 1969 issue. Coming as it did in that troubled time of civil rights disturbances and the war in Vietnam, the Digest's gesture in putting detachable flag decals in its 18,441,369 magazines was read as symbolic support for the Nixon administration and the forces of "law and order" by a number of people. Baseball player Jackie Robinson, then board chairman of Freedom National Bank in Harlem, was quoted by Jon Nordheimer in the *New York Times* as saying, "When I see a car with a flag pasted on it, I figure the guy behind the wheel isn't my friend." Robinson went on to explain that the flag had become for him and others, like Charles Morgan, Southern director for American Civil Liberties Union, a manifestation of opposition to social progress for minorities or support for the Vietnam war. DeWitt Wallace expressed himself as being "amazed" that such political significance was attached to the flag and added, "The display of the flag is one way to show that we know what a privilege it is to be an American. Don't you get a thrill when you see the flag flying outside a post office, a factory, or an office building? I do."

The Wallace instinct was, as usual, working well. In a followup study on the flag, the Digest learned that 78 percent of its readers removed the decal—almost twice the previous record set by a first-aid booklet—and half of those put it to use. Some 50 million more decals were ordered by various organizations and individuals. At least 10 million cars were found to be bearing little flags and another 5 million decals were pasted to the doors and windows of homes. There were either a lot of hard-nosed "patriots" out there, or, more probably, a great number of people as innocent as Wallace himself of the fact that certain forces were using the flag as symbol of reaction.

With support like this from readers, it's no wonder that the giant of Pleasantville generally just ignores the Lilliputian arrows its critics fire. The magazine got used to these light stings during World War II when, with Max Eastman's article on "We Must Face the Facts About Russia," Reader's Digest opened the cold war in July 1943, long before Churchill did. Russia was then our noble ally, painted in glowing colors by people like ex-Ambassador Joseph E. Davies, whose book and film, *Mission to Moscow,* were widely popular; hence, liberal voices berated the Digest for its stand. Another article in the same year by Republican Senator Hugh A. Butler of Nebraska whipped up an even greater storm that for a while threatened one of the Digest's most important and controversial editorial practices, the so-called "planting" of articles written to Pleasantville specifications in other magazines and then "reprinting" them.

The Butler article, reporting on a trip to twenty Latin American countries, charged that much of the $6 million being spent there to achieve hemispheric solidarity was being wasted. It so angered the Roosevelt Administration that Vice President Henry A. Wallace publicly apologized to the United States' good neighbors to the south. Democratic Senator Joseph Guffey of Pennsylvania took to the senate floor to denounce the Digest and to suggest that the Digest practice of signing contracts for exclusive use of material from other publications might be a conspiracy in constraint of trade. The senator's remarks were followed by a series of articles in the now defunct liberal newspaper, *PM*, making many of the same charges.

As in the late 20's when other magazines first learned that Wallace was making piles of money, a few now began to revolt against Pleasantville practices. One of these was the *New Republic* which set forth its complaints on March 6, 1944. After pointing out that, by farming out articles of its own origination to other magazines, the Digest was thereby ignoring the *other* writing in those magazines, the *New Republic* said:

"When it began 20 years ago, it did in fact reprint most of the best writing from current American periodicals, and it did so without any predetermined editorial policy of its own. Today it has such a policy, and it rejects a substantial amount of good writing in the magazines which does not conform to its specialized political and social views. That is one reason, and perhaps the chief reason, why the Digest finds it necessary to write articles and give them away in order to have them reprinted. And that is why the New Republic, which was closely associated with the Digest in its earliest days, and accepted a contractual relationship when it was first offered, will no longer use material which originates in the Digest office and is intended for eventual reprint there."

It's to be imagined that exposure in *New Republic* was no great loss to the Reader's Digest; there were still plenty of other publications willing to receive Digest articles. In any case, the Pleasantville motives for using the system had little to do with "specialized political and social views." DeWitt Wallace seems to have originated planting for two reasons: as a way of repaying the smaller magazines whose material he had freely used in the past, and as a way of maintaining the concept of a reprint magazine when he could no longer find enough articles of the quality (not the point of view) he needed elsewhere. The Digest's high pay was drawing the best professional magazine writers out of the market, and Wallace felt that, by letting their bylines and material appear first in a smaller magazine, he would strengthen rather than weaken other publications. Even *New Republic* admitted that no editor was obliged to print an article offered by the Digest and that 80 or 90 percent of them were non-political. As for contracts for reprint rights, Digest money kept many small magazines afloat. Eugene Lyons, editor of *American Mercury* before he went to the Digest, told me that Digest subsidies made all the difference for the *Mercury* which was "always on the ragged edge—even in glorious Mencken days it couldn't make a living."

Whatever the motives, the planting system did play a part in a much more important rupture of relations about the same time as the *New Republic* break. It was with *The New Yorker*, and it cost the Digest not only one of its major sources but also brought upon its head perhaps the worst storm of bad publicity in its half-century history. A man who should know told me that Harold Ross of *The New Yorker*, an editor to match Wallace in determination and eccentricity, decreed the break on two matters of principle: 1) that an article, as printed in *The New Yorker*, was the best possible product as to style and length and shouldn't be altered; and 2) that the Digest program of contracts and placement of articles in other magazines was theoretically dangerous in that a few people in Pleasantville could control what a wide spectrum of American magazines had to say. My informant admitted that the specter of Pleasantville control of American magazine publishing has not materialized—no magazine is obliged to use any article the Digest offers—but he did say that *The New Yorker* still holds to the Ross principles, particularly the first.

That the Digest editorial treatment of articles may have been the most serious offense in Ross's mind is confirmed by a story passed down by the late Ike Shuman who was at the time *The New Yorker*'s executive editor, or what was called Ross's "Jesus." As such, Shuman was the liaison between Ross and Wallace. In the late 30's, the Digest was picking up a great deal of material from *The New Yorker*, much to the liking of *The New Yorker* writers who often found Digest payments for reprinting higher than their original fee. This, together with condensation of what he thought to be perfect prose, galled the proud Ross. Shuman at the time was having lunch every Tuesday at the Ritz with Wallace, and on one such occasion, Wallace told him, "I greatly admire *The New Yorker,* but I've never met Harold Ross." Shuman promised to bring his editor along the next Tuesday. But it wasn't easy. Ross fussed, fumed, swore, asserted that he was too busy to have lunch. In the end, though, he went. Wallace was already at the table. When Shuman led Ross over to make introductions, *The New Yorker* editor's first words were: "Is the stuff in my magazine good enough for you?"

Not content with declining further republication by the Digest, Ross published a long profile on the magazine by John Bainbridge, "Little Wonder, or The Reader's Digest and How It Grew." A smoothly written, rather snide look at the Wallaces and their magazine—"The quality of optimism in the Reader's Digest is not strained. It drips from every issue as sweetly as syrup from a maple tree."—Bainbridge's book ripped into the placement system with the curious story of a magazine called *Living Age,* a story more recently confirmed by John Tebbel in *The American Magazine: A Compact History. Living Age* was bought in 1938 by Joseph Hilton Smyth, Walter Grey Matheson and Irvine Harvey Williams with $15,000 contributed by a Japanese diplomat who also supplied $2,500 a month to keep it going. According to their guilty pleas in court in September 1942, Smyth and his friends ran the magazine for the Japanese government between June 1938 and December 1941, taking in some $150,000. Bainbridge reported that, in the same period, the Digest reprinted thirteen articles from *Living Age,* most of them plants, including one in May 1940 entitled "How Smart Are the Japanese?" The evidence would suggest an answer: smarter than Pleasantville at that point.

W. A. Swanberg, whose biographies of Hearst, Pulitzer and Luce have qualified him as a leading critic of American journalism, took a swing at the Digest planting system in *Luce and His Empire.* Swanberg drew a number of parallels between the Time, Inc., publications and the Digest—both put out by sons of Presbyterian ministers who inherited missionary zeal, both simplistic by reason of catering to "the intellectual laziness of people seeking quick and easy wisdom," both showing "hostility toward the New Deal, hatred of Communism and some flirtation with Facism." Then he wrote: "Both magazines were marred by factual errors, exaggerations and inventions which did not trouble the proprietors because they were interested in successful journalism and politico-moral messages rather than mere information. Both were not above deception. Time in purporting to be a newsmagazine, RD in claiming to be a digest of other magazines when in fact it quietly 'planted' pieces of its own manufacture in other publications in order to go through the rigamarole of buying them back and 'digesting' them."

The furor over planting articles has largely subsided, probably owing to the fact that in recent year the Digest has been running more acknowledged originals, particularly in the areas of politics and economics. Still, as Tebbel writes, "There continues to be apprehension in many quarters about the Digest, and its satellite empire of record clubs, condensed book clubs, record distribution services, and other agglomerate assets. The power of a magazine whose total circulation is 18,000,000 is obviously great. Moreover, the Digest's international editions circulate in many languages all over the globe, spreading whatever word the magazine wants to spread. Some believe it is spreading the word of the CIA. Others regard it as a high-level propaganda agent for ultraconservative political groups. The Digest itself continues to insist it is not selling anything except entertainment and information.

"Unquestionably, however, it has a political point of view, and a social one as well, and both are reflected in what the various editions of the Digest print. Since each international edition has its own editors, these viewpoints can be pinpointed toward specific nations and areas of the world. In sum, the fear of most critics is that a great deal of power has been placed in the hands of a tiny group of men, who are free to use it in any way they wish."

Whether the "tiny group of men" in Pleasantville has the kind of power Tebbel suggests is open to question for a curious reason. The thunder from the right within the pages of the Digest seems to fall on deaf ears. While, for example, the Digest goes on reaching into more and more American homes, Democrats, who receive scant notice from the magazine, continue getting elected in disproportionate numbers. Perhaps this is because readers either skip or fail to take to heart the more ponderous political and economic preaching from the Pleasantville pulpit. Digest polls give highest readership popularity ratings to departments, jokes, corking good dramatic tales, nostalgic tear jerkers, how-to-do-it pieces on health, wealth, marriage, local civic affairs. A writer on political subjects conceded to me that he got more results from books that sold a few thousand copies than he did from a Digest article. "The influence of the Digest politically is nil," he claimed. One reason for this, in his view, is that "politically Wallace was often beyond his depth—he reacted to the surface which, of course, made him a good Digest editor" but kept him from being taken seriously by the real movers and shakers in political affairs.

Specifically, however, the Digest can have a powerful political effect. One case was the February 1971 article by Washington Editor William Schulz called "The Mob's Grip on New Jersey." The villain in this piece was, as it happened, a Republican, State Senator Frank (Hap) Farley of Atlantic City who was charged with being boss of one of the nation's most corrupt political machines. His Democrat opponent, Dr. Joseph McGahn, an obstetrician, mailed out 50,000 reprints of the Schulz article in the week before election and was swept into office with 60 percent of the vote. Schulz, understandably, likes to cite this case as proof of Digest effectiveness and denial of Republican bias.

Since Schulz's Washington office generates much of the Digest's current political material, his view of the magazine's stance is important. While he admits to a conservative bent, he states flatly that there is "no policy of laying off Republicans," that, in fact, he receives no specific political instructions from Pleasantville. He regards Digest reporting of the political scene as fairly close to down the middle. "If I were an idealogue of the Right or the Left," Schulz says, "I would be unhappy in this job." Still, the fact seems to be that Schulz and his colleagues are, by nature and/or conviction, somewhat right of the center: employing such people is the Wallace way of achieving political purity without the need for specific orders. My own sponsor for a job at the Digest went out of his way to stress to Wallace that I was—it was true, then—a Taft Republican, and I underwent considerable not-so-subtle questioning from the great man to confirm this fact. In this connection, a statement former Chairman Lewis made to a BBC-TV reporting team is illuminating:

"Our publisher and founder, DeWitt Wallace, has a consistent philosophy of life and philosophy of magazine publishing. He has expressed it in small meetings and constantly in the magazine. Each one of us who has been here over the years has acquired that outlook on life, agrees with it enthusiastically and communicates that in memoranda and conversation and in just the articles we accept and those we reject, even in passages in articles we accept or reject for reasons which don't fit into our basic philosophy. So that anyone with any sensitivity or intelligence who is around here for a few years really knows what we're about and becomes part of it."

The Wallace philosophy, of course, goes beyond political conservatism and free enterprise economics. Lewis articulated it this way: "Our basic thrust is our belief that people want to be better each day than they were the day before. It's a Puritan philosophy if you like, and we believe in the work ethic and the perfectibility of man, and we appeal to the individual in his better nature not his worst nature. And our great success comes from the fact that we do trust people's instincts to want to improve themselves. On every page of the magazine you will find something in there which will help you to be a better person."

This belief in perfectibility is the foundation of the Digest's positive thinking, its sunny optimism, which ironically has caused more continuing critical problems for the magazine than any number of controversial political articles. The Digest quite frankly avoids articles about problems which may have a number of conflicting solutions or no solutions at all; it tends to tackle a subject only when, in a few often oversimplified pages, it can leave the reader with the feeling that something definite and good will come out of it all. For example. I can remember being anguished that the Digest would do nothing about the interesting death of God debate, would not even pick up a well-done *Time* cover essay outlining the various points of view on the situation, an essay that I had recommended. Ultimately, the matter was handled by getting an article out of the late Harry Emerson Fosdick, then a very old and sweet divine, who reaffirmed the faith, to which I personally was able to contribute only a kind of classic Digest title, "Whose God Is Dead?" The Digest is even positive about being negative. As Assistant Managing Editor John M. Allen told BBC, "If we're writing about cholesterol, for instance, we want to go in and find out if cholesterol is good or bad and say that. There's nothing worse than the kind of article that leaves you up in the air." The result, according to BBC's own commentary on what it learned in Pleasantville, is that "people read it comfortable in the knowledge that when it drops through the letter box, it will be pretty much like last month's and with no nasty surprises about the world. . . . For all its authority and impressive range of subjects, Reader's Digest presents what seems only a partial view of the world, a view which sees a solution for every problem, which sees heroism rather than misery in every disaster."

Variations of this BBC reaction echo through the classrooms of high schools and colleges throughout America, and perhaps the world as well, where the Digest is often held up to ridicule as an affront to subtlety, ambiguity, skepticism and other essential virtues of the truly inquiring intellect. The result has been that young people between the ages of roughly fourteen and twenty-four, especially in the late 60's when the Digest stood foursquare against everything exciting that seemed to be happening in their world, tend to eschew the magazine. One of the few Digest failures was an effort to start a campus magazine to be inserted in college newspapers; several of the most

prominent publications, among them the *Daily Princetonian,
Yale Daily News, Harvard Crimson* and *Columbia Spectator*,
rejected the Digest's *Campus Courier*. Said Donald Morrison
of the *Daily Pennsylvanian*, "It's just another Reader's Digest.
It doesn't attack substantive issues that college students are
interested in." Along about the same time, I was doing youth
work in my home town of Darien, Connecticut, and was introduced at a meeting as a Digest editor only to have a pretty
blonde high-school senior put the matter more succinctly: "I
hate Reader's Digest!"

Braced with this sort of thing in interviews, Digest philosopher Lewis would coolly reply that the Digest will catch the
young people a little later when they get married, have homes
and jobs and are in need of the sort of practical advice the
magazine has to offer. Perhaps. Some other Digest editors
seem more concerned than Lewis over the defection of the
young and sophisticated. When another British writer, Anthony
Haden-Guest, was investigating Pleasantville, he found John
Allen struggling over the right answer to a letter from a college
student in Lamont, Illinois, that began, "Most students are well
aware of the shortcomings of the Reader's Digest; e.g., the
extreme prejudice in outlook, low intelligence appeal, general
defender of most establishment mistakes . . ." That some of
this irritation with such a single-toned publication has moved
abroad along with the magazine itself is demonstrated not
only by the questions foreign journalists ask but by the opening
remarks of one of the Digest's own foreign executives at an
international meeting. "The Digest has been characterized as
the bland leading the bland, and we've got to do something
about that," he said.

There are, however, many both inside and outside the Digest
who would disagree with him. One of these is the Reverend
Dr. Billy Graham, and no doubt so would his colleague in the
cloth, the Reverend Dr. Norman Vincent Peale, whose popular
pleas for positive thinking have been put into Digestese countless times over the years. "Don't you think when everything in
the last few years has been down beat that we need something

up beat?" Dr. Graham asked me. "You've got the devil and the occult and the monster pictures, all frightening, in the minds of young people for a generation, and we need something to encourage us. There's a wonderful world of news out there that's good news. We need a little bit of something to say that something's all right in the world and God is still in his heaven and he's in control. I think the Digest has given us a great deal of that and has been a great thing for America. I'd hate to think where we'd be without the Digest."

Since all this good news probably does induce placid expectations of pleasure in most readers, as the BBC claimed, they certainly do howl when they come across anything that upsets them, contrary to the *Christian Century's* supposition. True, the magazine does not publish a regular letters column—although it did for a while years ago under the heading "Speaking of That"—but it does often assemble excerpts from letters into a later article when the response has been strong enough. A look at the most provocative subjects over the years confirms the theory that the Digest does not arouse political passions, except on specific issues relating to the reader's personal life. The articles drawing the heaviest response lately were: "Safer With a Gun? Don't Believe It!" in February 1975—2,858 letters, of which 1,334 were cancellations; and "The Politics of Abortion" in March 1973—920 letters, of which 147 were cancellations.

Birth control in any form has always stirred up readers. Catholic response to "Margaret Sanger: Mother of Planned Parenthood," July 1951, caused the Digest to print a collection of dissenting letters that December. An article in February 1969 called "Parenthood Should Wait" was followed by another in June, made up of readers' letters and called "Parenthood Should *Not* Wait!" Even in a lighter vein, anything having to do with relations between the sexes is likely to touch off a similar explosion. Consider this list of titles which provoked enough good letters that the Digest felt obliged to run them: "The Hardest Working Women in the World" (American),

"The Power Men Have Over Women," "Time to Give Divorced Men a Break," "But Women *Are* the Favored Sex."

Such intense interest, of course, confirms the Digest's wisdom in being open, and even somewhat daring, about sex despite the fact that such articles have opened the magazine to the kind of teasing *Time* indulged in as long ago as 1958. Said *Time*: "What the sex manuals don't tell you, beckoned newspaper ads last week. The commodity on sale: a magazine article offering 'penetrating guidance' to 'anxious' husbands and wives with 'secret worries.' What lifted many eyebrows was not the subject of the article but the magazine that touted it: the staid Reader's Digest . . ." Among other things, the article in question, "The Act of Love: Woman's Greatest Challenge" by gynecologist Marion Hilliard, described climaxes ranging from "one so slight that it is a sigh to one so profound and deep that it results in an agonizing cry . . . a small death." Ignoring *Time*'s dig, the Digest has gone on to publish even more explicit articles in the last twenty years.

That the Digest is fair game not only for other magazines but comedians and public speakers may be a kind of backhanded compliment—people know the product so well that a whole mental set can be evoked by simply naming it. For example, nobody could have misunderstood what Secretary of State Henry Kissinger meant when he was quoted as saying, "Don't ever write anything more complicated than a Reader's Digest article for Nixon." In the same way, Roger Angell could evoke chuckles from *The New Yorker* readers in those unrestful days of 1969 with a reverse twist on the Digest outlook called "Life in These Now United States (The 'Readers Digest' is Captured by the Enemy)," ending with that common bit of fun—a take-off on Digest titles:

> *"Coming Next Month:*
> "Black Power: The Miracle of the Electric Eel
> "Playin' My Axe: Harold Stassen's New Career as a Rock
>   Musician

"Let's Get in God's Bag

"From Pot to Hash: Confessions of a Short-Order Cook

"Human Encounter Groups: New Hope for the Post Office?

"The Friendly Lepers of Katmandu

"Getting Busted: The Truth About Those Silicone Treatments

"And other articles of heartening credulousness!"

One of the most elaborate bits of tomfoolery at Digest expense was a column by Art Buchwald whose humor the Digest once felt obliged to explain to its readers. This column which, for obvious reasons, did not find its way into the Digest said in part:

"I can now reveal for the first time why President Johnson can't ask J. Edgar Hoover to resign. The reason is J. Edgar Hoover doesn't exist.

"He is a mythical person first thought up by the Reader's Digest, and over the years he has become such a legend that no President has dared reveal the truth.

"What happened was that in 1925 the Reader's Digest was printing an article on the newly formed Federal Bureau of Investigation and as they do with many pieces they signed it with a *nom de plume*. They got the word Hoover from the vacuum cleaner—to give the idea of a cleanup. Edgar was the name of one of the publisher's nephews, and the J. stood for jail.

"What they hadn't counted on was how successful the article would be. J. Edgar Hoover caught the imagination of the American public and became a household word. The FBI had no choice but to keep the legend going. Besides, a person who doesn't exist can't make mistakes. . . ."

After this column appeared, there was a cool breeze blowing on Buchwald from the direction of Pleasantville for quite a while. Despite all the jokes it publishes, the Digest tends to take itself seriously, and matters weren't helped by the fact that a good many of those people out there who have faith in Reader's Digest wrote in to ask if the Buchwald assertion was true and, if so, why had the magazine done this. In the end, the Reader's Digest survived the allegation of having invented J. Edgar Hoover as easily as it has the more serious crises of criticism.

As long as 18 million or so Americans keep buying the magazine, it is unlikely that any criticism will much affect it. It isn't that the giant is deaf; it's that a few dissident voices are hard to hear against such a chorus of satisfied subscribers.

VII

My God, How the Money Rolls In, Rolls In

In the *New York Times* a year or so ago, advertising columnist Philip H. Dougherty noted a report that The Reader's Digest had representatives in Vienna, Austria, proposing a $1.87 million to $4.53 million advertising program to members of the Organization of Petroleum Exporting Countries (OPEC) meeting there, while at home the magazine was already running a $1.2 million series of ads sold to the Business Roundtable. Said Dougherty, "Those folksy folk really know where the money is." Indeed, they do. At this writing, the October 1976 issue of The Reader's Digest with some $8.5 million in advertising set a new record for total volume in any issue of any magazine in history, surpassing, of course, only the Digest's previous record month. The forty-eight-page detachable insert for which the Bicentennial Commission of Pennsylvania paid $1,028,410 in March 1976 was so uniquely large that it was proposed by the Digest for inclusion in the Guinness Book of World Records. And equally unusual in magazine publishing, the money coming in from the Digest's 18 million circulation exceeds its advertising revenue. As a result, the little monthly is taking in, according to a *Forbes* magazine estimate, "probably as much as

Time Inc. will gross from the worldwide publication of its whole family of magazines."

Exactly what the Reader's Digest earns has become a periodic and fascinating guessing game for the financial press. The magazine is part of a large company, the Reader's Digest Association, Inc., which puts out numerous other products such as books and records and which is privately owned. All voting stock is in the hands of the founders, DeWitt and Lila Acheson Wallace; non-voting shares have been meted out to favored employees under arrangements where the company can repurchase it if they leave or die, others have been deposited in the charitable foundation. The Reader's Digest Association is thus not obliged to publish figures, and it doesn't. As Dun & Bradstreet, Inc., said laconically in its 1976 report on Reader's Digest Association, Inc.: "Financial statement declined."

Nevertheless, it is possible for an interested party with a pocket calculator and a good eye for reading between the lines of company admissions such as the fact that RDA is "half way up the *Fortune* 500 ladder," to come up with some "ball park" figures that at least reflect the truth. On this basis, the closest round figure for the gross income of RDA seems to be $700 million annually; of this, somewhere between a fourth and a third is brought in by the parent, or United States, edition of the magazine. But beyond that the financial waters in Pleasantville become so truly murky that perhaps it is no accident that the company's chief financial wizard, Executive Vice President Richard Waters, has been nicknamed "Muddy" in some circles. A true secret, of course, is what has come to be known as the "bottom line"—the profit extracted from this gross. It has to be assumed, however, from the ease with which the company seems to find money for new ventures and the enormous sums its chief beneficiaries, the Wallaces, have given away that the Digest would rank far higher among the corporate giants in profitability than in volume.

In view of the figures, it might be wondered why the bulk of this book is devoted to the magazine. More important than the fact that my own experience was within the magazine is the fact that, as elsewhere described, the magazine is *The Little Engine That Could,* the generating force of the whole enterprise. With some minor exceptions, all RDA business stems from skillful use of the magazine's list of subscribers, itself a secret as carefully guarded as the financial records. There are only three copies in existence—one in a computer, one in a bank vault and another hidden somewhere in the Digest's condensed world. The importance of this list was described to me graphically, if somewhat crudely, by a man with Digest experience both in business and editorial, at home and abroad, when he said, "With a list like that, you could sell shit in a paper bag." Though another senior Digest business official with vast experience in selling by mail agreed, he added, "But not twice."

Be that as it may, top business executives of the RDA who are as free with dispensing the organization's business philosophy as they are chary with figures repeatedly emphasize the primary role of the magazine. While they have almost equal faith in other products, they acknowledge that the initial sale is generally made to someone who has come to have, as their own slogan puts it, "faith in The Reader's Digest." In addition, it was the technique learned in selling the magazine by mail that served to sell the books, records, educational materials, home audio sets and the like that now make up the bulk of the RDA's ancillary business around the world. Indeed, if there is a "secret" to Digest business operations comparable to the "secret" of its editorial performance, it lies in its proven ability to get somebody, almost anybody, out there to open up a letter and respond.

Not surprisingly, the Digest's leadership in the field of direct mail selling is another reflection of the innate "genius" DeWitt Wallace brought to the enterprise he founded. From the Wallace biography, it would be difficult to tell whether he was more businessman or editor when, in 1922, he launched his little magazine. Interestingly, the first selling letter he was known to have written, the one that got him admitted to Mt. Hermon School in 1906, said, "Although I have not fully decided as to

my future work, I think it will be in some line of business . . ."
His jobs were all related to writing promotion letters, and it
was those first circulars about a totally unknown magazine, sent
out from Pittsburgh after he was fired from Westinghouse,
that made publishing possible. For the next four or five years,
Wallace himself so successfully promoted his product, as well
as editing it, that he was at last able to hire help in handling
circulation, but it is a safe assumption that the help absorbed
as much as they could of the magic Wallace touch.

As in editorial, the addition of more minds has over fifty
years brought new ideas and refinements to the basic Wallace
concepts. The Digest not only tried every device known to man
to get people to respond to letters but invented many new ones.
Innovation was physical as well as mental. In charge of purchasing promotional printing and developing equipment for direct
mail, George Lawrence saw his budget rise from some $3
million to $25 million in fifteen years—an almost perfect gauge
of expanding RDA business. "In the early days when we
wanted to run a piece where the envelope was too big for the
machine, we would go down there with a hacksaw and cut off
part of the machine," Lawrence recalls. Later, at a cost of
$200,000, the Digest developed a special press to, according to
Lawrence, "give the Digest a corner on the personalized letter
market which we had for quite a few years. The whole secret
of direct mail success was to do something nobody else would
do and capitalize on it until other people found out about it."

A Digest innovation more in the realm of ideas than machinery made direct mail history—and nearly caused panic at the
United States Mint. It began with the need to put more bite
into an aging Digest promotion letter which began, "An ancient
Persian poet once said, 'If thou hast two pennies, spend one
for bread and the other to buy hyacinths for the soul . . .'"
Somebody got the idea of sending out two pennies with each
letter, inviting the reader to return one against his subscription
to the soul-satisfying Reader's Digest. This involved sucking
out of the market 100 million pennies in return for one million
Digest dollars. The Mint got into the act when it appeared that

the Digest was stripping the whole New York area of pennies, and magazine executives had to make hasty arrangements to have 60 million pennies shipped into New York from other spots around the country. Meanwhile, the floor in the warehouse where the Digest pennies were stored collapsed under the weight. Nevertheless, the letter went out, pennies and all, and brought a return worth the effort and money.

But the most sensational and durable selling technique pioneered by the Digest has been the sweepstakes, launched by a young executive named Gordon Grossman who rose to vice president in charge of all Digest marketing before resigning a few years ago to go into his own business. Grossman recalls getting the idea from lucky number sweepstake ads the automobile companies were running in 1962 as "traffic builders" for their outlets. "What had not been done was adapting this to direct mail," he said. "We had a yes-no option mailing going out. We laid sweepstakes on top of this, and the results were sensational in terms of increased response. I won't talk about figures, but it was more than double."

Since then the Digest has stuck with sweepstakes through interminable Congressional hearings, actions by the Federal Trade Commission, state court cases and complaints from unlucky entrants. The Digest has so far won, or settled, all of its legal hassles and evidently regards the results as worth the time, effort, and unfavorable publicity. Indeed, by the summer of 1976, sweeps were bigger than ever with the grand prize lifted to $50,000. In that contest, prizes, ranging from a first-aid kit to the fifty grand and amounting to $11,107,174, were awarded to 682,234 winners—or, by Digest estimates, one in every 108 households in the United States. Interestingly, more than 60 percent of the winners sent their lucky numbers back in a "no" envelope which says a lot about the value the Digest puts on getting a new "yes" name to feed into that secret list. Even more interestingly, DeWitt Wallace himself, the old master of direct mail selling, has never really liked sweepstakes since he feels that they detract from selling the magazine on its merits alone. But the figures produced by his business associates have been so convincing that Wallace has been forced to go along, as indeed he has been more or less dragged into every major RDA venture outside of the domestic edition of the magazine itself.

Business, as such, at the Digest can be said to have begun with the arrival of a personality very nearly as powerful as Wallace himself, Albert Leslie Cole. Born in Chicago only five years after Wallace, on December 12, 1894, a dropout after whatever education the New York public schools afforded him, Cole went to work for the Frank Munsey publications in New York at the age of sixteen. After service as an ensign in World War I, he rose to become president and publisher of *Popular Science Monthly* and *Outdoor Life* by 1929, and vice president of the distributor, S-M News. The story goes that Wallace, who got to know Cole through putting his little magazine in the hands of S-M for newsstand distribution, arranged for Cole to act as outside consultant on circulation, the fee being based on an increase in business. Wallace soon found himself having to pay such large fees that he decided it would be more economical to hire Cole at a very substantial salary. However it happened, by 1939, Cole was installed as general manager of The Reader's Digest. Stocky, florid, handsome, sturdy of voice, decisive in manner, Cole was the Hollywood casting agent's dream of the typical tough, but genial, executive. He had passions to match—golf, the Republican Party and the Boys Club of America, in about that order. A perfect counterpart to his shy employer, Cole's name figures prominently in almost every decision to expand the Digest's business.

Undoubtedly World War II slowed Al Cole's drive toward diversification, except for moving into the international field, because it wasn't until 1950 that the Digest plunged into its first—and best—sideline, Condensed Books. Even circulation figures for Condensed Books are somewhat guarded since there is no advertising to require disclosure, but they are admittedly in the neighborhood of 11 million volumes per year in the United States and at least 17 million for all editions. Some years ago *Publishers Weekly* made an educated, and probably conservative, guess of $45 million as the gross for this operation, but a better picture emerges from a recent comment to me by a man who *does* know the figures and described it simply as a "money machine." Digest Vice President John T. Beaudouin, editor-in-chief of Condensed Books, has described The Reader's Digest Book Club in the United States as "by far the largest organization in its field," and said that, with its foreign operations included, the Club is "one of the largest publishers of hard-bound books in the world."

Fittingly, the idea for Condensed Books grew right out of the magazine itself and in the brain of the very first full-time employee DeWitt Wallace ever hired, Ralph Henderson. Wallace tried his first condensation of a book—Arnold Bennett's *How to Live on 24 Hours a Day*—in the second issue of the magazine, March 1922. By the 30's regular book condensations were appearing, and Henderson was in charge of the task of finding and editing them. He was by his own admission bothered by the fact that, because of space limitations, he had to pass up a number of good books and almost all fiction since one of Wallace's chief competitive selling points was that the Digest provided "facts" in a magazine world where fiction was supposed to be the main attraction. Beginning in the early 40's, Henderson began making proposals for separate use of books—his favorite, a magazine format containing two books and selling for the same subscription price as the Digest. Nothing much happened until Al Cole got into the picture, as Henderson tells the story himself in a memoir composed for the Club's twentieth anniversary.

"The idea lay more or less dormant," Henderson wrote, "until the summer of 1949 when I had many long discussions with Al Cole about the idea of a book club, using fiction along the lines I had tried out in the magazine. He was willing to back my editorial ideas, but for selling he preferred a volume in hard covers 'to look and feel like a book,' and at a necessarily higher price. We were to compromise on an expanded hard-cover quarterly volume—basically recognizable as the book that goes to subscribers today.

"One day that summer of 1949 Al and I went together to

present the plan to DeWitt Wallace. I was to state the editorial appeal and Al was to back me up with cost figures. But before I had properly opened my mouth, Mr. Wallace looked from one to the other of us and said, 'If you agree on this book club idea, why don't you try it out?' So that was it. In less than five minutes, Al and I walked out, all choked up with unspoken arguments, but with what I underestimated at the time as a million dollar decision."

The rest is, as they say, history—but history in pure Digest style, a story of unbroken success. Cole's business judgment would seem to be vindicated by a marketing expert who, having studied the CB audience for years, told me, "What it amounts to is selling hard-cover books to people who don't buy books; less than 10 percent of CB members buy one other book a year." As for the editorial expertise, Henderson simply brought it along with him, recruiting Beaudouin and Agnes Allen from the magazine staff and, a little later, Eleanor Hard Lake, who had written for both *Fortune* and *Reader's Digest* and whose brother was on the Digest staff. These people quite naturally adapted the magazine's assembly line of readers, cutters, check cutters, and the like to a new medium. Because they have more space for their final product and because the material with which they work—mostly fiction, until recently—is more fragile, CB editors tend to be more delicate in their approach. Publishers and authors rarely object to CB editing since the royalties they get based on the huge circulation are likely to exceed anything either of them could hope for in the market.

Since the earliest days of the operation, CB has recruited its own editors who sit apart from the magazine staff in a wing of the second floor of the Pleasantville headquarters. Except for hearing the bells at noontime and collecting their Christmas turkeys, they might well be in another world. One reason for this is that Wallace, perhaps because of his prediliction for fact over fiction, has paid little attention to this stepchild of his magazine, except presumably to rejoice in the profit figures. The one time he did interfere editorially was so notable that Henderson is forever recounting it. Caught without something better to read on a trip, Wallace picked up a popular historical novel, looked it over and sent Henderson a note to the effect that it might find a place in CB. It was *Love is Eternal,* a sentimental version of Abraham Lincoln's marriage that all the otherwise astute CB editors had rejected, unhappily in writing. Nevertheless, Henderson did run it—an almost universal reaction to a Wallace suggestion—and for many years it led the list as the most popular CB offering.

Condensed Books was virtually keeping RDA afloat financially by the time Al Cole extracted from Wallace the most momentous business decision he had made since the founding of the magazine—taking advertising. Although the decision burst like a starshell above Madison Avenue in 1955, it had been a long time in the making in Pleasantville. In *Journalism Monographs,* John W. Garberson, a former Digest advertising promotion director, examines this decision in detail. Although Cole first brought up the idea of advertising in 1940, it wasn't until the early 50's that rising costs made it a matter of serious discussion. "It was a matter of economics. We either had to start taking ads or the magazine would lose a million dollars a year. It was that simple," Cole told Garberson. "There may have been a possibility of getting readers to pay more for the magazine, postponing the necessity of advertising revenue for a while, but we did some research that certainly didn't give us any encouragement in that direction. Besides—and I was the fellow who was supposed to know something about circulation—we were already charging $3 a year and 25 cents a copy for the magazine, and I was absolutely sure that if we increased the price to readers, circulation would go down. I was nuts, but you never know that at the time."

Armed with his survey that showed some 90 percent of those questioned would rather have advertising than pay more for the magazine and with the experience of using advertising in foreign editions of the Digest, Cole kept talking to Wallace on and off for a couple of years. "By (the early fall of 1954) some of us were pretty sure that taking advertising was inevitable and that it would be good," Cole recalled. "I think Wally knew it, too. But we couldn't get him to say 'yes.' Or 'no' for that matter. One day—it must have been around the start of November in 1954—Wally and a few of the rest of us were in his office talking about various things, not advertising, as I remember. Sort of out of the blue, Wally said, 'By the way, Al, if you still think we ought to take advertising, I suppose the first thing we should do is tell the other magazines.' "

Wallace was undoubtedly revealing the real reason behind his caution about taking advertising—the perennial fear he had lived with for thirty years that a source of much of his material would be shut off. Although he had long ago outdistanced all other magazines in circulation, he hadn't yet competed with them for their most important dollar—the advertiser's. Given the job of protecting this flank, Cole called upon the major publishers—Curtis and Time—in one fast-shuttling day between Philadelphia and New York, and softening the blow with an offer of larger payments for reprints—such contracts for reprint rights to materials were running in the neighborhood of $100,000 a year—he managed to bring them into line; the rest followed, of course. The problem of coping with the avalanche of advertisers wanting to get into the country's widest-selling magazine was harder. There was no staff, and in the Digest tradition of bumbling through with "gifted amateurs" Cole turned to forty-year-old Fred Thompson, a sixteen-year veteran of diverse Digest business chores, as his advertising manager. Thompson, now one of the deans of the business as advertising vice president of the *New York Times*, coped spectacularly after a rough year or so of adjustment. From $12,012,520 in advertising revenue in 1956, the figure has risen steadily to a take in the $60 to $70 million range—$74 million in 1976.

The three men who were answering the phones that "started ringing off the wall" in the spring of 1955 when the Digest announced it wanted advertising—Wallace, Cole and Thompson—have been replaced by an impressive force which, under Publisher Charles D. Hepler, lists at least 100 names in the masthead. While they now have to sell aggressively, particularly against the heavy competition from television, the impact from

Digest advertising is very nearly as great as that from the articles it runs. In "The Best Advertisements from Reader's Digest," author Julian L. Watkins reports that one ad in 1956, "Suddenly Soap is Old Fashioned," caused readers to clip 1.8 million coupons and Lever Brothers to proclaim that it was "the best advertising response in all its history." A later ad for Cannon hosiery boosted sales by 44 percent over the previous years. Premium offers in Digest ads have drawn everything from 2,000 purchasers of a $79 ten-speed bike to 20,000 requests for a free set of coffee mugs.

No one, I'm sure, was less surprised at the reader response to advertising than Editor Wallace. He never did have a philosophical or professional objection to the use of advertising; on the contrary, he ran a piece in that historic April issue by Bruce Barton, partner in one of America's largest advertising agencies and frequent Digest contributor, extolling the place of advertising in American life. "I've always thought a magazine with ads in it—good ads—is better from the reader's viewpoint than it would be if the ads weren't there," he told Garberson. "Readers get a lot of valuable information out of ads." One reason he would not take cigarette and liquor ads in the United States (although they are accepted abroad) was that such advertising "isn't interesting." But there was more: "Ads are to get people to try new ideas, new things, and I don't think the magazine should be in such a position where liquor and cigarettes are concerned. I don't have anything against drinking or smoking, but I don't want to feel that we are taking an active part in introducing millions of people to them. Another thing, I have known lots of writers and other people with drinking problems. Some of them have told me that nothing makes them want a drink of liquor—a drink they shouldn't have—as much as seeing how delicious a high-ball or a martini looks in an ad. We won't be involved in that."

Four years after taking advertising, the Digest had evidently driven the wolf far enough away from the door to feel safe in venturing forth on its first offering that had nothing to do with the printed word—the making and selling of records. It was perhaps a natural assumption that the magazine's golden list of people avid for culture in the form of articles and books might also yield some people who liked music. It had to be the right kind of music, to be sure—music with universal appeal and just a touch of self-improvement, as titles of the first albums reveal: "Music of the World's Great Composers," "Festival of Light Classical Music," "Music That Will Live Forever." Once it was established that the market was there, somewhat more specialized offerings came forth—a superb "Messiah," and an equally well-done "The Swing Years." Now, nearly twenty years later, records, as well as the sale of a home audio system assembled in the United States from Japanese components, are a steady and lucrative part of the business both at home and abroad—how lucrative, nobody will say. The only mistake the company made in the record field, according to Walter W. Hitesman, Jr., the man mostly responsible for that development, was getting involved in selling the product of an outside record company. "We learned that it was better to make our own," he said. "The real Digest secret is giving good quality for a good price, and it is hard to control all that unless you are responsible for the whole product."

But there's another Digest business secret involved in the record club, as confirmed to me by both Vice President Waters and Chairman Kent Rhodes. When a new thing doesn't work, the Digest drops it. This was true, for example, in the 60's of the aborted publication to be inserted in college newspapers, of a brief ownership of Funk & Wagnalls publishing house, of an effort to sell mutual funds in Germany, of an experimental woman's magazine in Spain, of a recent effort to market reproductions of the great masters of painting. One reason the Digest can do this so handily is that it tends to stick to what's known in the trade as "software" rather than "hardware," following a dictum attributed to Al Cole that "we are publishers, not printers or manufacturers."

Unlike most publishers of its size, the Digest owns no forests, no paper mills, no printing establishments, no fleets of trucks, no television stations, no radio stations—no nothing, really, but some of the buildings in which its people work and the presses upon which it is printed. The presses are, of course, expensive propositions, and they are installed in the plants of printing companies in the United States and abroad with whom the Digest negotiates long-term contracts for their operation. A recent contract with Arcata in Buffalo was announced at $100 million for five years. The other major plant for the magazine is Dayton Press, formerly McCall's, in Dayton, Ohio, and for the condensed books, it is Donnelly in Crawfordsville, Indiana. The Digest keeps updating its presses and, as this is written, new ones are being installed in both Dayton and Buffalo that are a third wider and run so much faster that one will do the work of two older models. Among other things, letting others be responsible for operations in one of the nation's most tightly unionized businesses has freed Digest management from many headaches. Publication has never been curtailed by a strike, although it was slowed a few summers ago when the plant was closed at Dayton by labor troubles and the load had to be absorbed in round-the-clock operations by Arcata.

As a matter of fact, the Digest business department has been an equal beneficiary in the special blessing that seems to fall upon every Wallace enterprise. Chairman Rhodes, whose route to the top was through production, couldn't recall failing to get out a single issue of the magazine anywhere in the world in half a century, except for the first few months of an Arabic edition right after World War II. Aside from the strike in Dayton, there haven't even been many close calls. The worst Rhodes could remember was the time the Digest press in France exploded during a run. The job was farmed out to presses in England and Italy, and the French edition continued to roll. This incident, in fact, revealed a hidden Digest strength to which Rhodes admits. If something, either physical or financial, is going wrong somewhere in the world, something's probably going right somewhere else. "For instance, things are bad in England right now," he said, "but they're good in Germany."

The Digest's apparent wisdom in staying out of hardware may be as much a matter of structure as shrewd judgment. As

Waters explained it, the fact of its being a privately held company automatically prevents the Digest from raising large investment sums through the issue of new stock or from making large purchases through the trade of stock. New Digest ventures are therefore financed by excess cash. It's easy to see the threads of history in this policy. Once out of debt, DeWitt Wallace was determined to stay there. As one longtime associate told me, "As a businessman, Wally is a curious combination of courage and caution. You almost have to drag him kicking into something new, and when you do, you have to make good on the promises you made to him."

Although the Digest board has established a new diversification committee, it seems improbable that they will go far afield from the general Wallace formula of providing entertainment, information and education. A large operation in the last field has been in progress for years with special editions of the Digest for school use. It has recently been expanded to provide games and other educational materials, and a fairly new acquisition is the Partridge Press, renamed Firefly Press, which distributes books suitable for second to fourth graders, much like a small-fry Book-of-the-Month Club. The gambles of trade publishing have apparently proved a little too risky for the Digest. After unloading Funk & Wagnalls, the magazine moved cautiously back into the field with something called Reader's Digest Press—a small editorial force that developed and published, in cooperation with another house, some 20 titles a year such as Theodore White's *Breach of Faith; The Fall of Richard Nixon* with Atheneum. Then last winter the company issued a statement that is remarkably fuzzy for a publication so noted for clarity, to the effect that all Reader's Digest Press titles then in the works would be published but that the future of the operation was undecided.

But, in addition to Condensed Books, the Digest is beginning to take on its usual gigantic proportions in one other area of hard-cover publishing—special books. This operation feeds like a leech off that main artery, the magazine subscription list, and is perhaps the finest illustration of the Digest business department doing what it knows best. As usual in the Digest story, this development had logical, historical roots—the little collections of favorite articles or jokes the magazine used to throw out from time to time for bedside reading. Under Hitesman, a hard-driving ex-Marine who found out how easy it was to sell record albums tailored to the stated demand of Digest subscribers, those two very special Digest talents—the ability to get people to open letters and the ability to manufacture easy-to-read prose—were fused into one powerful current to generate made-to-order books. The idea is simplicity itself: just ask people who already like what they read in your magazine what they'd like to read in the way of a book, and give it to them. With some 18 million potential readers to play with, it's possible to be sure of a sale in the millions (10,000 is a good sale for your average trade book) before you publish. Here's how Lila Freilicher described the process in *Publishers Weekly*:

"The development of the just-published Reader's Digest Bicentennial contribution, *Story of America*, edited by Carroll Calkins from concept to finished product, illustrates the marketing process at Reader's Digest. The idea for the book was first proposed three and a half years ago by Calkins in a lengthy memo which outlined the contents in detail. Based on the information in this proposal, the potential marketability of the book was tested in a questionnaire along with about 30 other books. Given the tentative title, 'America 1976: The First 200 Years,' and a brief description, the reader was asked to state his degree of interest in the book at the price given.

"Reader response indicated that there was enough interest to go on to the next step, the so-called 'blue' book, or prospectus. Based on the contents of the original proposal and including sample pages, the 'blue' book spelled out exactly what would be in the book and was used to help design a full-color, fold-out brochure which was mailed to Reader's Digest subscribers about two and a half years ago. It asked readers to reserve a copy of *Story of America*.

"In terms of editorial design, the challenge, according to Calkins, was to provide 'as many points of entry into the book as possible.' When people go through an encyclopedia volume, he explained, they flip through pages looking for things that interest them. 'We didn't want people to turn more than two or three pages without finding something that stopped them.' Thus the heavy page-by-page use of illustrations, special boxed features and, every so often, full-color pages or spreads devoted to feature stories.

"As with the other Reader's Digest books, Calkins points out, the basic purpose is to deliver information as engagingly as possible without diluting it. Each chapter was written by an outside professional writer with background in the subject. As each chapter came in, it was checked for accuracy by an internal department of four editors who went over every date, name and event. Then each chapter was sent to an outside consultant who read everything for historical accuracy. Calkins was responsible for orchestrating the whole operation and, additionally, for editing the copy so that all articles had a common tone. As each manuscript was completed, designers began doing rough layouts, and, once the pictures were ready, page-by-page production began."

Presto—an instant best seller! Perhaps fittingly, this wondrous operation takes place in the towers of Manhattan, and there is little or no contact between these calculating editors and those in Pleasantville. Compared to the book operation, the seat-of-the-pants way in which Pleasantville editors have to guess what readers will want each month would seem as chancy as roulette. There is, however, one other form of gambling at the Digest: movies. For a while there, when the Digest decided to get "with it" in the new decade of the 70's by going into motion pictures and television, it looked like the old Wallace magic could move through the range of media as easily as it had through the range of language and culture. The first RD picture, a musical version of *Tom Sawyer,* produced with United Artists, was a success. But the sequel, *Huckleberry Finn,* and a musical filmed in England called *Mr. Quilp* and based on Dickens' *The Old Curiosity Shop,* bombed out. Hope is higher for others now in the can—a filming of the book, *All Things*

Bright and Beautiful, which was successful in Scotland under the title, *It Shouldn't Happen to a Vet,* and *The Incomparable Sarah,* a biography of Sarah Bernhardt—but for the moment the Digest cameras have stopped turning.

Executive Vice President Waters, guardian of the Digest vaults, has become Pleasantville's Sam Goldwyn, taking over from the creative types like Chairman Hobart Lewis and his assistant in the venture, Managing Editor Fulton Oursler, Jr. A more unlikely movie mogul would be hard to imagine. Tall, balding, with a pencil-sharp nose and mind for figures to match, Waters looks more like a character out of a Dickensian counting house than out of a Hollywood studio. But the idea seems to be for Waters to recoup the losses, and perhaps eventually to make a profit. When I talked to him, he seemed confident that this could be done in the long, long run, mostly by selling them off to television. "When we went into this," Waters explained, "everybody told us there was a great demand for G pictures. But when we produced them, it just wasn't there. Nobody wanted to book them, and nobody came when they did. Even Disney is having trouble with G pictures today. Take *The Incomparable Sarah,* which is PG because of its subject matter: everybody said they loved it but added, 'If you had only put her in bed a couple of times we could sell it.' Sex or violence, you've got to have one or the other, and we have neither. TV is the only market for G pictures."

The Digest's ventures into television have fared better—but not much. They've made animated fairy tales and films of some of the famous "I am Joe's (Whatsis)" articles in the magazine as well as rather glittering cultural things like the civilization series by Lord Kenneth Clark on educational television. However, according to Waters, the new and cautious guideline to Digest Television Director, Bertram MacMannis, another "gifted amateur" who switched from selling ads to television production, is that any future package must include a sponsor before production begins. In the works are four one-hour specials to be narrated by author James Michener on the predictable subjects of Israel, Iberia, Hawaii and the South Pacific.

Whether Reader's Digest can make it in visuals as it has in print is still debatable at this point, but there is one use of electronic communication for which Waters can hardly wait—delivery of printed materials. "It's already happening in Japan," he said. "There you get a special attachment for your television set, and during the night when transmission costs are low, it grinds out a facsimile copy of your morning paper and drops it on the living room floor." Such a wonder is ten to fifteen years down the road here, according to Waters, but its advent might help to solve the company's single most pressing financial problem everywhere, the rising cost of mail.

"Since 1971, postal rates for magazines have gone up 150 percent—and will probably double in the next three years," said Chairman Rhodes. Although along with other publishers, the Digest is heavily into experiments with alternate, private delivery systems in metropolitan areas like Los Angeles and San Francisco, it seems that for the most part the company will have to grin and bear the postal increases. This is hard to do, when you consider that the Digest, in 1975, paid $46,545,000 for 591 million pieces of mail of all classes in the United States, and that its worldwide mailing bill comes to $100 million a year. The fact that this cost accounts for well over 10 percent of the company's gross revenue and is subject to astronomical fluctuation with the smallest change in rates no doubt accounts for the number of postal articles appearing regularly in the magazine as well as the company's lobbying efforts in Washington more than reader interest.

Digest representatives testify at every conceivable congressional hearing or postal conference here or abroad. In the offices of Coleman W. Hoyt, the Digest's mail specialist, reposes what may be the most comprehensive library on mail to be found anywhere in the world. The acquisition of Melvin R. Laird, former Secretary of Defense and, more importantly, a former congressman felt to be popular with his cohorts, for a salary in the neighborhood of $72,000 a year, for a job called "senior counsellor" on the business side of the masthead, may have had something to do with efforts to persuade old friends on Capitol

Hill to be reasonable about mail. It was to be hoped so since bringing heavyweights in from the outside is contrary to all Digest tradition of promoting amateurs from within to whatever new task or opportunity falls open. (A body of opinion about the Laird appointment was reflected in the comment of a Digest writer who told me, "Well, there goes my favorite line. I was going to describe somebody as having all the charisma of Melvin Laird.") But, in all truth, it must be reported that despite its obvious self interest, the Digest has done a great deal toward shoving the post office into the twentieth century by pushing and/or pioneering such things as workload-sharing in which the customer gets a discount for presorting mail, more efficient material handling with forklifts, and palletized mail replacing the old canvas sack on the back, said to have been invented by Benjamin Franklin. The philosophical basis of the argument that not only the Digest but other publishers put forward against rising postal rates is that some sort of government subsidy for the dissemination of knowledge was, and should be, intended by the people. Rhodes points out that despite the numbers involved, higher postal rates are, in fact, harder on the marginal, specialized magazines than on the giants like the Digest.

The Digest, in Rhodes' view, will survive whatever the post office might do, or any other foreseeable calamity. He does not subscribe to the popular pessimism about so-called mass magazines despite the failure of *Collier's, Saturday Evening Post, Look, Life* and others. "Look at the record," says Rhodes. "Since 1968, *TV Guide* has added six million, *National Geographic* 2.7 million, *Family Circle* 1.5 million, Reader's Digest 1.25 million, *Playboy* three million. There's plenty of business around for mass magazines." In this connection, Rhodes is a firm believer in the fact that the principle business of RDA is the Reader's Digest—"mother," as he calls the magazine. The company tries to see that the magazine stands on its own feet, no matter what happens to the other businesses, but it can be a tough problem in accounting. "Take Pintchman here," he said, referring to the RDA's manager of press relations, Charles Pintchman, who was sitting in with us, "should his salary be charged to the magazine—or what?"

However the accounting is done, it is evident from talks with Rhodes, Waters and others that the heads of present Digest management have not been turned by the quick money opportunities in fields other than publishing. Actually, RDA is involved in only two such schemes. One, the Foreign Study League, an educational travel program that ships Americans abroad and brings foreign students to this country, hasn't, in Waters' phrase, "turned the corner yet." The other, a door-to-door selling scheme called QSP, Quality School Products, is a small diamond mine. Though what the Digest gets out of it is, of course, secret, Waters admits that it grosses $80 million a year and that no QSP representative earns less than $20,000. The idea is to organize young people in school classes, scout troops, Little League teams, or whatever, to peddle magazine subscriptions (virtually all but *Playboy*), candy (from a company in which the Digest has an interest), placemats and other products to raise money for some such project as buying uniforms or a trip to Washington; profits are split with QSP which supplies the products and know-how.

Very nearly all of RDA's ancillary activities have moved abroad (QSP is going in Puerto Rico, Mexico, Canada, England, so far) with varying degrees of success. Some do better than here; the brightest prospects for the Foreign Study League, for example, are in Japan where students seem to have the yen (in both senses of the word) to come to the United States. On the other hand, the sale of copies of great paintings which has proved a mainstay in Japan failed in a United States trial. In fact, the only successful imports from foreign pioneering to date have been book ideas, such as the *Do-It-Yourself Book* which is causing the Digest to experiment with a whole new distribution system through hardware stores. It's inevitable, however, that with growing sophistication, there will be more and more cross-fertilization within the Digest's rich fields of endeavor everywhere.

From the serene vantage point of Pleasantville, the possibilities for proliferation seem limitless. Those "folksy folk" who "really know where the money is" have proved that they can sell almost anything by mail, or on foot, in any language and in any place. If there's a self-limiting factor built into their business, they haven't found it yet. Isn't it possible that people out there, not excluding mailmen, might one day get one letter too many and revolt? When I put this question to Rhodes, he said, "The amazing thing about soliciting people by mail is that, if you find a person who is an expired subscriber and can somehow or other get him to buy something, even if it's the magazine all over again, he's likely to buy a book from you. The interesting thing is that he is more likely to buy books if he's just bought the magazine than if he's just sitting there. If he buys a book, he's more likely to buy something else. Sears, Roebuck calls this 'recency of purchase.'" After all, the Digest only reaches one in four households; there are three left to go.

The best summary of business at the Digest was given to me unconsciously by a high Digest executive, now retired. I was telling him about a friend of mine who had left the Digest in his youth to seek his fortune elsewhere. Ultimately, he went bankrupt by buying into quick money schemes, by looking for what he called "the money tree." My sage old friend shook his head. "If he'd wanted to find the money tree, he should have stayed at the Digest," he said. Having a better grasp on this fact than my friend, most people do stay on in Pleasantville even though there are times when life in this most curious organization belies the name. Quite obviously, for most people in any aspect of publishing, monetarily there's nowhere to go from Pleasantville but down.

VIII

Pleasantville, U.S.A.

Is there really a Pleasantville? Well, yes and no. There is a town in Westchester County, New York, some forty miles from Manhattan, called Pleasantville and characterized by, among other things, an outsized post office to handle the flow of the tons of mail that link the Reader's Digest with its millions of subscribers around the land and with its offices all over the world. There is also an experience called "being in Pleasantville" which the thousands of people who work for the Digest share. But, oddly, neither the Digest nor its people have actually been in Pleasantville for nearly forty of the magazine's fifty-five years.

If a town called Pleasantville hadn't existed in 1922 when the Wallaces started looking for a suburban location, it seems likely that they might have been forced to invent it, so perfectly does its name match the aura of the little magazine that put it on the world map. The Wallaces did actually live and work in Pleasantville until 1939, by which time the facilities and address for their large mail enterprise were so thoroughly established that any change would have been difficult. In any case, they moved only a few miles up the road to an amorphous political subdivision by the name of North Castle Township, the main village of which is Chappaqua, a word almost designed to drive computers and uncertain spellers crazy.

As might be expected with a Digest move, the one from Pleasantville to Chappaqua seems to have been in the right direction. This January in an article on the snob appeal of Westchester suburbs, Betsy Brown, writing in the *New York Times,* called Chappaqua the "in" town—"a place for the upward striving professional, with a respected school district and a downtown lined with boutiques." As for Pleasantville, "it is an 'old shoe' of a village, homey unpretentious, where people walk to school and stores." Digesters who don't live too far afield inhabit such places as Armonk ("open space, pretty village"), Katonah ("subdued elegance"), Bedford ("huge estates, horses and a hunt club"). Thus, in a physical sense at least, Digesters, both at work and at play, have dwelt this half century in one of America's pleasantest places.

Some years ago, a Digest editor showing guests around the company grounds, was moved to say, "Shows you what God could do if he had money." The remark was probably not original and certainly injudicious since the Wallaces, when they heard about it, didn't think it was funny. They are quite justly proud of company headquarters, a true pioneering venture in locating a major business in the suburbs and mostly the work of Mrs. Wallace. Indeed, while the Wallaces have been publicly shy and even secretive about their personal lives and details of the business they privately own, they went out of their way some years ago to show off their grounds and buildings to 100 million people with a feature in the Digest itself called, "Pictures From Pleasantville, An Armchair Visit to The Reader's Digest." The article ended with this: "Thus, in the truest sense, our home belongs not only to us editors, but to you readers, wherever you are. We hope that this armchair travelogue will serve as an invitation to visit us in person." The earnest type of readers who favor the Digest took this quite literally, and for months the halls were jammed with visitors, somewhat to the distress of those of us trying to work and enduring with suffering smiles all the variations on the classic exclamation of people who first see the Digest, "I just don't see how a person could ever do any work in a place like this!"

The reaction is forgivable since the Digest's 155 rolling acres, lying between Route 117 to the east and the Saw Mill River Parkway to the west, has been variously described as looking like the campus of a small college or a large suburban high school, depending on the viewer's frame of reference, but never an office. The central building is a three-story Georgian structure which, when it was built at a cost of $1.5 million in 1939, was thought to be big enough to house so small a magazine. Since then low-lying wings, carefully designed not to detract from the ivy-encrusted main building, have been added periodically until the whole complex now sprawls over some five acres. One of the wings shelters ever newer generations of winking and blinking computers that can keep track of 40 million Digest accounts at the rate of about a million names an hour—and provide a touch of wonderland for gaping visitors.

But the chief attraction remains, as intended, the main building where on the first floor, along corridors squared onto flowering courtyards, sit the editors of the magazine in wordless confirmation of the fact that their work is still held to be the heart of the enterprise. Insofar as it is compatible with the necessary steel desks, filing cabinets and typewriter tables, the place is furnished to give the atmosphere of the most luxurious English manor house. Fresh flowers, prepared by a special employee in a special cutting room off the reception rotunda, are set out every day, and in season an outsize Christmas tree jollies the rotunda with the scent of pine. On the walls of the corridors and editors' offices, painted in muted Williamsburg colors, hangs a collection of paintings, mostly impressionist, that the *New York Times* recently called "the county's most valuable outside the Rockefellers' at Pocantico Hills." Like most financial figures in Pleasantville, the value of the Wallace art works has not been officially revealed although author Felicia Warburg Roosevelt estimated the collection, which includes originals by such as Modigliani, Cezanne, Bonnard, Soutine, Picasso, Chagall, Corot, at $5 million.

This estimate is probably conservative. Once not long ago an editor we'll call Joe was walking through the Pleasantville halls when a friend cornered him and said, "You'd better get back to your office; I just heard Mr. Wallace asking where you sit." On Joe's level, the prospect of a personal visit from the founder and owner was fraught with horrendous possibilities, not excluding firing, and so he hurried back to sit sweating at his desk until the great man appeared in the hall outside his open door. Mr. Wallace did not come in; instead, he stood staring at something on the wall and then remarked, "I just wanted to see what more than a million dollars looks like," and walked away. Checking up, Joe discovered that somebody had told Wallace the current value of a painting, the location of which was identified as "hanging next to Joe's office." Indeed, Wallace who was happy putting out the Digest all alone in a pony shed has always seemed a little astonished at what his wife has wrought. A Digester who was present when Wallace first gazed upon his large corner office, then decorated in white leather by a fine feminine hand, heard him say, "All this stuff would go well at an auction." Evidently it did since Wallace's office was soon turned into everyman's dream of a paneled study, not excluding an antique secretary with secret drawers and a huge and startling Chagall over the fireplace.

Given a free hand, Mrs. Wallace has dominated the physical development of the Digest not only with loving care but with what somebody once described as "a whim of iron." As she told author Roosevelt, "If I want something done, I always get my way." This must have been trying for architect John Mackenzie. When his minions were laying up brick, Mrs. Wallace suddenly decided that she didn't like it, searched New York state herself until she found an old brick factory making a product with the right patina. She didn't like Mackenzie's proposal to decorate the cupola atop the building with spread eagles, either. As Ms. Roosevelt reported it: " 'Suddenly,' she said, 'I woke up in the middle of the night and thought of Pegasus, the winged horse. When he stomped his feet he was supposed to have inspired men to write.' " Thus, the front half of winged horses protruding from the cupola not only provided decoration but a symbol for the magazine.

Since Digesters don't normally mount to the cupola, one of them, gazing at it daily as he came back and forth to work, began speculating on what it must be like inside. This led to a drawing depicting the rear ends of horses. Though it's doubtful that this drew whoops from Mrs. Wallace, it did provoke an instant reaction from Al Cole, then the magazine's general manager. "My Gosh!" he said when he saw it, "All the vice presidents in one room!" Perhaps to remove further doubt as to what was behind the horses, a few years ago an electronic carillion—inspired as so many Pleasantville matters are by a Digest story and costing some $35,000—was installed in the cupola. Played either manually or automatically with rolls, the carillion makes the skies over Chappaqua ring with light melody for fifteen minutes every noon and longer on special occasions. Although a Digest survey of neighbors found more appreciation than resentment of this innovation, the reaction of a good many people right under the bells can best be defined by an old joke. "Aren't those pretty bells?" one fellow asks another. "Eh?" "I said, aren't those pretty bells?" "Can't hear a thing you say because of those goddamned bells!"

At least in the early days, a few gaffs from the new gadget were to be expected. There was the time, for instance, when the bells saluted a visiting Army general with the Marine hymn, or vice versa, much to the embarrassment of the host, Digest Vice President Paul Thompson, himself a noted graduate of West Point. The worst mistake, however, occurred at 4 a.m. on the Sunday after Christmas 1969, when the bells suddenly began pealing "Jingle Bells" into the silent night. A watchman had inadvertently pressed the button programmed to make the bells ring at 4 p.m., but bells can't tell night from day.

Whatver people may think of them, the ringing of the bells intensifies the campus atmosphere as do the landscaped grounds. As interested in the outside as the inside of her creation, Mrs. Wallace added to the architect's headaches by insisting that he position the original building so as not to harm two ancient oaks, one just outside the front door, facing east, and the other down the slope behind toward the parkway. The pay-off for her care came thirty-seven years later when in 1976 the National Arborist Association and the International Society of Arboriculture designated the Swamp White Oak in front of the building as a "Bicentennial Tree." The citation explained that "at the age of 250 years this tree is a living witness to the Revolution of 1776." Some 80 feet tall with a breast height diameter of 54 inches and a spread of 100 feet, the tree has been equipped with a protective lightning rod and carefully fed and trimmed over the years by grounds keeper Bill Rodriguez and his crew of half a dozen or so men.

The oak is only one of the more evident wonders on the Pleasantville campus. Dogwoods line the walks, formal gardens grace entryways and courtyards, literally thousands of blossoming bulbs light the woods lining the main driveway in spring. Early on, Mrs. Wallace personally involved herself in gardening. A prospective employee for the New York art department was sent to Pleasantville to get the approval of Mrs. Wallace who has over the years personally supervised the art department the way her husband has the editorial; the applicant's apprehension at passing muster before this grand lady was somewhat eased when he found her poking around in the gardens like any suburban housewife. This Wallace concern for gardens led some years ago to one of the more bizarre incidents in the magazine's history. Touring the grounds one night, local police picked up a man who seemed to be wandering aimlessly and suspiciously around the buildings. On the way to the station, the man protested violently that he was a hired "tulip watcher" to prevent small animals from devouring the new growth on hundreds of recently planted bulbs—an unlikely story that the police didn't buy until they confirmed it by a call to the Digest's business manager.

Despite such precautions, a species of wildlife did succeed recently in upsetting Digest calm. Evidently headquartered on one of the ponds in a posh housing development across Route 117 from the Digest, a flock of geese began invading Digest grounds to eat apples dropping from the trees of a miniature orchard alongside the main driveway. (This orchard, incidentally, appeared full-grown and overnight some years ago, lending some credence to the story about God.) Whenever the geese appeared a Digest executive charged with the care of grounds and buildings would rush personally from his office overlooking the orchard and shoo them away lest their noted capacity for defecation ("Quicker than grass through a goose") might sully the greensward. Noting this, nature lovers on the staff felt that he might somehow be upsetting the delicate natures of the geese. A couple of impish editors composed a letter which they sent to another high-ranking Digest business executive. Purportedly from a woman in the housing development who had come to love the geese and complaining in no uncertain terms of such inhumane treatment of God's creatures, the letter said, among other things, "I was so mad at your Mr. So-and-so that I wished that those geese would peck him on his you know what." Circulated widely by its gleeful recipient, the letter did the trick, and the geese were left undisturbed.

Beyond the orchard, on the eastern edge of the grounds, is the other important building, the Guest House, where most high-level wining and dining takes place. Built somewhere around 1800 in colonial style—and since enlarged in the same style—the building served as a farmhouse and country store during its long history. When the Wallaces acquired the property, the building was first used as construction headquarters, then rented until 1950 at which time it was renovated to provide three dining rooms of various sizes for official entertaining and bedrooms for Digesters coming to headquarters on temporary duty. The place is fitted out even more like a home than the main building, abounding in priceless antiques, Oriental porcelain and paintings, including two Corots and a Lépine. Despite its elegant coziness, some foreign visitors, left alone at night in the creaky old building in what amounts to the middle of nowhere, have come firmly to the conclusion that it is haunted and dubbed it the "ghost house." A German editor who braved out three months there swears that he finally saw the ghost on a bright moonlight night—an Indian hoeing corn in the field behind the house. Since there wasn't any corn there by daylight, his story was widely doubted.

Though probably not invaded by Indians, the Digest grounds were once the scene of a killing so famous that Fulton Oursler, the human writing machine, turned out a whole book about it called *The Reader's Digest Murder Case.* The event took place on the rainy afternoon of April 3, 1950. A Digest truck, William Waterbury driving and Andrew Petrini, a messenger, sitting beside him on a short ledge facing the rear, left the front door about 3 p.m. with a load of checks and cash for Chappaqua. Suddenly a battered old truck pulled across their path on the driveway leading to Route 117. When they stopped, a man wearing large spectacles and a rubber nose appeared at the right window, fired a revolver into the cab, killing Petrini. Two other men seized Waterbury and bound him. The gang drove both trucks to a side road nearby where they transferred themselves and the loot to a waiting car and took off. They must have been disappointed when they examined their haul: some $40,000, of which $35,143.26 was in unendorsed checks, leaving them only $4,960.91 in cash, or less than $1,300 each. Apprehended later, the criminals proved to be three parolees from Dannemora State Prison, who were convicted of murder, and a friend who turned state's evidence.

Guarded now unobtrusively around the clock by uniformed Burns Agency men, the Digest has since been remarkably free of violence or vandalism, considering the treasures in art and the flow of cash within its walls. Aside, no doubt, from the usual business pilfering of small quantities of supplies and fictionalizing on expense accounts, the only crimes I ever heard of in my time were a gentlemanly act of embezzlement on the part of an employee exposed to too much cash and a heist of ladies' purses by a man, presumably an outsider, posing as a telephone repairman. So there certainly is a Pleasantville in the physical sense, at least. Yet, whatever visitors may think, work goes on there, and where there's work, there's the inevitable daily drama of struggle and frustration, success and failure, joy and misery, perhaps even intensified by the placid background against which it is played and the patriarchal benevolence that is supposed to take the sting out of work.

Everybody who comes to work for the magazine or its parent organization, Reader's Digest Association, Inc., is handed a sheaf of booklets setting forth the benefits they can expect beyond salary. Among the titles: "The Reader's Digest–Blue Cross, Blue Shield," "Your Major Medical Plan," "The Reader's Digest Retirement and Long Term Disability Plans," "Reader's Digest Profit-Sharing Plan." This last is illustrated throughout with cartoon figures of a man and woman (there are some 1,162 male and 2,130 female employees on the company's United States staff) whose supposed dialogue sets the tone and purpose of the policies. Man: "This makes me practically a stockholder"; woman: "You and me both." Woman: "Now, I'm working for me"; man: "And I for me." Man: "It stimulates us to help boost *profits* . . ."; woman: ". . . and keep costs *low.*" A last cartoon shows a contented woman sitting alone and musing, "Working for the Digest is a plan of life."

Profit sharing is only one of the Digest employee benefits which, taken all together, must honestly be called impressive. In addition to a good pension and medical program (there's also an in-house dispensary with nurses on duty and a doctor on call), some very special things are laid on. Every employee gets every Friday off in the merry month of May, presumably chosen by Wallace for its beauty and, possibly, the suburban need to to get outdoors and help spring along in yard and garden. At Christmas every employee gets a large frozen turkey, and on his or her birthday, can claim a free lunch in the cafeteria where all food is regularly sold below cost. The company underwrites cheap bus transportation for those who don't wish to drive, gives away free Condensed Books and magazines and offers reduced rates on other RDA products such as records, tapes, special books. There is even a modest cafeteria sweepstakes to make up for the fact that company employees are ineligible to compete in the big subscriber lottery. Each employee gets four weeks paid vacation a year to rest up from the ardures of showing up five days a week between 8:30 a.m. and 4 p.m.—35 hours in all, if you count the prescribed half hour for lunch; less, when coffee breaks are taken into consideration.

There are probably many reasons for the Digest's deviation from the normal nine to five business hours, but the main one would seem to be that it is a kind of "country time" (the Digest's New York office keeps regular hours), allowing Digesters to enjoy the gifts of suburbia in the late afternoon light. Real pioneers who worked above the banks and stores in Pleasantville during the 30's recall that Editor Wallace often closed up shop for everybody as early as 3 p.m. on days that looked promising for golf and tennis. Even in the new building where a growing staff dictated more regimentation, DeWitt Wallace seemed almost a fanatic about getting people to go home on time. A man who was there during the days Wallace came regularly to the office recalls how the boss would walk down murderer's row precisely at 4 p.m., stick his head in a door and say, "Come on, Fritz (Managing Editor Dashiell), time to pack up and get out. . . . Time to go home, Bun . . . (subsequent Managing Editor Mahony)" and so on. "These fellows would gather up all their papers, stuff them into a briefcase and go out to the parking lot," my informant told me. "When they saw Wally's car leave, they'd turn around, come back into their offices and go on working."

On the executive level of the Digest work almost around the clock was expected; Wallace himself was known to spend most of the time away from the office laboring in his tower room at High Winds. So this chicken shooing act would seem almost incomprehensible except that Wallace would explain that he didn't want people sitting around there burning the lights— and mean it. Like many of the rich, Wallace has a kind of string-saving mentality; at one point during a recession, he canceled free newspapers for the editors, ordered that the Guest House stop giving away cigarettes and change the cocktail nibblies from cashews to peanuts while, of course, the million-dollar executive jet kept making the rounds of the nation's golf courses for the pleasure of advertisers. In truth, though, lighting at the

Digest tends to fly higher than the plane in terms of costs as a study at the worst period of the oil shortage revealed—in fiscal '74, the company used 275,000 gallons of oil for heating purposes and generated 11,484,500 kilowatt hours of electricity.

Aware of all of this, Wallace plunged personally into the battle to save energy. He not only decreed that people turn off their lights when they went to lunch but sent an agent around to identify offenders. Like as not, one of these would return to find a personal note of admonishment from "DW" on his desk. Though most culprits caught in this crime suffered in shaky silence, Managing Editor Fulton Oursler, Jr., proved that he inherited some of his father's writing talent by responding with a note that Wallace saw fit to broadcast: "I have tried to believe that the noontime light in my empty office was only the afterglow of editorial brilliance, a misplaced halo, the trailing sparks of a phosphorescent wit, or the nimbus that always brightens my life when a Digest springtime approaches. But, alas, my secretary confirms your report. I will not make light of it. Those shocking figures from Con Ed prove that this is indeed a burning issue among current events. Now that I know watt's what, I will do an instant volteface, and I hope in the future that you can report that the Digest, at least at lunchtime, is ohm free."

If Wallace insisted that hours not be overkept, he was equally demanding that they not be underkept. In the early, informal days, he often decreed on the spur of the moment what came to be called "editorial Fridays" off after an issue had been put to bed. Apparently some editors got the wrong message and took to decreeing their own Fridays, or perhaps Tuesdays or Wednesdays off, too; whatever, Wallace instituted a form throughout the editorial department that came to be known as the "laundry list"—a sheet with blank spaces for arrival and departure of every day in the month. Times of these events were to be entered daily with excuses for deviation duly noted, such as "ice storm," "wife sick," "in New York office," etcetera, and they were collected monthly. Whether anybody up there studied these sheets was not known for sure, but one girl in the New York office, pressed for time on collection day, simply scribbled 9 a.m. to 5 p.m. into every appropriate space. Back came a note from Wallace congratulating her on perfect attendance which leads one to believe that he either had his tongue in cheek or had editorial reasons for encouraging the writing of fiction. For at least the last quarter-century, or perhaps longer, this annoying and somewhat demeaning procedure prevailed. Not long ago the straw boss in charge of collecting and filing laundry lists asked Wallace what he should do with them. "Oh, is that still going on?" Wallace said. Even with this obvious disinterest at the top, the straw bosses kept the thing going, perhaps because, like any bureaucratic growth, the laundry list had taken on a life of its own, and would be missed.

Aware as he must have been that the laundry list was a fairly wide-meshed net and that, in any case, it was thrown over only one department in the business, Wallace from time to time conducted what came to be known as "bed checks" in some quarters. A man we'll call Tom arrived on the dot of nine in his New York office one day to hear the phone ringing. When he picked it up, a voice said, "Hello, Tom, this is Wally . . ." Still hardly awake and totally unused to hearing voices from on high, Tom said somewhat uncertainly, "Yes . . . ?" "I just wanted to see how you are getting along," said the voice. "Fine, sir, fine," Tom replied, and the phone went dead. Immediately, the phone started ringing in the still empty office next to Tom's which was, by coincidence, occupied by a man also named Tom. Our Tom rushed over, picked up the receiver and heard the same voice ask, "Is this Tom?" "Yes, this is Tom . . ." "Well, this is Wally; I just wanted to see how you are getting along . . ." The bed check could work in reverse, too. About nine o'clock one evening, the phone rang in the home of a friend of mine. It was Wallace, and my friend's wife informed him with some bitterness of tone, no doubt, that her husband was still in his New York office. Minutes later my friend picked up his ringing phone in the office to find Wallace on the other end ordering him to go home.

For nearly everybody with any amount of responsibility within the company, the eerie feeling that DeWitt Wallace had his finger right on your pulse was conveyed not only by the phone but by the mails. Evidently equipped at all times with a little black book listing names and home addresses of key employees, Wallace was prone to drop a card or letter from wherever he might be in the country or the world. Generally they were welcome messages like the one I got from Williamsburg or some such place congratulating me on a "spot"—finding a usable article in a magazine from which we rarely printed. What shook you, though, was the fact that if he somehow knew that, he was probably equally aware of your errors. Indeed, Wallace was not above setting up rather elaborate watching devices to make sure he was getting his money's worth from his employees. Paul Reynolds reports on such an operation in his book:

"Wallace . . . was the questioning, hardheaded businessman. In 1939 he hired an author whom I shall call Smith at $600 a month for three months, to read some twenty current magazines and to report personally to Wallace in his home as to which articles in these magazines Smith thought worthy of Digest reprint. Wallace phoned me at my home to explain that checks could not be made out to my agency for fear that his office might get wind of what was going on. Wallace was conducting an independent check on his editors. For the sake of their morale he did not want them to know what he was doing.

"A year later, seeing Wallace at a Dutch Treat luncheon, I asked him how the Smith matter came out. Wallace said, fine. He added that he was convinced that his editors were doing a fine job in selecting pieces from other magazines for reprint. To check on his editors this extraordinary man had involved himself with great pains in an unusual sub rosa activity."

An insight into why Wallace would suffer these pangs of doubt about his employees comes from an editorial associate of mine. Like everyone else, he had to be interviewed by Wallace before he could go on the staff. At the end of this trying meeting, Wallace sighed and said to him, "I don't really know what you are going to be doing. I'm not sure what anyone does around here—I used to do it all myself, you know."

Having done everything himself, Wallace not only kept his eyes open but focussed them "on the sparrow," so to speak. The same interest in homely detail that made him such a genius as an editor carried over into other matters as well. A fascinating glimpse of this side of DeWitt Wallace comes from Harry Morgan who for a long time directed the World Press Institute at Macalester College, a charitable enterprise in which Wallace had great personal interest. So keen was the interest, in fact, that Wallace would call Harry in St. Paul several times a week to chat about it. After a few months of this, he suggested that the calls were costing a lot of money and that it would be more economical for Harry to send him a weekly report. So every Friday Harry would dictate a report and get it into the mail in St. Paul in time to reach Wallace at his High Winds home in Mt. Kisco on Saturday. This worked well until one busy Friday when Harry forgot the report.

"At seven a.m. Saturday," Harry relates, "my secretary called and said, 'Harry, we forgot the report.' Half an hour later we were down at the office where I dictated the report, and we mailed it airmail, special. On Monday morning, I got a phone call about eleven o'clock from Wally. 'Harry,' he said, 'I could really lose my temper, but I thought this over, and I decided that all of us, even young people like you, learn from mistakes. I enjoyed reading your report, but do you know what happened to it?'

" 'No, sir . . .'

" 'Did it ever occur to you what went on between St. Paul and rural Westchester County?'

" 'No, sir . . .'

" 'It was postmarked Saturday morning, and it arrived in Westchester probably some time Saturday night or Sunday morning. We don't have rural deliveries even for specials. So you wasted the special delivery stamp, and you wasted money sending it airmail because if you had sent it regular mail it would have arrived at the same time as it did on Monday. So let's just remember the waste of special delivery plus the difference between first class and airmail. This I can forgive. But do you know what really concerns me and should concern you?'

" 'No, sir . . .'

" 'Let's just think for a moment what might happen between St. Paul and Westchester County . . .'

"I said, 'Wally, you'll have to tell me.'

" 'Up in the left-hand corner it says Macalester College, St. Paul, Minn. Imagine the number of people who handled this letter realizing the money wasted by a nonprofit college. In terms of public relations, what does this do?' "

Within a week, Harry received from Wallace a full page of 100 first-class stamps, as well as a packet of old, used envelopes to replace the new manila ones in which he had been mailing his reports.

Knowing the keenness of the Wallace eye and ear, the "sparrows" in Pleasantville tend to fly low and chirp softly. There's a curious quiet about the place as compared to other editorial enterprises which, by their nature, bring together highly verbal and opinionated people. "It's a kind of neutral atmosphere," one writer who came in out of the cold to work a dozen years as a Pleasantville editor told me. "Very provincial. Nobody was really excited about anything. I'd come in all worked up about some big political story or something that had broken in the morning papers, and nobody would even mention it. Intellectually, I didn't make any friends there; it was just as if I were working in a clothing shop. In fact, I don't think there were very close friendships among any editors, and if there were, they had nothing to do with the magazine but were based on skiing or hunting together or something like that. When you'd join them for lunch, that's all they talked about."

Coming up from New York, I had almost the same impression. I put it down partly to the fact that these people had worked so long in harness together that they had exhausted the need for any communication below the level of daily trivia, as is often the case in long and stable marriages. When I and a couple of other young men were hired, they were still speaking of one editor in his mid-30's who had been on the staff for seven years as "new." We were the first editorial people hired in all that time; the rest had been around for twenty or more years, an almost unbelievably long warming of editorial chairs. So suspicious were the old hands, or maybe Wallace himself, of new blood that there was a saying in those days descriptive of the "breaking in" period—"seven years before the masthead." It was true. The "new" man's name went on the masthead—a decision Wallace alone could make—just after we arrived, and it was almost seven years to the day before my colleagues and I joined him. Now with Wallace letting others have their way on details, names go on the masthead almost before a new editor gets his pencil sharpened—O, tempora! O, mores!

In addition to familiarity, a kind of futility dampened the expression of opinion. Except in the most technical sense as to whether an article was or wasn't usable in the Digest, editorial opinion was rarely sought. For one thing, perhaps on a cue from the top, there were no meetings of any kind, an almost unheard of practice in editorial enterprises (or almost anywhere else in modern business) and one that must have saved the Digest incalculable man hours over the years. Most communication was carried on by note, but doors were always open so that it was possible to drop in on anybody from the executive editors on down for a quick snatch of dialogue if necessary. About the only thing resembling an editorial meeting was the Guest House lunch, an internationally famous institution which has hosted such past or future heads of state as Brandt of Germany, Rabin of Israel, Nixon of the United States, among others. Many editorial projects do come out of these luncheons. Hobart Lewis liked to cite as a stellar example Cornelius Ryan's *The Longest Day* which was born at a luncheon during which the author was asked what he'd like to write, given all the time and expense money he needed, and Ryan said, "The story of D-day."

But Guest House luncheons were most emphatically not occasions upon which Digest editors were expected to express their own opinions. Though they were seemingly informal, protocol was as rigid as that of a state dinner. The person who was supposed to do the talking was, of course, the guest. Since most guests were selling something, whether a specific article, a political point of view, or their own sparkling personality, they would oblige. As a result, only the most skillful at talking with a full mouth ever got much lunch. Truly experienced guests like Leland Stowe, the Pulitzer prize-winning reporter who became a Digest roving editor, didn't even try. He would arrange quietly for the Guest House steward to pack a sandwich for him to eat on his way back to New York, prop his notes against an empty plate and deliver a steady monologue to the chewing editors. No matter who had arranged the lunch, the host was automatically the senior Digest person in the room—Wallace, of course, then Lewis, then Harper, then Mahony and on down. The host's function was to keep the guest talking with appropriate questions, and the other six or seven editors present were supposed to leap to his rescue if he faltered. If you were quite junior and didn't feel moved to expose your brilliance to the boss, you could get in some steady, satisfying eating at these affairs. Should the subject of the luncheon seem to call for a decision, such as an assignment, all eyes would turn to the host. Only with Wallace or Lewis present could a project get a firm yes or no; the others would have to hedge their bets in case Wallace or Lewis felt otherwise. Thus, few guests departed any wiser than they were when they came with respect to the ultimate fate of their project.

Obviously, such an atmosphere was not conducive to anything like discussion. The guest, being a guest, was treated as such, regardless of his views. The guest, being also a salesman, delivered his message in a way he felt would be most pleasing to Wallace personally, or to Wallace as represented by his editors. For an editor who was invited along as window dressing to plunge in and challenge the guest—and, by implication, the host who was leading him along—was unthinkable. One editor, new to Pleasantville, more or less did this in ignorance at a Lewis lunch. His first lunch at the Guest House became his last, for he was shortly thereafter "let go" on the grounds of incompetence, not only groundless grounds as those of us who knew his work could attest but, even if true, grounds he held in common with a number of colleagues who remained. On the other hand, failure to perceive the Guest House protocol might legitimately be held to be a form of incompetence, as it would certainly be in the case of a person pursuing a diplomatic career.

I can personally testify that it could be a kind of torture to sit through one of these performances when you were graced with a special knowledge of the matter in hand. Because I had spent the war years in Asia, had made several return trips to the area and had generally tried to keep up with events there, I was often included when Wallace's personal Asian advisor, Dr. Walter Judd, the former congressman, came to lunch. A thoroughly likeable man of great personal charm and unmatched forensic ability, Judd would propose to a nodding Wallace yet another diatribe against Red China and communism in general even at a time when the most Republican of Republican administrations was plotting to open the door to China, a venture that any dispassionate observer of the area knew was inevitable and necessary. I can't imagine what would have happened if I had questioned Judd's "expertise"—after all, he was twenty years my senior and had been a missionary in China; moreover, it was abundantly clear that Wallace liked what he was hearing. Interestingly, though, at one lunch when none of the editors present had either the power to fire any of the others or the authority to buy what Judd was saying, the good doctor was an entirely different person. He freely revealed an understanding of the complexities of the Chinese experience that never appeared in the simplistic message he sold to DeWitt Wallace and delivered from the platform.

The futility of expressing one's personal views was underscored by the fact that two of the highest editorial executives during my time were known to be liberal Democrats, yet their political opinion was never reflected in the magazine. An incident involving one of these men was instructive. He came into the office of a younger editor who worked with a good many writers and, pacing up and down, outlined a glowing, optimistic article that the Digest would like on what was right with

America, citing all the positive points that could be made in great detail. "Do you think you have anybody who could write a piece like that?" he asked. "Well," said the younger man, "you've got it so well in mind, why don't you write it yourself?" "Because I don't believe a word of it," the older man said.

Only in the passions heated up by the Vietnam war, when the Digest strongly favored the war and blasted American protestors of every stripe as unpatriotic, did private editorial opinion boil to the surface. Several young editors, mostly in New York or the book department of the magazine, wrote memos of protest to Hobart Lewis about one article which resulted in very minor modifications, such as altering the proposed signature from "The Editors" to a line describing it as "An Editorial." They got similar small concessions on another piece, but when the dust settled, at least three editors had resigned, including one Kenneth Gross who had been at the Digest only three months. In a long piece for *Newsday* about his experience, Gross quoted a friendly senior editor nearing retirement as telling him, "I think you behaved well. But you must remember where you are. These people aren't interested in what you think or what you believe." Gross goes on to report: "There were many tormented editors that Christmas season. Urgent meetings and angry conversations were held in pine-perfumed offices and hallways. But many had already spent their annual 15 percent Christmas bonuses. They had counted on it and it was part of their budgets."

Indeed, this bonus ranks so high among the Digest employee benefits that the company broadcasts it annually in press releases like the one for 1975, beginning: "For the fiftieth year in its fifty-four year history, The Reader's Digest will pay its employees a year-end profit-sharing bonus. The bonus, which will amount to 15 percent of each employee's base salary, will be paid early in January . . ." What isn't included in the press release is the fact that, since the bonus has been paid so continuously, salaries for people going to work at the Digest are negotiated on the assumption that it will go on being paid. This means 15 percent, a heavy share, of everybody's income derives from a payment that the company can withdraw at will. In addition, a fairly large number of "key employees" throughout the company are annually rewarded with "special bonuses" sent to their homes along with letters from the top advising them to keep both the amount and receipt of this favor secret. These bonuses as well as stock options depend solely upon the pleasure of the giver and can amount to a third to a half of an employee's total income. After a person is on the special bonus list—he generally doesn't know how or why he got there—for a few years running, he naturally begins to commit himself to expenditures, such as mortgage or college tuition, he might not otherwise afford and, of course, loses interest in getting involved in any gaff or controversy that might cause his name to be scratched by the unknown hand that put it there in the first place.

Salaries above the clerical worker's hourly-rate level are a Digest secret more carefully guarded than the subscription list or the bottom-line profit figure. Owing to specific admonitions of secrecy, Digesters, even when drunk, are more close-mouthed about discussing income among themselves than they are about politics. While hourly rates at the Digest are known to be no more than competitive with other businesses, salaries are held to be spectacular—and in some cases they are (that is, salary plus bonus), as any astute observer of size of houses, age and quality of automobiles, duration and distance of pleasure trips and other manifestations of conspicuous consumption can guess. One of the few published accounts of the Digest salary structure appeared in *Time* some twenty-five years ago. Since it went unchallenged and since Wallace is still in full control of the company, it is worth repeating with all due allowance for inflation.

"The Digest's senior editors reportedly get anywhere from $20,000 to $50,000 a year, and sometimes half as much again in bonuses," *Time* reported. "Salaries and bonuses vary widely. Wallace keeps his staff guessing on their pay. One year Executive Editor Payne drew a salary of $34,000 and a bonus of $87,600; in a later year, he got a salary of $84,500 but no bonus.

In one year, Al Cole got a salary of $99,500, two years later got $84,500."

Since there is no reason to suppose that Digest salaries have, on the whole, gone down, it must be evident to anybody in the business that a Digester—or a good many Digesters depending on the base from which they started—on the senior editor level and above makes more money than he could possibly hope to make in any other place. This is presumably true for the business department, too. Not only that but the accumulation from stock options, profit sharing and the like can make a person in a relatively modest job truly wealthy if he lasts out the course. Hence, few people ever quit the Digest voluntarily, resulting in a rather remarkable display of company loyalty.

How far this loyalty goes in the other direction is an interesting question. Not long after I reached Pleasantville, primed with stories to the effect that it was a place from which nobody was retired or fired, a senior executive told me laughingly, "You know I was hired on a temporary basis, to see how it worked out—that was fourteen years ago." Within a year, the man was gone, probably after getting the golden handshake; from tales about separation payments, in those days at least, it might more nearly be described as platinum. In any case, evidence abounds that the Digest, aside from more liberal use of money to assuage its conscience, is capable of pursuing the perhaps necessary ruthlessness of any successful business, and this can be hard on those true believers who opted for it as "a way of life."

A recent case in point has to be that of Walter B. Mahony, Jr. For thirty-nine years Mahony labored in Pleasantville virtually around the clock, seven days a week, and as a result rose to executive editor and vice president. Since he had a few more years to go before retirement, Mahony was the logical contender for the top editorial spot, editor-in-chief, in the executive reshuffle following the departure of Lewis. What happened instead was revealed in a memo signed by Wallace and Editor-in-Chief Thompson that speaks for itself: "Bob Cousins, Editorial Director of General Books, has long felt the need for a Chief Text Editor. Recognizing this significant opportunity, Bun

Mahony has resigned as Executive Editor of RD to fill this important assignment . . . It is with real regret that we accept Bun Mahony's departure from the magazine. He has rendered notable service to the Digest for 39 years. Bun's dedication and loyalty to the magazine have not been surpassed by anyone. He will be truly missed both professionally and personally by his colleagues. But certainly the entire editorial staff joins us in the hope that Bun's high expectations of satisfying accomplishment in the new opening will be fulfilled . . ."

Thus beneath the placid surface of Pleasantville boils a well of competitive struggle that may actually surpass that in organizations where a divided power structure gives a beleagured executive a chance to enlist allies. Another man who left the organization in frustration told me, "Wallace just doesn't believe in organization, and he doesn't know how to handle people. I don't know whether he likes competition or just thinks it's the right way to do things, but he certainly uses it." Proof of this was what happened when Mahony was elevated from managing to executive editor. Not one, but four, men were appointed to fill his spot. This not only made it hard on the men in contention but on those of us below seeking clear directives. "A horse race like this sure makes it hard on us ass kissers—we don't know which one to kiss," said a friend of mine. Reaction was swift. One of the new managing editors met my friend in the hall and said, "Say, I hear you called me a horse's ass." Since the offender is still there, it is to be assumed that his sin has been forgiven, but the bite of his words lingers on as a more accurate description of real life in Pleasantville for a good many people than that in the company booklets.

While this may not be evident to visitors soaking up the tranquil physical surroundings of Pleasantville, it shows itself to the observant eye. When a friend of mine was leaving the rat race of New York journalism and boasting to his erstwhile colleagues about the peace and prosperity he'd find in Pleasantville, one of them responded, "Yeah? Then why in hell do they drink so much up there?" Whether Digesters drink more than, say, their counterparts in IBM headquarters a few miles across the Westchester hills in Armonk, is to be doubted, but they probably drink as much. Sadly, I've personally watched good men who lost earlier Digest horse races go the route of alcoholism. The disease is rampant enough, as it must be in any company of such size, that a new personnel benefit is the Reader's Digest Employee Alcoholism Program which stresses that "employees with alcoholism will not have their job security or promotional opportunities jeopardized by a request for help."

High spirits, whether "under the influence" or not, are in fact viewed with remarkable tolerance by Digest management, which is to say, Wallace. There's a Digest tradition of pranks and practical jokes, called "capers," that are so widely known as to authorship and so pointedly overlooked that it almost amounts to an acknowledgment of the need for release of tensions that cannot be dissipated in more creative ways. In any event, the tradition is well founded since Wallace himself was fond of stunts in his younger days, as in the two reported by *Time*: "Once, on his way to a Halloween party, he sent word that he had been hurt in an auto accident. Then he tottered in, in Mercurochrome-splashed bandages. On another occasion, calling on a Digest editor to meet his new bride, Wallace broke the ice by starting a game of leapfrog with her on the lawn." A story handed down to me had to do with a Wallace discipline by way of a prank. When the Digesters were moved from Pleasantville into their fancy new building, a couple of editors displayed their disdain for such elegance by wearing old clothes and growing beards. As the story goes, Wallace summoned them one day into his own office where they were confronted by the entire remainder of the staff wearing false beards. They not only got the message but, until the last year or so, beards were known to be anathema to Wallace and were seldom seen in the halls of Pleasantville.

Recent pranks, like the letter about the geese, have sometimes had the bite of protest, usually against the stuffiness of privilege. The Digest's vast parking lots—they hold 1,000 cars —were long democratically open to everyone on a first-come, first-spot basis; Wallace himself often parked the farthest from the building. When, however, reserved spaces were suddenly assigned to favored employees, one of the best of them to a rather fussy and precise woman, the pranksters took action. One dawn, a decrepit rowboat salvaged from the mud flats of Long Island Sound was found in the lady's place, securely tied to the designating marker. If Wallace heard about this, it's to be presumed he enjoyed it, because he himself had taken to playing a game with the parking. No longer coming regularly to the office, he would often show up about noon, cruise the reserved line and put whatever car he was driving into an empty spot. One executive returning from lunch and finding his space occupied, marched to the reception desk and demanded that the guard be summoned to haul the offender away. "Did you notice the license plate?" the receptionist asked cautiously. The man went back, saw that the plate was LBW (Lila Bell Wallace—Wallace often drove his wife's car), and found another place to park. Despite this much discussed game, nobody seemed to get, or want to get, the hint. The end came one day when Wallace was walking out at lunch time with a much trusted, though low on the totem pole, employee. As they reached the reserved line, he said, "I'll walk along with you to your parking place." "But I don't have a parking place," the man replied. Wallace returned to the building and made a phone call. By the end of lunch that day, the markers on reserved spots were gone—and are still missing as of this writing.

Aside from such fun and games, the more usual diversions resulting from a mingling of the sexes are no more unknown in Pleasantville than in any other large organization. Even back in the 30's it was, in the words of one woman who was there, "a swinging place." The women, she asserts, frustrated by the bucolic surroundings and the often low reward for their services, sought satisfaction in catching men. Since most men come to the Digest in mid-life and encumbered with wives and often children, the games going on were for rather high stakes. While it is unlikely that the Digest divorce rate is statistically higher than that of the population as a whole or that of any other comparable corporation, a significant number of Pleasantville partings have ended for the man in remarriage to a woman who knows her way around the Digest and who, therefore, is presumably more understanding of his trials, tribulations and triumphs. I can recall hearing of one first wife who could never get it through her head that mowing the lawn herself was small sacrifice for allowing her husband to compile a "laundry list" record of departures at 5:30, 6, 7 or later. In any case, keeping it "in the family" may mollify to some extent the genuine distress that the long-married Wallaces have often expressed over the fact that members of the Digest seem to have as much trouble as anyone else with an institution they so celebrate in the pages of the magazine.

Of course, as almost any issue will reveal, the Digest is far from being philosophically opposed to seeking joy in sexual activity. Both of the Wallaces themselves exhibit, within limits of a decent restraint, a lively interest in members of the opposite sex, and Wallace has been known to encourage his employees to do likewise. In fact, at a Guest House party for foreign journalists enroute to the World Press Institute, the Wallace interest in seeing romance flower got a little out of hand. Girls from various Digest offices had been recruited to dance with the young men from abroad. Dropping by the party on his way to dinner, Wallace told the assembled group: "Young men, I'm going to give you a good piece of advice. These girls are here for only one purpose—so that you can have some fun. And to you girls, I'm going to tell you that these men have a reputation for being fine men in their countries. If you are going to be raped, you might as well relax and enjoy it." As in the case of some Digest articles, the Wallace humor was taken too literally by men who may have had trouble with the language and girls who may have been awed by the boss. "It happened everywhere," one of the young journalists who was there told me, "upstairs, downstairs, outside. Some guys came in with mud all over them."

But maybe the incident was more illustrative of the sort of cultural problem that can arise in an international institution than anything else, as another, more private Guest House frolic suggests. A young editor from a Latin country making his first visit to Pleasantville was evidently lonely in the Guest House, having left behind not only a wife and children but a mistress. He used his evident charms to rectify this situation almost immediately after meeting the daughter of a lofty Digest executive at a party. Aroused by odd noises in the night, the Guest House manager looked out and saw a car that he recognized as belonging to the executive. Suspecting a delicate problem, he called his superior, the man in charge of grounds and buildings. This grounds keeper, no friend of the other executive, seized upon the opportunity gleefully. He phoned local police and told them that somebody was evidently trying to steal Guest House art works and asked them to accompany him in an investigation. Equipped with flashlights, the police and the grounds keeper stole up the stairs, flung open the young editor's door and bared, in the most literal sense, the liaison. This exposure was embarrassing for the executive and his daughter—but worse for the philandering editor. Shipped back home, he was fired reluctantly by a boss who also possessed a Latin temperament. "What's the matter with you?" he asked the editor. "Don't you know what motels are for?" The editor was incensed. "It's all your fault," he said. "It was my first trip to America, and you never told me." To open the cultural gap a little wider, consider this footnote to the story: the young editor was, according to his boss, distressed not so much by losing his job, not so much by what his wife would think, but by what his indiscretion might do to his relations with his mistress.

Whatever they might find in the way of romance, and despite the fact that Lila Wallace's name has been forever listed at the top of the masthead with that of her husband, women at the Digest have been a rather distressed lot. They have been branded by the old saying that the Digest is put out by "little old ladies in tennis shoes." And for some time their generally meek demeanor and ladylike dress gave a little credence to the quip. Styles, like everything else at the Digest, tend to filter down from the top. When I first went there in the days before air conditioning, Wallace would come to work on hot days in a sports shirt, a comfort quickly adopted by the rest of us. In the air-conditioned Lewis regime, a tie and jacket became the unspoken order of the day since it was impossible to know when you might be included in a sudden conference or luncheon where you could be an embarrassment to the well-tailored editor-in-chief. Interestingly, the first time I saw Thompson after his elevation to Lewis's old job it was midsummer, and he was wearing a sports shirt.

Digest women had no such example since on her rare appearances Mrs. Wallace was usually elegantly turned out for luncheon or cocktails rather than for labor at a desk. They had to wait for another one of those intercultural exchanges to liberate them. Coming from fashion-conscious Paris, a young woman editor turned up one day in what came to be called her "gangster suit"—black pants with a wide pink stripe, black blouse with stripes and a tie. She was unaware that pants weren't worn to work in Pleasantville until she observed the stir it caused. A male editor watching her walk down the hall whistled and yelled, "Hey, are you our little old lady in tennis shoes?" But the other women editors were, of course, even more fascinated. At the end of the day, one of them came to her and said, "Now that you dare, I shall dare." And she did.

Getting into pants, however proved easier for Digest women than getting into better jobs. Despite the fact that women outnumber men nearly two to one in the total Digest community, most of them above the lowest clerical level have had the feeling that the Digest does not take them seriously, as a woman who worked there more than forty years complained to me. This feeling was captured by Gross with his fresh—in more ways than one—eye when he wrote: "Women, too, were forced to play an essentially comic role. For example, it was regarded as a breach of etiquette to invite female editors to lunch. This despite the fact that Lila Wallace occupied a lofty position. The men simply did not take women seriously. I knew of several women doing comparable work who made considerably less than I did." A chilling tale confirming Gross's perception involves the time an executive with an all-female staff set up a

Guest House lunch to introduce them to DeWitt Wallace; as part of the proceedings he had all the women line up and hike their skirts so that the boss could admire their legs.

More serious to Digest women than such indignities is what they feel to be professional slighting. The number of regular female writers for the magazine can be counted by the fingers on one hand, even today; a rather astonishing situation in view of the progress women have been making in other forms of publication and, of course, television. A recent Digest masthead shows only two women writers—Roving Editors Jean George and Virginia Kelly. Only one woman, Assistant Managing Editor Mary Louise Allin, appears among the top command; those women listed as senior staff editors are performing essentially the same functions they always did in the all-female departments of copy desk, research and excerpt editing. On the business side of the masthead, one has to travel a long way down the columns of fine print to find a single feminine name. This is somewhat of an irony in view of the fact that the first edition of the Reader's Digest had a masthead containing the names of one DeWitt Wallace and three women (two of them fictional). Even today's limited mention of women in the categories from senior editor on up is less a reflection of new enlightenment in Pleasantville than a rather hasty response to a serious charge of discrimination filed by a number of Digest women in the early 70's and still in the courts.

First brought before the New York State Human Rights Division and dismissed, the complaint is now before the United States District Court of the Southern District of New York where the case has been ordered to trial in the spring of 1977. Filed on behalf of eight specified women, the case is a "class action" complaint under Title VII of the Civil Rights Act of 1964, claiming representation of more than 2,000 women—"all women employees of the Reader's Digest Association, Inc., and all those who recently have been and/or will be in the future employed by the Reader's Digest Association, Inc., excluding those women, if any, who hold unskilled jobs on the building and maintenance staff." The suit, according to Harriet Rabb, the plaintiff's principal attorney, is calling for equalization of pay between men and women, including retroactive additional pay for those women whose salaries were lower than those of men in comparable jobs, and "a declaratory judgment and injunction to restrain defendants from maintaining practices, policies, customs and usages which discriminate against plaintiffs and members of their class because of their sex with respect to hiring, placement, promotions, and other conditions of employment."

Among the last "conditions" cited by lawyer Rabb are complaints from women in all-female clerical pools that records are kept and admonitions given on such things as frequency of visiting the ladies' room and/or length of stay therein. On a loftier level, women are charging rigged conditions to inhibit or block promotions, vast discrepancies in pay (particularly in the category of special bonuses and stock options), lack of opportunity for training, and the like. "The company offered us a heap of money to go away," Ms. Rabb told me," but we turned it down. In the first place, this suit can't be valued in money. There is a pervasive sense of fear in that company, and we want to put an end to it. It's incredible, but, of all the witnesses we've interviewed, not one has ever had the nerve to ask for a raise. We want to open the company to some accountability, to get an injunction that will demand some sort of organization chart so that people will know what kind of jobs they can hope to get and how to prepare for them. And we want the judge to say, 'I look at the top jobs in your company, and there isn't a woman in one of them—go out and get some.' We're hoping that as a result of this suit, if we prevail, people—men as well as women —won't have to tremble in their boots anymore."

How do you "open up" a privately owned company, particularly in the face of the well-known Wallace generosity, however he chooses to distribute it? Doesn't Wallace have a right to run the place any way he sees fit? Lawyer Rabb's response to these questions was swift and to the point: "The way he runs the place is in violation of the law."

Whether or not the suit actually goes to trial, as scheduled, it has already altered the conditions of life in Pleasantville, as a glance at the changing masthead between 1972 and now will confirm. It seems safe to predict that there will be fillies in future Digest horse races and that some of the secrecy and inequity of a paternalistic, structureless organization will disappear. If so, working for the Digest may lose a bit of magic, the way Christmas did when you stopped believing in Santa Claus. In the end, the real difference between "being in Pleasantville" and being in any of a number of similar places or organizations is the dominating presence of a uniquely gifted and humanly unpredictable man named DeWitt Wallace.

IX

"Me Go Now"

One of the literary products in shortest supply for any publication is humor. Despite its vast resources and millions of unsought submissions, the Digest may have more trouble striking the right humorous note than any other magazine. The reasons are both internal and external. The funny bone in any human being is almost as unique as his fingerprint, and the Digest's editorial structure, in which the last word on everything goes to the man highest on the masthead, obviously limits the selection in any given issue to what tickles one particular person. But an even more severe restriction may be, ironically, the huge audience to which the magazine is addressed. Like everything else in the table of contents, humor must have universal appeal and be immediately clear—a very difficult standard by which to measure something with as highly individual characteristics as humor.

My first lesson in handling Digest humor came in 1958 when, as a father of young children, I was moved to laughter by an Art Buchwald column called "Don't Be a Pal to Your Son." It was an interview with the acerbic cartoonist Al Capp, the tone of which can be gathered from the following quotations:

"It is my humble belief that we should make American children feel neglected, insecure, unwanted and unloved. In return we'll get courtesy, obedience, good scholastic records. They'll be so eager to be wanted that they'll do everything in the world to please us . . . Don't be a pal to your son. Be his father. What child needs a 40-year-old man for a friend?" This, remember, was at a time when all those postwar babies were just beginning to flower, when a child-centered philosophy dominated the schools, when "togetherness" was supposed to rule the home.

A few days after I proposed the Buchwald piece, Alfred S. ("Fritz") Dashiell, the Digest's impressively calm and sturdy managing editor, came in to see me. He had the article in hand and was chuckling over it, a very encouraging sign. He'd like to use it, he said, but Capp came on so strong and deadpan that he wondered if all those millions out there would realize that it was funny. Wouldn't it be better to tell them so in an editorial precede? At the Digest you don't argue much with a managing editor who has the determined look of a kindly bulldog, so it ultimately ran with this italic note: "When a humorist asks a famous cartoonist about the state of American youth, the answer is likely to be explosive. In this case, the element of truth that underlies all good wit puts a bite into the tongue-in-cheek words of Al Capp, Li'l Abner's creator."

With this experience behind me, I wasn't too surprised at what happened when I proposed that we reprint an article from *Today's Living* by Bill Conklin called "Me Go Now." I laughed so loudly when I first read this article that a couple of my fellow editors heard me and came in to share the fun. They liked it, too, and I was sure that I had a winner.

In the piece, Conklin, describing himself as a copy writer in an advertising agency, recounted a number of encounters with his new boss, Glenn Gordon, the creative director. On one occasion, for example, a secretary had her purse stolen, and thinking the thief might have ditched it in the men's room wastebasket, she asked Conklin to look for it. While he had his head in the basket and was pawing through the refuse, Gordon walked in. Another time Conklin, returning from a meeting outside the building, stepped into the elevator on the ground floor at 4:20 p.m. and came face to face with Gordon. All he could think of to say was, "Hi, just getting back from lunch?" As Conklin wrote, "Convene all the authors of all the articles on how to succeed in business. Ask them to select the one phrase *not* to be uttered to the boss at twenty past four in the afternoon. 'Just getting back from lunch?' would score an enthusiastic victory by acclamation . . ."

Nevertheless, Conklin finally did manage to have what he thought was a very reasonable conversation with Gordon. "I decided to quit while I was ahead," he wrote. "I stood up quickly and leaned toward Glenn to say good-by. A simple 'So long' or 'Nice talking with you' would have sufficed. But as I searched for the appropriate farewell, my mind (never very stable) gave way completely. My mouth began to move wordlessly. Finally I managed to speak. 'Me go now,' I said hoarsely, and walked away. Why I said that—like most of the things I do—had an explanation, but it's the kind that never can be given without adding to the confusion. I had been reading about Robert Benchley. Once, during a bad play involving a character who spoke pidgin English, he had said, 'Me go' and had left the theater. I suppose that the phrase stuck in my subconscious until that terrible moment."

When "Me Go Now" was tossed into the editorial hopper, whoever was issue editor that month scheduled it right away. But the older and wiser heads above him shook negatively and took it out of the table of contents. Considering the enthusiastic reaction to the piece by so many of my contemporaries, the verdict baffled me until it dawned on me that those longest at the Digest probably felt that "Me Go Now" struck too close to home. It was an almost exact description of the foot-in-mouth disease that afflicted nearly everybody in the organization, quite probably (or especially) those closest to the top in the presence of DeWitt Wallace. I knew for certain that it was true of me, and I decided to make publication of "Me Go Now" a cause. The fact that an editor could consider such a matter a cause, the winning of which would provide psychic gratification, in itself says a lot about the organization. In any case, the record shows that I burned for almost three years before I resorted to the solution that applied to every problem of frustration at the Digest—go to Wally.

Until the mid-60's, at least, DeWitt Wallace was in such daily touch with Digest affairs that his initials—and editing—frequently appeared on copy. It was official policy then that any decision could be appealed to him; indeed, Executive Editor Payne once told some of us, "If you don't like any of my rulings, by all means go to Wally." Although I'm sure that Payne, a rather sweet and self-effacing man who seemed content to take his hundred plus thousand dollars a year and let the credit go, meant what he said, an appeal to Wally wasn't a thing you did lightly in practice—you were almost sure to make somebody in between mad. So I waited for an opportunity to make this daring act seem logical. It came at a poker game. From time to time we younger editors would gather for an evening of imbibing and low-stake poker, an acceptable practice even though it sent us bleary-eyed to the office next day since Wally himself was addicted to the game as well as to out-of-office fraternizing among members of the Digest family. At one of these games, I recited what I could remember of "Me Go Now." It evoked such hilarity from my colleagues that they encouraged me to push it. Next day I sent it along to Wally with a note leaning heavily on the circumstances of the poker game and received a response to this effect: "I don't think it's so funny, but if you all do, I don't see any reason not to use it." With this tepid endorsement, I managed to get it through at last—and was gratified by the number of people who confirmed my suspicions that it spoke for them in their relations with the big boss.

Whether DeWitt Wallace is aware of the shivering awe he inspires in underlings would be hard to tell. His modesty is legendary and may be part of the problem. He would come and go at the Pleasantville headquarters with such little panoply that many of the thousands of persons working there had no idea of who he was. On one memorable occasion shortly after the bells were installed in the tower, Wallace drove Mrs. Wallace down at noon and parked in front of the building to hear them play. Not recognizing the elderly couple, a guard asked them to move on—and they did. Wally deplored the executive habit of communicating through a battery of secretaries as either wasteful or pretentious and made and received phone calls himself. Not one for small talk anyway, he even dispensed with introductions, leaping right into the subject at hand, so that it behooved anybody likely to have contact with him to learn to recognize his high, reedy voice at once. Nobody in the company was beyond reach of Wallace's phone, and the embarrassment caused by his surprise calls could be devastating. In a fairly typical situation of this sort, the secretary of a minor executive who had worked years at the Digest without ever hearing or seeing the legendary founder picked up her ringing phone.

"Hello, is Bill there?"

"May I ask who is calling?"

"This is DeWitt Wallace . . ."

Suspecting a joke, she said, "Oh, yes? Well, this is the Queen of Sheba!"— and hung up.

Although Wallace dialed back and patiently explained that he really was DeWitt Wallace, it took several paychecks before the girl was sure she wouldn't find the proverbial pink slip in one of them. Another lady, even longer in Digest experience and farther from the throne, had a much worse experience. It didn't help that this lady was of such a nervous temperament that once when she was eating an ice-cream bar at her desk and the phone rang, she stuck the ice-cream in her ear and the phone in her mouth. Possibly because of her nerves, the lady was wont to take one or two cocktails too many at large gatherings such as the company party where she first encountered DeWitt Wallace. When a tall and distinguished man came into the room and began shaking hands, the lady whispered to a colleague, "Who's that?" Aware of the number of drinks she'd consumed, he replied mischievously, "The company psychiatrist. Be nice to him, because he's very important." Thus when the lady's turn to shake Wallace's hand arrived, she looked up at him, batted her eyes and said, "Baby, I'd love to get on the couch with you any day." Regardless of his reaction to "Me Go Now," Wallace reportedly found that one funny, but when the lady learned the sobering truth her nerves were not improved.

Although increasingly common in the years since Wallace has been doing most of his work at home in High Winds, such incidents of mistaken identity are comic opera compared to the dramas played out when the employee knows all too well who Wallace is. The dialogue is not made easier by the great man's enigmatic character. At one of Wallace's very rare public appearances—a speech in the White House thanking President Nixon for bestowing the Medal of Freedom upon him and Mrs. Wallace—he went to the trouble of denying the "old myth that DeWitt Wallace is a shy and modest person." Nevertheless, these are the adjectives most often applied to him. Twenty-five years ago, *Time* described Wallace as "bony, angular and shy"; five years ago, Joyce Hergenhan, writing in *The Reporter Dispatch* of White Plains, said, "Throughout the meeting, he constantly showed the modesty and shyness always attributed to him by his colleagues." Whether from shyness or shrewdness, Wallace has the disconcerting habit of keeping the conversational ball in the other person's court, occasionally scoring a clean passing shot with a pointed or unexpected question. This can result in very odd behavior on the part of tense people almost always hoping to find favor in his eyes.

One editor who had almost daily conversations with Wallace in the way of business found himself left alone with the great man at a party. "I didn't think bringing up business was appropriate under the circumstances, and I couldn't stand just saying nothing," he told me, "so I started to tell him the filthiest joke I ever heard. By the time I realized what I was doing it was too late to stop. It wasn't even funny, and he just looked at me as if I had crawled out from under a rock." My own first memorable meeting with Wallace tied my tongue in a knot. My wife and I were taken to the Wallace home, High Winds, by the editor sponsoring my hiring on a Saturday afternoon for a social drink and, of course, inspection. With so much at stake, my nerves were so taut they were singing. But things went well at first. The Wallaces met us at the door like any suburban couple greeting newcomers, and the day being cool, Wallace led my wife to the fire burning on the hearth of their surprisingly cozy living room and twirled her around to warm her up. Then we all sat down, and Wallace, fixing me with his searchlight eyes, asked, "Mr. Schreiner, why were you born?" I may have opened my mouth, but absolutely nothing came out. Just before my nerves actually snapped, Mrs. Wallace saved the situation by graciously suggesting a look at the birds they kept in the house.

Though an entirely different personality than her husband— "dainty, cheerful and forthright," according to *Time*—Mrs. Wallace can occasionally evoke the foot-in-mouth disease, too. It is no secret that her opinion can have as important an effect on a Digest career as Wallace's; one man's success is said to have followed a party at which he sipped champagne from her slipper. In view of this, it's not surprising that a colleague of mine nearly worried himself into a nervous breakdown after a lapsus linguae at a party at High Winds. Several cocktails to the good, he was leaving when he encountered Mrs. Wallace speeding her departing guests on their way. A master at finding something nice to say, she looked up at him and exclaimed, "My goodness, I never realized you were so tall!" My friend rose to the occasion, squaring his shoulders and lifting his chin. "Why, I'm six feet two when fully erected," he said, and then tore into the anonymity of the night.

Whether his conversational style is deliberate or whether he simply makes the most of a natural reticence, Wallace has learned to employ it very effectively in pursuit of his purposes. Over the years he has been almost abnormally resistant to personal publicity of any kind; he permitted *The Reporter Dispatch* interview only in celebration of the Digest's fiftieth anniversary. In this light, Ms. Hergenhan was almost naive

when she wrote: "Characteristically, he was more interested in
learning his interviewer's opinions on a wide range of subjects
than he was in talking about himself."

Wallace has a way of keeping the talk running along his own
particular track. This can make things difficult for somebody
who wants to put across a point he doesn't want to hear. During
a time when unfavorable rates of exchange had effectively
cut salaries of people in the Digest's Paris bureau by more than
10 percent, one of them happened to be in Pleasantville. All of
her colleagues had primed her with facts and figures to present
their plight to Mr. Wallace when she met him. Her account of
the vital interview—vital to her and the other starving wretches
in Paris, that is—is a perfect picture of Wallace in action.

"He greets me, asks me to sit down, inquires, 'How's the
Paris office?'

" 'Fine, but we have a few problems . . .'

"He looks at me and says, 'That's a very beautiful suit you
are wearing. I like women who wear colors.'

"I say, 'Oh, thank you very much. I bought it in Paris, you
know. I'm in the Paris office, and . . .'

"He goes on, 'That suit is beautiful, but you, yourself, are
beautiful, too . . .'

"So where do you go from there? I smile; he has thrown me
completely off course. Finally, I don't know how, we end up
talking about New York state and the dogwood trees. Mr.
Wallace says, 'I understand there are no dogwood trees in
Europe, and I think you are missing a wonderful thing. This is
the time of dogwood trees, and you should drive around New
York state and admire them.'

"I think this is a very nice, old gentleman, but how do you
make a transition from 'a beautiful suit' and 'dogwood trees' to
'I'm starving'? You don't; you go away frustrated."

Another visitor from Paris—John D. Panitza, the Digest
bureau chief there—had an even more historic meeting with
DeWitt Wallace in the "Me Go Now" manner. The subject was
the same: money. Although he had been heading up the bureau
for quite some time, Panitza was then, in 1959, making only

$360 a month. In the best Digest tradition of never asking for a raise, he suffered this situation silently until it became evident that nobody in the home office was thinking about him, as to salary at any rate. Using what he could scrape together from his meager earnings, he took some vacation time and paid his own way to the United States with the intention of pleading his case before Wallace personally although he had only met the man once.

Everything went well at first. Ushered into the presence on the very day of his surprise arrival in Pleasantville, Panitza, a man gifted with Bulgarian emotion, described his condition of near starvation with tears in his eyes. Wallace listened sympathetically, cautiously promised to look into the matter and give Panitza an early answer. Relieved and elated, Panitza set out for New York to celebrate what he was sure would be a raise as a guest of his brother at the championship bout between heavyweights Ingemar Johansson and Floyd Patterson. Panitza's account of the rest of the evening goes like this:

"At Yankee Stadium we are in the second row in $100 seats. Low and behold, before the fight starts, who sits in a chair smack in front of me but DeWitt Wallace. I practically collapse. I had been telling him that I couldn't pay the rent, could barely eat, and here I am in a $100 seat. He hasn't seen me, so I decide to get up and leave. But my brother says, 'You so-and-so, if you go, I'm going to kill you; I could have taken somebody else to this fight.'

"While we are still arguing, the gong goes and the fight starts. Johansson starts swinging at Patterson and Mr. Wallace stands up and yells, 'Hit him! Hit him!' In the first round Johansson knocks the other guy out. End of fight. Wallace turns around and sees me. I don't know who is more embarrassed— he or I. All I can remember is that I push my brother forward and say, 'I want you to meet my brother who paid to bring me to the fight . . .' In his turn, Mr. Wallace says, 'I'm sure you know that I don't usually behave this way in public places.' I got a very handsome raise—and ever since he has recalled that night with a chuckle."

The difficulties of communicating with DeWitt Wallace often gave rise to misunderstandings. A person in the grip of tension and a burning desire not to irritate the man from whom all blessings flowed would sometimes miss the message when Wallace did speak. Asking him "What do you mean by that?" could exhibit a flawed intelligence, an undesirable attribute in an editor or writer or even an ad salesman, while going back to him for clarification could reveal an impaired memory. Under such circumstances, the best procedure was often to make an educated guess as to the boss's intentions and carry on in hope. Sometimes it didn't work, as in the case of the firing of Roving Editor James Stewart-Gordon.

Already a free-lance writer of national reputation, appearing frequently in *American* and other magazines, Stewart-Gordon was invited to Pleasantville to meet DeWitt Wallace. Recalling that interview and subsequent baffling events, he reports:

"First of all, I never really knew I was hired. Wally told me what the terms were—one thousand a month retainer plus two thousand a story—and then introduced me to Merle Crowell. (An aging, taciturn man from Maine, Crowell was a sort of personnel-business manager for the editorial department.) Crowell took me around and introduced me to people but nothing was said about where I should work or hours or even where to send stories. So I went back to Princeton, New Jersey, where I was then living and played golf every day. A month or so went by during which I sent a few clippings suggesting stories in to Wallace and got my retainer check in the mail. Suddenly I was summoned to Wally's office. He showed me a letter he'd written and asked me to read it in his presence. It indicated he never wanted to see me again, alive or dead, and if I weren't out of there in two minutes he'd put the dogs on me.

"I went out of there lower than a lapis lazuli in a diamond setting. While I was driving home, a New Jersey cop stopped me and said, 'You're speeding.' So I showed him the letter and said look what just happened to me. He said, 'Boy, drive on.' During the next few years, I had other jobs, and I'd meet Wally all the time. He'd call and say I'm going to be walking down

Madison Avenue on the right side between such and such streets in twenty minutes, and I'd meet him there for a walk and talk, or we'd meet in a bar for a drink. But nothing was said about my job.

"After about five years, I went back to the office to talk to one of the assistant managing editors whose judgment I valued, Bill Hard. *American Weekly* needed an editor, and I showed Bill some of my ideas and asked if he thought they were any good. 'You used to be a professional wrestler, didn't you?' he asked. I said, 'Yes' and jumped up on his desk. (Stewart-Gordon, a short, powerful, barrel of a man was quite capable of doing this.) He said, 'Well, if you want to do a story on professional wrestling, go ahead and do it.' I said, 'Gee, I was fired here; I don't know if Wally wants me to come back.' So Bill wrote a note to Wally who replied, 'Treat him like any other writer. Give him $1,800 a story.' So I wrote that story, and in the next three issues it was bing, bing, bing. Then I got a letter from Wally which said, 'Glad to see your byline more frequently lately.'

"Ultimately I was restored, but Wally has refused to admit to this day that I was ever fired. I think I know what happened. He probably tried to reach me one business day and was told, 'Oh, he's out playing golf'—and you know how he is when he can't find someone who works for him. But, you see, he never told me where I was supposed to be when, and nobody else seemed to know either."

DeWitt Wallace is probably unconscious of the comedies, and near tragedies, provoked by the "Me Go Now" syndrome. Certainly, his style is not intended to intimidate. He issues orders in the most diffident fashion—"Don't you think you ought to have a look at such-and-such article?"—and he is about as far from the Hollywood stereotype of the thundering, desk-pounding executive as you could get. So the mind-numbing tensions in these encounters are all on one side, as it always must be when one man holds absolute power over the fortunes of another.

X

Old Writers Never Die, They Just Go to Pleasantville

In a new book, *Smart Aleck*, about Alexander Woollcott, writer, wit, founder of the Algonquin Round Table and most famous as the "Town Crier" on radio in the 30's, Howard Teichman writing'." If this were nothing more than another Woollcott first approached Woollcott to write for the magazine, Aleck contemptuously told a friend, 'Mr. Wallace has destroyed the pleasure of reading; now he is about to destroy the pleasure of writing." If this were nothing more than another Woollcott witticism, it wouldn't be worth quoting. Unhappily, though, it summarizes very aptly the attitude of a great many, if not all, writers who have finally found themselves going through the Pleasantville wringer. A Digest researcher who has worked for a dozen years with countless writers of all stripe told me, "I have never worked with a writer who has not been apologetic at some point about why he is writing for the Digest."

Nevertheless, from the moment Wallace opened his gates to Pleasantville about 1935, writers began coming through them in a steady stream like repentant sinners filing to the altar in a Billy Graham rally. The acerbic Mr. Woollcott was one of them. For all of his fame, including playing Sheridan Whiteside in the fabulously successful "The Man Who Came to Dinner," he was in need of money and signed on as a Digest roving editor at $24,000 a year to write something called "Twice Told Tales." Unfortunately, he was also in failing health. On Saturday, January 23, 1943, he lunched with Mr. and Mrs. Wallace, stopped afterward to have a dozen yellow roses delivered to Lila in thanks, went on to the radio studio to appear on "The People's Forum" during which he collapsed and died. A rather ironic last day in view of his bitter comment.

The explanation for Mr. Woollcott's behavior is, of course, money. "The standard apology," said the researcher, "is money. Mr. Wallace is a great person; he makes it just like Christmas, they say." If this seems crass, listen to George Kent who had just retired after one of the Digest's longest and rovingest careers that took him to some ninety-two countries in thirty-three years. By the time he stumbled upon the Digest, Kent was already a seasoned free-lancer whose work was appearing regularly in *Collier's, American, Country Home,* among other magazines.

Kent's first knowledge of the Digest was when the magazine picked up two articles he'd written for *Country Home* and sent him checks, out of the blue, as it were. He had to go out to a newsstand and buy a copy to see what the Reader's Digest was. Then when he was working on an article about Stevens College in Columbia, Missouri, Pen Dudley, the Wallace's former landlord who through his public relations contacts had become a kind of unofficial talent recruiter for the Digest, asked Kent to send the piece to Pleasantville. What happened thereafter astounded Kent, as he tells in his own words:

"The next thing I knew was that I got a call and a shy, trembling little voice said, 'This is Mr. Wallace.' And I said, 'Yes, Mr. Wallace?' The name didn't mean a thing to me. He said he was editor of The Reader's Digest and liked the piece, but he said it needed more work and made a date to meet me at the Commodore Hotel. An hour later, Pen Dudley called and said, 'It's in the bag, George.' But there was no mention of money.

"When I met Wally at the Commodore where we had a cup of coffee, he handed me a check for $1,400. I nearly fainted. You've got to understand how things were then. I was normally getting about $300 an article. The biggest amount I'd ever earned—$1,200—was a fluke. I ghosted an article for Ed Wynn, the old Fire Chief, for *American.* Wynn didn't want to see me and wouldn't even look at the article, but *American* said it was the funniest thing Wynn ever wrote and paid me $400. Then Ed Wynn wrote me and said he enjoyed the article very much and turned over to me the check for $800 they had sent him.

"Well, after Wally gave me the check, he asked me to go back out to Stevens to get more material—for which he paid expenses and more money. After that, he asked me to take on an assignment. It was a cheesy assignment and not very successful, and I thought this guy's just a flash in the pan. Still, I had gotten the feel of money. So I went on doing piece after piece. . . ."

The feel of money; there you have it. Writing's always been a precarious profession, and writers are generally temperamental and unstable people. It's hard to tell whether the conditions of the work provoke the personality, or vice versa; it may be one of those chicken-and-egg questions. In any case, when DeWitt Wallace began working with writers, he seemed to have the same gutsy grasp on their natures as he did on their products he had been seeing in other magazines. So he developed a rather diabolical, carrot-and-stick system. Instead of putting them on the staff as so many magazines did, he offered them the illusion of freedom, which is supposed to be one of the great psychic gratifications of the writing life, by giving them enough of a retainer to keep them from starving and article fees higher than they could get anywhere else in the market. Thus, the sky was the limit to what they could earn, and there were at least a couple of boards stretched across the hole to keep them from falling into the cellar.

Once again, instant success. Even in the heyday of the general magazine when such well-paying rival markets as *Collier's, Saturday Evening Post, Life, Look* and *American* were flourishing, an amazing number of famous names began turning up almost exclusively in the Digest and on its lengthening masthead. Here are some: William Hard, J. P. McEvoy, Max Eastman, Fulton Oursler, Donald Culross Peattie, Paul de Kruif, William L. White, Eugene Lyons, Alexander Woollcott, J. D. Ratcliff, John Gunther, Stanley High, Noel Busch, Cornelius Ryan, James Michener. Because he had the money, Wallace didn't have to opt for training the young tigers; he could tame the old lions instead. It seems natural that Wallace would want the men whose work he had admired—indeed, the stepping stones leading to the Digest were the articles a man had had reprinted in the magazine—and he went after them.

He got some curious characters in terms of the Digest's rather pious and certainly conservative public image. For one thing, many of them had been more than "a little liberal," as W. S. Gilbert would put it, in their youth. For his espousal of socialism, J. P. McEvoy had once been known as "the young Debs"; Max Eastman, editor of *Masses* and prolific author, was once a world famous friend of communism; William Hard was a socialist-leaning muckraker until, according to his daughter, he saw the light so clearly after an all-night argument with a banker friend that he ended up a member of Hoover's "medicine ball cabinet"; Stanley High was a top speech writer for FDR who transposed his talents into a different key to perform the same chore for Eisenhower. Like reformed alcoholics, old socialists are the most articulate enemies of economic sin, and Wallace capitalized on this fact. In any case, a closer look at two of the most colorful of these men, McEvoy and Eastman, whose records clearly qualified them to be classed as writers— that is, people whose talent and joy lay more in the felicitous use of words than in the subject they tackled or the information they conveyed—is illustrative of what was going on as Gulliver began toying with the Lilliputians.

McEvoy had a dizzying career. An orphan found on the steps of Catholic Foundling Hospital in New York on January 21, 1895, McEvoy was given his name (Joseph Patrick McEvoy), nationality and Catholic religion by an Irish schoolteacher in New Burnside, Illinois, who raised him. He grew into a chunky, vibrant man who, because of a flattened nose, looked, in his son Dennis's words, "like a pugilistic Einstein." McEvoy left home at fourteen, never to return, was tossed out of a number of schools, including Notre Dame University and began newspapering in Chicago in the wild and inspiring days of Ben Hecht, Charles MacArthur, and Carl Sandburg. A column he wrote called "The Slams of Life" was turned into a Broadway hit, *The Potters,* in 1923, and he went on to write other hits, including sketches for the Ziegfeld Follies. He teamed up with an artist to do the comic strip, "Dixie Dugan," and wrote for such magazines as *Saturday Evening Post.* A flavor of McEvoy comes through in a comment he made after a visit to Russia in 1931: "They are breaking their necks to build just one Gary, Indiana. At home we have dozens of them."

McEvoy's life was a great deal like his career. "My father's private life was turbulent to the point of low comedy," writes Dennis in his unfinished autobiography. "He was married three times—but the stream of unofficial 'mothers' I knew seemed almost endless. They were of every variety and nationality. He was drawn to women as a flower is drawn towards the sun—pure heliotropism. And they to him." What drew a man like McEvoy toward the Presbyterian confines of Pleasantville seems to have been another kind of glitter—that of gold. "One year, he made approximately a million dollars from his writing, most of it from a successful Broadway musical which was sold to the movies," says Dennis. "The next found him going about our house at night, extracting coins from the little clay piggy banks which belonged to my sister and me to pay the milkman—credit having been temporarily suspended." If this seems extreme, compare the memory of Eleanor Hard Lake to the effect that, in pre-Digest days, her father, William, and her mother, both free-lance writers, would be entertaining ambassadors at dinner in their Georgetown home while they couldn't pay the bill at the corner grocery.

Whatever Wallace paid McEvoy, he got more than his money's worth. Long gone from the ranks of straight reporting,

McEvoy wrote fabrications that were full of humor and pathos and truer than truth. One of them, "Charlie would Have Loved This," became a kind of Digest classic. It was a simple piece about a group of widows, gazing for the first time upon the Eden of Waikiki in Honolulu and recalling how they had planned to go there with their husbands in retirement before the poor work horses dropped dead in harness, leaving them the money for the trip. When my wife and I went to Waikiki, we sat next to a table of just such women, as we could detect from their loud conversation, and I found myself telling her McEvoy's piece from memory—the surest sign of "lasting interest."

Nobody appreciated McEvoy's contributions more than Wallace. The lifestyle of a man who can make a million one year and be broke the next is hard to change. One winter more than twenty years ago, when a dollar was still more or less a dollar, Wallace, pleased with a McEvoy article, told him, "J. P., I want you to take a week's vacation—you and Peggy—and the Digest will pay for it." According to then editorial business manager, James McCracken, Wallace had in mind, considering the season, a jaunt to Florida that might cost $600 or $700. But the curious McEvoy, who had never been skiing, went north instead, taking not only his third wife, Peggy, but their two daughters as well. They holed up in the finest Canadian ski resort, rented boots, skis, lifts, instruction. "McEvoy, of course, put it all on the expense account," McCracken relates. "It came to $1,700, probably the equivalent of about $5,000 today. When I looked at it, I thought, 'Holy Mackerel—Wally will be furious!' He came to the office every day then and approved all accounts, so I called him and asked if I could bring this one to him personally. He stared at it for a while and shook his head and said, 'This is just amazing. I've never seen anything like it. But J. P. is such a fine writer, I can't do anything but OK it.' "

Like so much else about him, DeWitt Wallace's tolerance of the foibles of writers is legendary. George Kent recalls a more legitimate expense-account story arising out of a long trip he took to do a tear jerker on the kidnapped children of Greece during which he had to hire cars, planes, interpreters and other costly aids. He mailed his manuscript along with his expense account from Athens and was rewarded with a furious letter from Wallace, complaining about the expenses. Before Kent had time to reply a cable arrived, saying: "Ignore my last letter. Wonderful story." Even though writers, until recently at least, had no pension rights as regular employees, many of them, aged and infirm and long past sitting up to a typewriter, received Digest checks in gratitude for past performance until their dying day. But Wallace's understanding often went beyond money. One writer, accused of assaulting a research girl, emerged from a conference at High Winds, which everybody thought would be a royal dismissal, with an increase in article rates; another, indicted for misappropriation of public funds in an earlier career, found Wallace coming to his defense. Wallace's measure of writers was what they could put on the pages of his little magazine. This undoubtedly accounts for his recruiting of that maverick Max Eastman, poet, socialist, atheist, pacifist, Don Juan.

About the same age, Wallace and Eastman had similar beginnings except that both of Eastman's parents were Congregational ministers in upstate New York. They even looked a little alike—tall, spare, handsome. But that was all they had in common. A graduate of Williams College, Eastman was editing *Masses* in New York while Wallace was peddling *Getting the Most Out of Farming* through the tank towns of the West. Eastman was tried—and acquitted—on charges of "conspiring to cause mutiny and refusal of duty in the military and naval forces" while Wallace was preparing to go into combat as a foot soldier in France. Eastman was acting as biographer, agent and translator for Leon Trotsky while Wallace was putting together issues of a magazine extolling democracy and free enterprise in a pony shed. Eastman was living openly "in sin" with actress Florence Deshon while Wallace was dwelling in Presbyterian wedlock in Pleasantville. Boasting of making twelve amorous conquests on one lecture tour in his book, *Love and Revolution*, Eastman writes: "I suppose I am a rather 'sexy' person—and I judge it is true of the whole tribe of lanky, dark ministers and deacons from whom I derive. Although bent, most of them on religious sublimation, I think *lecherous* is not too strong a term for the natural instincts they wrestled to hold in check. The term has been applied to me more than once and not without reason. Perhaps I can best summarize the facts by saying that I experienced no glimmer of surprise or disbelief when Dr. Kinsey published his book of statistics about *Sexual Behavior in the Human Male*." (By contrast, Wallace assigned a writer of noted religious bent—a convert like the socialists and, hence, fierce—to do a hatchet job on the shocking Dr. Kinsey, but it died in research.)

By 1940 when the paths of these two men crossed, Wallace's magazine had outdistanced all competition and was thrusting abroad; Eastman was justly famous, in literary circles at least, for his poetry, critical essays, lectures, and many books, including *The Sense of Humor, The Enjoyment of Poetry*, and *Leon Trotsky, the Portrait of a Youth*. But Eastman was broke. Knowing this, his literary agent suggested that he try writing up an "unforgettable character" for Reader's Digest. Eastman did an essay on his ministerial mother, sent it along and was rewarded by a telephone invitation to Pleasantville from Wallace—"the first hospitable message I had ever received from a magazine that paid big money." Despite his personal poverty, Eastman had decided that he no longer believed in socialism and had written an essay to that effect which he called "Socialism and Human Nature." During the course of talking about his mother, he asked if Wallace would like to see the piece on socialism.

" 'I should say I would,' he exclaimed in so delighted a tone that my heart sank a little. (The renegade complex makes cowards of us all.)" Eastman wrote. "I stipulated that I should see and revise the proofs of my essay the last thing before it went to press. 'To you it is just another article,' I said. 'But in my life it is an event of momentous importance. I want every word in it to express my thought exactly.'

"He agreed. And he kept his word, telephoning me to come over to his office late one April afternoon. The proofs were lying

on his desk and he left me alone with them. I found my
thoughts, although somewhat compressed, carefully unaltered
in the process. I fixed the proofs to my satisfaction, and went
home to await, with what courage I could, the storm that would
break over me from the Left.

"I had seen every word that was to appear over my signature,
but two things I had not seen. One was a brash new title invented by the editors: instead of 'Socialism and Human Nature'
—'Socialism Does Not Gibe with Human Nature.' That would
go off like a bomb in the minds of my astonished colleagues.
And far worse than that: a 'box' had been prepared with loving
care to stand at the entrance to my article and give it prestige—
a veritable shout of welcome from Wendell Willkie, ex-head of
a capitalist corporation and rightwing candidate for President
of the United States. Wendell Willkie! The Southern Light and
Power Company! The Republican Party! That would prove I
had 'sold out,' if my words did not.

"I don't know whether DeWitt Wallace knew, or even
suspected, what a blow that was to me, and what a boon to
those who would assault me. I never spoke of my misery to
him or to any of his editors, but I was sick for two weeks. The
Socialist Call held a three-column funeral service: 'In Memo-
riam—Max Eastman.' Dwight MacDonald, an editor of *Partisan
Review*, wrote: 'Max Eastman, hero of the old *Masses* trial . . .
publishes an attack on socialism which Wendell Willkie im-
plored every good American to read, and which is the low-water
mark to date in such affairs for vulgarity and just plain foolish-
ness.' Even the *Progressive*, a liberal magazine, permitted my
old friend Harry Elmer Barnes to denounce me as a 'renegade.'
'What Has Happened to You, Max?' was his title, and in the
next issue I tried to tell him. But that millstone, Wendell
Willkie, around my neck had drowned me. There was no use
explaining."

Still, money evidently meant more than pride to Eastman
then, so he tried turning an old essay on "The Folly of Growing
Up" into Digestese and sent it in. Meanwhile, he went to his
friend, Max Schuster, looking for a job as an editor in a publish-

ing house. Schuster said the only job he could think of that might fit Eastman's free lifestyle was a new one Wallace was creating at The Reader's Digest called roving editor. These lines merged, as Eastman reported:

"I was then still in touch with DeWitt Wallace. Indeed I had a date for a luncheon with him and a selection of his editors— a kind of obsequy, I imagined, or post-mortem, on my little essay, to see if I could understand what, from their standpoint, was the matter with it. I thought I understood too well, but during that luncheon Mr. Wallace said something that rather put my thoughts to shame.

" 'You write so beautifully,' he said, 'that I'm sure you can write for us.'

"In answer I said something like this: 'If anyone writes beautifully, Mr. Wallace, it is because he is writing straight out of his own head and heart. You can't do it at the bidding of an editor, or a tableful of editors, no matter how charming they are and how much you enjoy lunching with them.'

"There was a pause after I said this, a smiling pause, during which I summoned the courage to bring forth an idea I had thought up as a result of my conversation with Max Schuster.

" 'I think perhaps there is one thing I could do that would be pleasing to you and at the same time spontaneous with me. I could write a whole series of articles like the one you liked about my mother. It might be called 'Men with Ideas.' I would pick out people who stand for something and go and get acquainted with them—not just interview them, but get to know each one well enough to write a biographical portrait—and then weave into it an exposition of the thing he stands for.

"Wallace's answer came so fast, and with so little motion of his lips, that I could barely hear it.

" 'I agree to that, and I propose that you become a roving editor of The Reader's Digest. We will pay you a living wage, and we won't tell you whom to write about. You pick your own subjects, write as you please'—he paused—'and send us your expense account.'

"I don't know what I said—I think I merely gasped. When

I came into our apartment after the trip home, Eliena [his wife] said: 'Max, what's the matter with you, you look pale?'

" 'I'm a roving editor of *The Reader's Digest!*' I answered, and dropped into a chair."

The series Eastman proposed was forgotten, but in the next years, he certainly roved, doing articles in Greece, Switzerland, Latin America. Indeed, for the rest of his life Eastman struggled, not always successfully, to write Digest articles, for the stick part of the Wallace scheme was that retainers and article rates were reviewed annually with a kind of performance rate often governing upward or downward adjustments, if not outright dismissal. Unusual performance was often rewarded with an unexpected bonus; writers got handwritten notes from Wallace on Christmas cards, some carrying ominous messages that ruined the Yuletide like, "I hope to see more of your byline next year." Although he was an unabashed Digester, as proclaimed monthly on the masthead, Eastman, too, felt called upon to apologize in his book: "When you are addressing many millions of readers, it is hard to stick by your own arrogant judgment as to how a thing ought, on eternal principles of symmetry and beauty, be said. Instead of either art or journalism, I have thought of it as *teaching*, when writing for these millions. I *am* a teacher, and I love to teach."

Why this apologetic attitude? Although everything that's written and published gets a certain amount of editorial direction as well as copy polishing, Digest articles get far more of it than most. Not only are they cut by a half to two thirds but, especially with originals, the sequence and even the wording is often altered to the editor's taste. In the Digest distilling process, the Scotch the writer served up may well become Drambuie —same base but a different product. This can't help but cause suffering to a sensitive person with pride in his craft, if not art, as is the case with most writers. Says one experienced Digest writer, "An article goes through many hands, each with an obligation to cut something. So what the hell do you cut? You can't cut fact, so you cut color. You cut the very things that make an article distinctive and reflective of the author. So it's turned out to be a standardized product. But the public doesn't mind; they like it."

This problem was probably not too obvious to the first writers flocking to Pleasantville. They were used to having their material appear pretty much as they wrote it somewhere else, thus gratifying their egos; when the Digest reprinted it, and sent them a check, it was like found money. This still applies to authors whose shortened books appear either in the magazine or Condensed Books and whose laudatory statements about the editing process are often used in promotional literature; their real work is being published elsewhere. It's only those who are locked into first submission to the Digest by their arrangement as roving editor, staff writer or whatever, who truly suffer the frustration. Even those articles that are "placed" in other magazines are given a heavy going-over before they are sent out.

But, being adept with words, writers are better rationalizers than most. Those who send in flattering notes telling the editors how much their copy has been improved can probably be written off as people who no longer care or who should be employing their talents in the creation of fiction. More believable are the resigned ones like a friend of mine who always tells people, "Well, the Bible was written by a committee." This same writer once complained of the editing of a book another publisher was putting out for him. "I'm sure you get much worse at the Digest, so what's the difference?" the editor shot back. "The difference," said my friend, "is that they pay me for it."

But an even more potent rationalization than money, insofar as the psyche is concerned, is this one: "Where else can my name reach 100 million people around the world?" Reflecting upon the publication of an article called "To Collaborate Successfully We Must Face the Facts About Russia," which the Digest ran at an unbelievable seventeen pages during World War II, Eastman said: "I might be from the standpoint of pure aesthetics a 'demi-prostitute,' as Cummings once laughingly called me, but there are other standpoints. There are other passions in a man's heart. I at least am not only an artist. And everything else that I am is royally glad to have my most specialized political knowledge and understanding unburied from the recondite pages of *Modern Monthly* and issued like a trumpet blast to millions of people."

While Eastman's message may have gotten across, it's likely his name—a most valued possession of most writers—didn't. The late Fred Sondern who was one of the Digest's most prolific writers used to tell this story about himself. One day, in the very small Connecticut town where he had lived for years, he was standing in the local news store beside a rack holding the current Digest, on the cover of which was not one, but two, articles listing his name as author. After trading comments on the weather with him, a local citizen said, "Say, Fred, what are you doing for a living these days?" Oddly, appearing in the most widely read magazine in history is no guarantor of fame to a person *as a writer*. *Who's Who* lists many of those Digest writers who have produced books and appeared in other magazines, none whose product has been published only or chiefly by the Digest. (It does, however, include some Digest executives—one of its shortest entries being supplied by that master condenser, DeWitt Wallace.) My rationalizing friend who *is* in *Who's Who* explains it this way: "The writers are little known, because their style is so flattened out that it doesn't make much difference who wrote an article."

Precisely. At the core of the Wallace genius was his discovery that the mass reader doesn't care who wrote what as long as the information is useful or interesting to him. As a result—and in contrast to magazines that scream "The New Norman Mailer" on the cover—Digest writer's names appear in the smallest acceptable print both on the cover and inside. The Reader's Digest is, as it has always said it was, a reader's service rather than a writer's outlet. This fact may account for another old and, in some quarters, dishonored practice that the Digest has lifted almost to the level of art—ghost writing. Since the information or idea is everything and it doesn't matter much to the reader who wrote it (after all who really knows who set down the books of the New Testament, or the Old, for that matter), it seems logical to run articles by presidents, members of congress, ambassadors, actors, prize fighters, corporation chiefs and even ministers—whose style, if any, would prove too murky for the Digest reader—without any acknowledgment of the "help" they receive.

Perhaps the outstanding writer of this kind in recent years was President Eisenhower. After he left the White House, he was signed on by the Digest for a rumored $25,000 an article, believed to be its highest rate as of then. Writer Eisenhower was worth every penny since nearly everything he said in the Digest became instant front-page news across the country, a form of public relations that can't be bought for any amount of money. But the Eisenhower fee was only the tip of the iceberg of Digest costs for his services since the late Ben Hibbs departed as helmsman of the sinking *Saturday Evening Post* to come aboard the Digest as a salaried senior editor to be Eisenhower's "ghost."

The process, according to Hibbs's description in the Digest's *Courier*, began with a discussion between him and Eisenhower on an idea either proposed by the general or sent down from Pleasantville. Once the broad outlines were decided, Hibbs would assemble information from the Eisenhower files and Digest research. After another talk session, Hibbs would write a manuscript which the general would attack "with gusto," often tearing the manuscript apart, making deletions and insertions and rephrasing paragraphs. "Let there be no mistake," Hibbs concluded, "The article, when it finally appears, is Eisenhower, inside and out."

Ghosting for people who have made their names in other careers—politicians, generals, businessmen—seems now to be widely accepted; in fact, it would stretch credulity even more to pretend that such personalities had the time and talent to be top-flight writers as well. The wicket becomes a bit stickier, however, when the practice is extended to people who are primarily famous for their production of words such as Lowell Thomas, Norman Vincent Peale, Billy Graham. The

helpers for the preachers are sometimes referred to in Pleasantville as the "holy ghosts," and the two men who have worked
most closely with evangelist Graham, the late Stanley High and
Clarence Hall, did have suitably ministerial backgrounds. On
the whole subject of ghosting, Graham is as refreshingly forthright as he is in his preaching.

"What I do I want people to know. Otherwise, I couldn't
keep my integrity as a clergyman," he told me. "I have help on
my newspaper column which has appeared six days a week for
twenty-five years. Until his death, a lot of it came from my
father-in-law. I answer questions in the column, and once a
year I make up a question to myself: Do you write your own
column? I always answer no. I do edit each one, and a column
won't be accepted unless it has my personal signature. In my
book on angels, I tell in the preface who helped me."

Graham explained the need for ghost writing in terms of the
demands modern life puts upon its personalities. Old-time
evangelists, he said, could get away with a few sermons over a
lifetime, but "when I give one on TV, I've got to throw it away."
Graham said he knew of one prominent radio minister who
kept three sets of writers—in New York, Chicago and St. Louis
—laboring to provide him with enough material. As for presidents, Graham, a frequenter of the White House, said, "I've
seen President Johnson—because I spent twenty-three nights
with him—go make a speech. They hand him the speech on
the way, and he's reading it walking down the hall in the White
House for the first time. There's no human way a president
could write all those speeches."

On writing for the Digest, Graham says: "I know they want
anecdotes—that's the hardest thing for me to come up with.
The ones I use in sermons come to me as I'm talking, because
I believe I am under inspiration, that they are brought to my
mind. Articles I have written for the Digest, I have written in
long hand, because then I can think slowly and deliberately
about what I want to say. Then I dictate them and do some
cutting and rewriting on the typescript and send them off to
Clarence Hall or whomever I am working with. Then they send

their version back for more editing and approval by me. Sometimes the editors want—you know, I'm always putting in as much religion as I can—to pull out some of my strongest points. And I can see why: being in a pluralistic society, they don't want the magazine to become a medium of evangelizing or proselytizing.

"I think the Digest has developed a style and presentation of great simplicity, and the use of anecdotes that hold people's attention—that I have to keep in mind. But I don't think you can get too simplistic today. For example, the vocabulary of the average clergyman is 5,000 words; the vocabulary of the average working man is 600 words. And so the people who read the think magazines are a small minority, and the people who read the popular magazines like the Reader's Digest are a large majority. One of the secrets of the teaching of Jesus Christ was that the common people heard him gladly. He said many profound things, but he said them in great simplicity. I have to work in my preaching to keep it simple—I mean, I deliberately work to keep it simple, and I'm almost embarrassed to stand up in front of television and talk as simply as I do. I try to do the same with my writing."

Graham, who has also written for *Life*, the *New York Times* and other prominent lay publications, admits to a writing problem peculiar to the Digest: because of its heavy editing, he doesn't labor hard enough on his articles. "I really don't, and that's bad," he says. "I always know somebody else is going to help me on it like Clarence Hall, and I always know they're not going to put it out unless they make it good. And I think that if it were all up to me, I would labor much harder. I really don't send them in as polished a manuscript as I would to another magazine." Sad to say, Graham shares this problem with a number of old pros in the business whose bleeding over lost or altered copy seems to have drained the heart out of them. But, of course, thanks to Digest editors, the readers would never know.

If Digest writers spend a great deal of time licking the wounds to their psyches, many of them are also given to licking the hand that feeds them; the "feel of money" is the sort of sensation you want to go on enjoying indefinitely. Woollcott's flowers constituted the mildest of gestures, compared to that of one writer who buried his first wife with a copy of the Digest in her hand. A picture of the loyalty evoked in the breasts of writers by Digest generosity emerges from the book, *Behold This Dreamer!*, an autobiography of Fulton Oursler as edited by his son, Fulton, Jr., now a Digest managing editor. By the time Oursler, another school dropout, joined the Digest in 1944, he had written some thirty books, including mysteries under the name of Anthony Abbot, and many movies, plays, radio shows, in addition to editing *Liberty*. Oursler had just converted to Catholicism, and veritable writing machine that he was, used his new understanding to rewrite the Bible into *The Greatest Story Ever Told*, a property that made millions. Described by a woman colleague as "a forceful person who looked rather like a witch," Oursler was a semi-pro magician and fond of such theatrical touches as keeping a long candle burning on his desk while he was engaged in the act of com-position. "He had a touch of Barnum," said Digest Roving Editor James Stewart-Gordon. "The candle on his desk, the sudden magic tricks—he made the commonplace dramatic and put theater into life." Oursler employed these talents well in relation to the Wallaces.

At Sandalwood, the Oursler Cape Cod home, according to the book, Fulton put on a magic show for the Wallaces, among other guests. Describing it, he wrote to a Baltimore friend: "I did the milk pitcher trick, using the *Reader's Digest* to pour milk into. (Naturally, when the milk disappeared, I said it had been condensed.) I forced the Queen of Hearts on Mrs. Wallace and then did the rising-card trick. But instead of the Queen of Hearts rising from the pack, a card rose with her photograph on it—and was this not proper, since she was the queen of our hearts?" Perhaps even a higher tribute was recounted by young Oursler who, acting as an assistant to his father, was summoned to the writer's study. "I hesitated as I entered the room," Fulton, Jr., writes, "for I saw that he was lighting the tall candle that stood on his desk. No one—guest, family or servant —dared enter when the flame burned; it was his signal that he was writing and not to be disturbed, except for a call from DeWitt Wallace, or the announcement of a new World War."

Is it any wonder that DeWitt Wallace has been heard openly lamenting in recent years that they don't make writers like they used to—wondering aloud where today's McEvoys, Ourslers, Eastmans, de Kruifs can be found? Because they weren't actually on the payroll and, therefore, exempt from the Digest's mostly mandatory sixty-five-year-old retirement and because they were, even in their seventies and eighties, still younger than Wallace himself, the old pros stayed on the masthead and sometimes appeared in the magazine until death did them part. Until recently, that is. The current editor-in-chief, Edward T. Thompson, has made arrangements to "retire" what's left of them to make room for the new breed of Digest writer who, like his editor, is virtually home grown.

Though this might prove a less exciting "service to readers" than the Digest offered in the days when Wallace captured the greats of his time, it is probably an inevitable result of the historical developments in the large world out there, as reflected in writing and journalism, since World War II. Material put out by the writers who have earned critical acclaim and/or established themselves as personalities in these years simply doesn't lend itself to a magazine retaining the Wallace imprint. Moreover, it's doubtful that many of these men and women would themselves care to be identified with the Digest point of view, even for money.

The practitioners of the "new journalism," for example—such as Tom Wolfe, or Mailer in his non-fiction—with their blending of fact and fiction rely heavily upon style to get their message across; digesting would literally murder their work. But in any case, their rather jaundiced view of the world around them is clear around the compass from that of the Digest. Also their use of language. Not only in its free-swinging employment of four-letter words but in its subtlety and sophistication, its allusions and insinuations, such language would certainly be shocking and probably incomprehensible to a very large number of loyal Digest readers, and converting it into digestese would probably prove unacceptable to the authors. In the field of print communication at least, the Digest now stands almost alone in its attitudes about nearly everything from what constitutes acceptable language to the American defense posture to the use of drugs to the causes and cures for the sexual and racial revolutions to the kind of God who exists, if he does. Thus, it seems highly unlikely that the personalities of today's literary world will appear in the Digest with the exception of book condensations in the magazine or Condensed Books.

But it would be plausible for Pleasantville to argue that, since it publishes the most widely-read magazine in the world, the real stars of today's journalism are, in fact, its own writers. In some ways this may be true. Much like the anonymous men who have served the CIA since the war, as compared to the "glamor boys" of the OSS, present Digest writers have acquired an unusual professionalism that deserves recognition, and the personal lives they lead may well be more exciting than those of their more publicized contemporaries.

XI

Just Give Me
the Facts, Ma'am

Back in the good old days when life was less formal at the Reader's Digest, the editorial staff put on a show for what basically was an audience of two—Mr. and Mrs. DeWitt Wallace. The skits were light-hearted spoofs of life at the Digest. The one that lingers longest in the memories of Digesters who were there has been recounted to me in versions as various as the stories of witnesses to an accident. But the way Eugene Lyons remembers it will do. A man comes on stage in what is meant to be the Gobi desert, or the Sahara, or some such out-of-the-way place, sets up a typewriter and starts pounding away. Presently, another man comes on stage and does the same thing. They get to talking and discover that they are both doing the same assignment for the Reader's Digest. Then a third man joins them, then a fourth—all doing the same story for the same magazine. At the time, this little drama was meant as a mild criticism of the lack of organization in an editorial staff just beginning to develop original articles. While the Digest system for making assignments has since tightened up considerably, the skit is still true in one important regard: The

Reader's Digest will send a writer anywhere at any time to get any story that it wants.

It is, in fact, the Digest's unstinting support in terms of expenses, time and research assistance that in the end tends to overcome for today's Digest writers such psychic wounds as having half their copy cut away and laboring in personal anonymity. The spirit of Digest support comes through in this story from Roving Editor Joseph P. Blank, somewhat of a Digest specialist in covering fires, floods, famines and other disasters that fail to daunt the human spirit. Arrived in New Orleans to do an article on hurricane Camille, Blank found himself grounded in the airport; every available rental car in the city had been preempted to take relatives, relief workers and government agents to the site of the disaster some fifty miles away. When Blank phoned his Pleasantville editor, then Ed Thompson, to see if there might be a Digest person in the area from whom he could borrow a car, Thompson said at once, "Buy a car." Fortunately for the ulcers of the man who handles expense accounts, Blank finally located a rental car in a suburb which he remembers as being a twenty-two-dollar cab fare away from town.

In pursuit of a story they know to be good, Digest men simply don't worry about money. In Saigon, Roving Editor David Reed was offered a man's first-person account of an attack on the American Embassy, the only catch being that the man wanted money. "I'll give you a thousand bucks," said Reed without hesitation, getting the story and knowing that Editor-in-Chief Hobart Lewis back in Pleasantville would back him up. As former Digest Washington editor Charles Stevenson once explained Digest reporting: "No expense, no effort is too great if it results in new, significant revelations. Dig for the facts such as no one else has the patience and the time or the money to do."

With this kind of blank check in hand, Digest writers lead lives that belie David Reed's statement that "the days of Richard Harding Davis are over." Perhaps owing to the speed of modern transportation and the proliferation of conflict in a splintered world, Reed's own adventures quite probably surpass those of that legendary reporter. Reed has thus far covered stories in seventy-five countries in all of the world's five continents; among these have been upfront reports on eight wars, not to mention assorted revolutions, guerilla strikes and other civil disorders. Yet Reed neither looks nor acts like the trench-coated foreign correspondent of the silver screen. Of medium height, slight, neatly tailored and trimmed, eyes owlish behind dark-rimmed glasses, Reed in his late forties still looks like a serious sophomore on his way to class. Abroad, he could easily pass for an earnest foreign service officer which, indeed, he once did to save his neck.

The event took place in 1971 when Reed was researching a story on East Pakistan, now Bangladesh. Hiring a car, driver, and interpreter, Reed travelled through the countryside observing at first hand the atrocities being committed by West Pakistan troops and their East Pakistan allies, the Razakhars. "I never saw one village that hadn't been burned," he said. On his way west again to tell a story that the authorities didn't want published, Reed was stuck for hours one night on a Ganges ferry with a group of West Pakistan soldiers. High on hashish, they raped women aboard and then got curious about Reed. They seized his pack, found a whiskey bottle and broke it, drink being against their religion. At this point, Reed joined the foreign service and began screaming that he was "the American consul from Dacca." It worked to get Reed and his companions off the ferry intact, but down the road a piece a band of Razakhars rose out of the bushes and flagged their car down with rifles. A bald-headed man jumped into the car and stuck a .45 revolver into Reed's ribs.

Ignoring Reed's protests that he was the American consul, the man said, "I'm taking you to my officer. You have violated the curfew."

At a schoolhouse, the man ordered Reed's driver to stop. Taking Reed with him at gunpoint, he banged on the door until a sleepy officer appeared. As Reed puts it, "I figured he was about a major, so I immediately promoted him. 'Colonel,' I said, 'what is the meaning of this outrage to the American consul?'

"He said, sighing, 'I am not a colonel; I am only major. Powers that be in Rawalpindi have denied me promotion.'

"Though I never served in the army, I said, 'Major, I am a military man myself. I also retired at the rank of major because I was denied promotion as I deserved. I understand completely.'

"He said, 'You are a nice gentleman. You must stay the night with us.'

"Then I said, 'Consul's business cannot wait. I must get back now and wire Washington about how all is so peaceful in the country here.'

"He said, 'No, my friend, you are staying with us tonight; otherwise, my men will kill you.'

"I said, 'Major, I accept the invitation.'"

Once, going directly from an assignment in Africa to Belfast, Reed found himself unprepared for the change in climate. As soon as he checked into his hotel, he went out to buy a—yes, trenchcoat. When he got back to the hotel, he found that a bomb had exploded, and the lobby was full of guests moaning and bleeding from the wounds inflicted by flying glass. But Reed's closest call, the one that almost changed his religion, came in Biafra in 1969.

Reed and Senior Editor Denis Fodor from the Digest's Paris office were having lunch with Fr. Seamus Foley and some of his colleagues at a Holy Ghost mission station on top of a hill outside Umuahia, the last capital of Biafra. "Everybody has always said you can't hear a MIG coming, but I did," Reed relates. "I dived into a corner. Denis and the priests followed me. Seconds later, the MIG came roaring over the building, firing rockets, machine guns, cannon. Each time the plane made a pass over Umuahia, it would wheel back and take a blast at us. During one lull, I said to Fr. Foley who was lying beside me, 'Seamus, do you think it's time I converted to the Catholic faith?' The wise father replied, 'Why don't you wait three weeks and see if you still feel that way?'"

In view of his experiences, Reed still relishes the tip he got from a Digest writer of another generation, O. K. Armstrong. Once a conservative congressman from Missouri and an acquaintance and staunch supporter of the late Chiang Kai-shek, Armstrong was on a globe-girdling mission to see whether the world could be saved from communism, and they met for dinner on the roof of the Embassy Hotel in Saigon. It was in 1967, at the height of the war, and the nightly fireworks across the Saigon river began as soon as they sat down. There were explosions everywhere; helicopter gun ships zoomed back and forth, firing rockets. To be heard over the racket, Armstrong said in the stentorian tone he had developed for the political hustings, "Dad burn it, Reed, you young squirts don't appreciate the fact that communism is an aggressive philosophy!"

By now rather philosophical about aggression in any form, Reed is also philosophical about the fact that, despite his many Digest articles and several books, his name is not, as they say, a household word. Once, he claims, his own mother told him all about a marvelous Digest article she had just read; she was not aware that he had written it. Indeed, if heavy-handed editors don't keep Digest writers humble, their mothers do. William Schulz, the Digest's Washington editor, told me that, like other writers, he bled profusely over the condensation of his first article to appear in the Digest—all that marvelous prose gone. Then his mother, calling to congratulate him after she saw his work in the Digest, said, "My, it's amazing how your writing has improved!" Reed's point of view is that the name of the Digest opens more doors than any personal reputation would do. In one eleven-month period, for example, Reed interviewed four heads of state—George Papadopoulos of Greece, Sekou Toure of Guinea, Juan Bordaberry of Uruguay and Richard Nixon of the United States—which he regards as rather heady stuff for a man who started his career, fresh out of the University of Chicago, as a copy boy for Chicago's City News Bureau.

Reed says that he has yet to meet a head of state who is not fully aware of the Digest's immense worldwide circulation.

Though many, if not most, of them differ politically, either on the Right or the Left, with the Digest's point of view and are fully aware that an article is likely to be critical, they nevertheless seem eager to have their names in its pages. Says Reed, "These guys are consummate politicians, more than politicians. They're dictators, Napoleon types. They know everybody is opposed to them, even their own people. Every one of them has a Praetorian guard. They don't want to be loved so much as respected and feared. So if they feel they can use you, they don't care."

A case in point might be General Omar Torrijos Herrera, leftist strongman of Panama, whom Reed visited in the course of researching his article "Should We Give Up the Panama Canal?" for the May 1976 Digest. Conducted by the general's press officer to the Torrijos home on the Pacific coast, Reed was greeted with these words: "I don't really want to see you. The Digest is against the progressive forces in America."

"If you identify the progressive forces as the KGB and the Communists, yes," Reed said. "But if you're talking about people like Betancourt or Bellande, no."

"Well, I don't see it that way," the general shot back. "Have you ever been in Vietnam?"

"Yes, five times."

"Did you support the war there?"

"Yes," said Reed, "mainly because our people were there. They were our army. I'm on their side, not the enemy's."

Torrijos seemed to like that answer, according to Reed, because he said, "Well, since you're here, I'll talk to you. Want to take a dip in the river?"

Reed agreed—and there followed an unforgettable twelve hours. A bluff man who, though white, likes to call himself a *cholo*, the brown-skinned majority of the Panamanians who are of mixed Indian and Spanish blood, Torrijos wears a military field uniform, complete with combat boots, an automatic pistol slung gunfighter style on one hip, a canteen full of whiskey on the other. Hustling Reed into a jeep which he drove himself,

Torrijos tore off to an airstrip where a DeHavilland STOL plane was warming up. Along with the press officer and a cabinet member, they flew to a small village that Torrijos was trying to develop. The place was a literal sea of mud. Reed, dressed to visit a head of state, paid a peon a dollar to borrow his horse to keep his feet out of the slime. Sitting on the horse, he watched Torrijos walk down to the river, unstrap his pistol and jump into the water otherwise fully dressed; his colleagues, though immaculately turned out for work in the city, jumped in, too.

"Boy, that's a hell of a way to earn a living," Reed said to the cabinet minister as they emerged dripping.

"Reed, are you suggesting that we only jumped in the river because the general jumped in?"

"That's exactly what I'm suggesting."

"Reed, you've got it wrong. We like swimming."

Back on the veranda of his oceanside home, Torrijos broke out the whiskey, and he and Reed drank together until midnight. Little of what they said to each other appears in the article, but the opening sequence gives the "feel" of the man as Reed experienced it that day. "I usually don't quote heads of state," Reed says. "I know what they are going to say; you get all that from the middle echelon people. But I like to see them to get that feel of them, to get a sense of the kind of people they are."

Drinking with their subjects, by the way, may be an occupational hazard for Digest writers, though few of them seem to mind it. Reed asserts that his father gave him two valuable pieces of advice—"never eat on an empty stomach" and "always drink with someone—or alone." The ability to drink was virtually a lifesaver for Reed in Ireland. "If I had to have favorite guerillas, it would be the Irish Republican Army," Reed says. "They are so charming and so full of blarney that it's hard to stay mad at them. There's only one army in the world composed of greater publicity hounds than the American army and that's the IRA. You're in grave danger of being killed—by kindness. Or perhaps by rounds of Irish whiskey which they keep on offering you. In fact, some reporters swear that the IRA will even force whiskey through your clenched teeth." On another continent and in another time, now retired Roving Editor George Kent got one of his most unusual stories by getting "very, very drunk" with a lonely, reticent Canadian mining engineer, John Thorburn Williamson, who loosened up enough to tell him about discovering a great diamond mine in Tanganyika—thus providing Kent's "Contender for the Diamond Throne" in the June 1947 Digest.

Digest writers have a tradition of getting to their man, wherever he is, almost as strong as that of the Canadian mounties, and often time proves more important in this quest than either whiskey or money. In the case of Williamson, for example, Kent sat around for weeks as the only guest in a small Tanganyikan inn with nothing but the West African Export catalogue to read until the diamond king returned from a trip into the bush. On another occasion, Kent got his greatest scoop by biding his time. It was during World War II, and Kent, looking for articles in neutral Portugal, heard that Dino Grandi, a former member of Benito Mussolini's Grand Council, had escaped and was hiding in Estoril under an assumed name. After cultivating an attache at the Italian embassy in Lisbon who introduced him to Grandi, Kent moved to a hotel in Estoril where he gained Grandi's confidence by visiting him daily over a period of weeks. The result was "The Last Days of Mussolini" in the October 1944 Digest—an article of such news value that it made the front pages of newspapers all over Allied Europe. Interestingly, when an excited Kent cabled Wallace that he had a "red hot story," he got this reply: "OK, but make it short."

While generally an ally, time can prove a problem, too, for Digest writers, as in the case of Watergate. With a lead time of more than eight weeks, Washington Editor Schulz and his colleagues had to sit by in frustration as events unfolded. "It was a daily breaking story," Schulz says. "Participants were leaking the story immediately for their own particular reasons to affect the course of events. So we wound up with the Teddy White book on Watergate and the Nixon failure."

Like Reed, who rose through the ranks of the City News Bureau, the *Chicago Daily News* and a five-year stint on *U.S. News & World Report,* Schulz and his Washington colleagues are the new breed of Digest writers—more professional journalists than artful essayists in the manner of McEvoy and Eastman. Schulz himself, a rumpled man with a wild mane of graying hair who could pass for a young senator or an aging poet, was a Washington columnist; his predecessor, Kenneth O. Gilmore, now a Pleasantville managing editor, came from the Newspaper Enterprise Association; Senior Editor Eugene Methvin is a graduate of *The Atlantic Constitution* and *Washington Daily News* and Senior Editor John Barron was a *Washington Star* investigator. Writing their heads off, the Washington staff supplies the Digest with an average of three articles per issue, many of them "signers" for senators, congressmen and the like. "The only political figure I've dealt with in three years who insisted on writing the article himself was former Secretary of Defense James R. Schlesinger," says Schulz. "The rest are content to let us do it."

Although almost all Digest Washington articles are staff written, Schulz & Co. occasionally recommend reprinting an article from another publication when they know it to be good and accurate and sometimes work with an outside writer who has an inside track on a subject. In addition to Schlesinger's "The Continuing Challenge to America," a few other titles from a recent Washington list gives an idea of their range of reporting: "Let's Stop Undermining the CIA," a signer by Melvin Laird; "Colleges Under the Federal Gun," by Senior Editor Ralph Kinney Bennett; "U.S.-Soviet Military Balance: Who's Ahead?" a signer by General Daniel Graham; "Big Government vs. the Little Guy," a signer by Senator James Buckley; "Workers Rights and Union Wrongs," by Senior Editor Kenneth Y. Tomlinson. "Ninety-five percent of the ideas come from us; the rest from Pleasantville or somebody who has a story to tell," says Schulz. Even during the time when Digest Editor-in-Chief Hobart Lewis was known to be one of President Nixon's close friends, Schulz says he had no communication whatever with Lewis about editorial matters.

This feeling of independence, coupled with almost unlimited time and expense (being on a salary, Washington staffers are spared the carrot of having to sell a lot of articles to boost their income through fees), makes Digest reporting almost a dream job in Schulz's view. Instead of hanging around Capitol Hill or the White House as most Washington correspondents do, Digest writers follow the threads of their stories out into the boondocks or even abroad, often for months at a time. Not being part of "the club," and frequently hiding behind "signers," Digest Washington staffers miss some of the personal glamor of being counted publicly among the Washington press corps, but their freedom to, in Stevenson's words, "dig for the facts such as no one else has the patience and the time or the money to do" more than makes up for it. This passion for fact is perhaps the chief characteristic of Digest reporting. Editors along Pleasantville's murderer's row can cut adjectives but seldom facts, and the Digest writer of today gets his satisfaction from seeing in print that telling detail nobody else could get.

While a half-century or so of "fact-minded" American journalism has made this kind of reporting, if not easy, at least understandable to most people in the United States, it is still a novelty abroad. In doing his first Digest article from Japan, English writer Christopher Lucas and his researcher, an American girl versed in the Japanese language, had to exercise considerable ingenuity to get that telling detail. Lucas was writing about a Japanese all-girl theater, known as the Takarazuka girls. Among other facts a Digest article on such a subject would be expected to have was the amount of money the girls earned. It was an unthinkable subject for Lucas to raise in Japan while interviewing one of the girls in front of the group's press agent, a representative of management. So by prearrangement, Lucas began feeling around for cigarettes in the middle of the interview; finding none, he asked the research girl to go out and buy some. Minutes later the press agent was summoned to the phone, and during the time the research girl, who had put in the call, could delay the press agent, Lucas pounced. The Takarazuka girl freely told him not only her salary but a number of other details that he could never have got otherwise. Of course, to protect the girl, Lucas did not reveal the source, reporting the facts on his own authority.

As the Lucas story illustrates, Digest writers are seldom alone in their search for the facts. Over the years, research has been elevated to the level of a fine art by the Digest, both in the United States and abroad. Under Staff Senior Editor Gertrude Arundel, a group of more than twenty young women and a couple of men works out of the Pan Am offices in New York. Each foreign edition has some research staff, and the Paris office under Staff Senior Editor John D. Panitza rivals that in Washington with three senior editors and four associates. Each of the editors in Paris, who develop stories on their own as well as give aid in research, speaks at least three languages, and they go along with writers to interpret. The research departments keep reference libraries as well as clippings on almost every conceivable subject, so that few Digest writers set out on a story in ignorance. When Reed, for example, was assigned a story on the Tupamaro guerillas in Uruguay, a country he'd never seen, research came up with what he called "a handy, twenty-five-pound press kit" on the subject before he ever left New York.

In addition to getting the writer started, research can nearly finish him since every fact in every Digest article is checked before it is printed. This checking process is, in the words of Editor-in-Chief Ed Thompson, "the harassment and salvation of each issue of the magazine." In a typical issue, 4,300 facts are checked; in one recent article alone, 573 facts were checked; in one two-page collection of humor, 32 facts were checked. Researchers do their checking by reference to their own files and the resources of the public libraries as well as by phoning authorities on the subject or persons mentioned or quoted in the piece. They underline each fact or quote in an article and either mark it OK or append a note explaining to the editors why they quarrel with it and giving their source of information. Often they suggest a more accurate rewording, and it is then up to the editor, usually the issue editor, to decide how the final copy should read. Researchers also point out potential libel as well as inaccuracy. I once saw a story go through in which *every* fact was either radically changed or slightly altered by research; an exasperated executive editor had circled the author's name and put a question mark beside that, too. It must be said, however, that it was the writer's adjectives and sense of anecdote that made the facts of an otherwise unremarkable story palatable.

It is peculiarly in this area of checking a completed article that the cultural and journalistic differences between reporting in the United States and other countries are most dramatically demonstrated. "When you get a cabinet minister in Europe on the phone and ask him if his eyes are really blue, he's just irritated," says one researcher in Paris. In one instance, this foreign annoyance with the American passion for fact was lifted almost to a diplomatic rupture. This involved a small filler, all of which are checked as solemnly as articles. To understand what happened, it is necessary to read again this little item that appeared under the heading of "Notes From All Over" in the October 1966 Reader's Digest:

"Life in Dogville, Spit and Fool may never be the same. The residents have suddenly found themselves living in Spacious, Little Cherry and Sunny. It's part of a campaign in the Soviet Union to spruce up the names of ancient villages, labeled before the revolution by the local population who couldn't stand the places. The program has already transformed Belly-Button, Rotten-Hole, Stinkeroo and Cockroach into names resembling U.S. suburbs—Bankside, Oak Grove, Happyville and Hillside. —UPI."

Since this obviously originated in Europe, it was sent to the Paris bureau for checking. (Note, by the way, that its being reported by United Press International was not considered proof of authenticity by the Digest; articles picked up from such prestigious sources as *Time* or the *New York Times* are as thoroughly checked as originals.) The filler was not received with joy in Paris where relations with the Soviet embassy, the most obvious source to consult, are often strained at best. In an effort to apply a rather universal grease to the grinding machinery of United States-Russian relations, a glamorous young researcher who had met the first secretary of the Russian embassy at a party was chosen to do the checking. When he came on the phone, he was rather testy since, unknown to her, he had been summoned from an important meeting to take the call. After she read the item to him, he really blew up. "Look, I've met you once, but that will be the last time. Why does your magazine write about silly things like this instead of the terrible massacres in Vietnam?" He slammed down the phone, and the cold war, in Paris at least, went into a deeper freeze. "People from Eastern Europe think you're making a fool of them with things like that," said a member of the Digest's Paris bureau.

Sometimes, though, the shoe is on the other foot, and Europeans try to make fools of Digest editors as one early, classic Digest research story shows. Shortly after the war, the Digest somehow acquired an article by a famous French stylist on the Johnny Appleseed of France, a peasant shepherd who was said to have caused a stand of 10,000 oak trees and a scattering of maples, lindens, birch to green the barren land he trod in the mountains of Provence. On instructions from Pleasantville, Panitza, then getting his start as a Digest researcher, set out to see this marvel for himself. While the shepherd was dead, some who knew him would surely still be there. The journey from Paris involved taking a train, a bus and finally a horse. Arrived at the site, Panitza could find neither trees nor folk who recognized the alleged name of the shepherd, though one villager he talked to was over ninety. Enraged, Panitza took the horse, the bus, the train back to Paris and presented himself at the home of the famous author. Flashing his most urbane and charming smile, the author said, "You never thought that was true, did you? What difference does it make? Isn't it a perfect Digest story?"

This experience not only reveals the tradition of rather careless, personal journalism that the Digest bucks abroad but also the extent of effort Digest researchers have learned to put into their checking. The magazine has been badly burned on a number of occasions. Back in the 50's before book condensations were subject to research checking, the Digest published a corking good yarn by Quentin Reynolds about a Canadian's experiences as an undercover agent in occupied Europe. The whole thing proved to be a fraud of such proportions that I was even assigned to do a story about it for *Parade*. On another occasion, one of the Digest's most dramatic First Person articles, set in the remote and hard-to-check jungles of Asia, proved to be an artful fabrication—after the fact of publication. The whole First Person program, which brings some 30,000 manuscripts of various degrees of accuracy and astonishment into Pleasantville every year, is a kind of booby trap for lovers of fact, and the sort of routine research needed to authenticate just one of these is worth recounting.

It was a tender little story called "Truce in the Forest" for the January 1973 Digest. Written by a man who had been just a boy in 1944, the article told how he and his mother had been living in a little cottage in the Hürtgen Forest, near the German-Belgian border, trying to escape the fighting. But the Battle of the Bulge broke virtually over their heads, and on Christmas Eve that year, three lost American soldiers, one of them wounded, knocked on the door asking for refuge. Courageously, the boy's mother took them in, killed the chicken she was saving for the return of her soldier-husband and prepared a meal. Just then three lost German soldiers also knocked on the door. Pleading Christmas, the mother got both the Germans and Americans to put down their arms and join together in what was a feast for all of them. The next morning, they parted amicably, each group heading toward its own lines. The story ended: "When I returned inside, Mother had brought out the old family Bible. I glanced over her shoulder. The book was open to the Christmas story, the Birth in the Manger and how the Wise Men came from afar bearing their gifts. Her finger was tracing the last line from Matthew 2:12. '. . . they departed into their own country another way.'"

Talk about a perfect Digest story! But was it true? The then First Person Editor James Finan wrote Paris. His letter landed on the desk of Ursula Naccache, an editor raised in Switzerland who could speak both German and French. Finan's letter described the author as a baker in Hawaii named Fritz Vincken who had told him on the phone that his mother still lived in Essen where his parents had had a bakery; Finan didn't quite catch the address, but finding her should be no trouble. Ms. Naccache got on the phone and called everyone in Essen by that name, inquiring whether they had a relative who was a baker in Hawaii. Negative. "On any other magazine, I'd have quit right there," she said. Instead, she started to think. People living in Essen wouldn't have a cottage in the Hürtgen Forest; what town sounded a little like Essen? Aachen, perhaps. A series of calls to Aachen finally located the bakery; Mrs. Vincken, who had sold it to the owners, still lived upstairs— they'd bring her to the phone.

The old lady proved to be so deaf that about all Ms. Naccache could establish by phone was that she did, indeed, have a son who was a baker in Hawaii. There was no other way of checking the story's details but to go and see her. In Aachen, Ms. Naccache discovered that the woman was not only old and deaf but ill and fuzzy memoried. So Ms. Naccache set out to study the locale of the cottage in the Hürtgen Forest, crossing and recrossing into Belgium. In the process, she befuddled border guards and finally got arrested by German police for unauthorized walking on government property when she tramped the railway line to see if it bridged the river. Although she had to pay a five-mark fine in addition to her other expenses, Ms. Naccache was satisfied that the events could have taken place as related and so notified Pleasantville. "In my experience," she says, "I find that people generally don't go around making up stories. Besides, I had researched with Connie Ryan on his war books, and I knew that lots of strange things happened between soldiers in battle. If somebody had made this one up, they would have tried to make it seem more spectacular."

Researching the Ryan war books, in fact, was typical of the kind of all-out Digest effort that multiplies a writer's eyes and ears a dozen times or more. For *The Longest Day,* the story of D-Day, fourteen Digest people dug into the records in five different countries; researchers also sent out 3,000 questionnaires and interviewed 700 eyewitnesses. Another massive effort was mounted to get the facts for Ryan's story of the fall of Berlin. As usual, some of the best stories never got into the book. One that Ms. Naccache recalls with relish was her interview of a German woman who claimed to have been sorely used by the Russian conquerors. Then young and living with two other girls in an apartment in the sector the Russian troops took over, the woman said that she and her friends had been surprised in their nightgowns early one morning by three Russian officers knocking at their door. The girls hadn't eaten for about as long as the Russians hadn't seen women, so the Russians went away and came back with eggs, coffee and the other makings for a breakfast. "You got up and got dressed?" "Well, we were so hungry we just cooked the food." And then? "Well, we all had breakfast together." And then? "Well, we put a record on the gramaphone and danced." And then? "Oh, and then, we were *brutally* raped."

To get the German side of the stuff that did go into the book, the Digest's Paris bureau established an outpost in Berlin under Senior Editor John Flint. It was his first Digest assignment for Flint, a lean, gentle man with the look and, as it turned out fortunately, the patience of a doctoral student. After spending his first six years in his native Vienna, Flint moved with his family to New York where he became a naturalized American and graduated from Columbia. Back in Europe, he worked in Paris for the wire services, then in the London bureau of McGraw-Hill before joining the Digest in that year of 1962. Sent off almost immediately to Berlin for what was supposed to be a six-week research stint, he had to brush up on the German he had learned as a child. By the time he returned to Paris a year later, Flint not only had regained his facility in using the German language but had amassed 3,000 pages of interviews and facts about the momentous events of those last days in the smashed capital of the Third Reich. He had also developed something like awe for Digest reporting. "Everyone who comes in contact with Digest research methods is taken aback by the extent to which the magazine goes into detail," he says.

"Getting this detail about the fall of Berlin was harder than covering D-Day," Flint claims. "Then you had a functioning military apparatus and a civilian bureaucracy that kept records. This was total collapse. Records either weren't kept or were destroyed or dispersed." With an office and secretary loaned by the Digest's German company and the part-time help of American students in Berlin, Flint hunted down not only what records there were but through ads in the newspapers and word of mouth what people he could find who had been in Berlin and had a story to tell. "It was a snowball operation," Flint recalls. A great map of Berlin on the wall of his office began to sprout pins identifying the location of action and people; files started to bulge with interviews, ticketed to indicate those characters writer Ryan called "travelers" whose activities could be stretched through the length of the book. From time to time, Ryan, who was also covering the Russian and American aspects of the story, would appear in Berlin to join Flint in interviewing these important characters in depth. How do you know when to quit on a thing like that? "Finally," says Flint, "you just make an executive decision that you have enough."

Though it is hard to separate specific costs of Digest Research from the general accounts for salaries, rent, phones, mail and the like, a few figures in Flint's Berlin file for expenses beyond these basics give some idea of how large the whole could be: November 1962, $533; February 1963, $985; May 1963, $1,676. Obviously, the Digest is, as advertised, unstinting in its efforts to get the facts. Yet, with all that, there are some things even the Digest can't learn. When writer William Warren turned in a piece on the temples of Bangkok, research

was asked to find the exact height of the famous Emerald
Buddha in the Wat Phra Keo on the palace grounds, a tidbit
Warren had omitted even though this statue was a centerpiece
for his story. Since the nearest Digest researcher to Bangkok
was in Hong Kong, the request was sent to Warren himself. The
writer didn't know. A second instruction went out: go and
measure it. Can't be done, replied Warren; the only person in
Thailand allowed near the sacred image sitting high atop an
altar is the king himself who changes the Buddha's golden
robes at the beginning of every season in a truly royal cere-
mony.

Despite such lapses, Digest reporting can nearly overwhelm a
writer. When I last talked with Roving Editor Blank he was
struggling with the job of reducing 57,000 words of raw research to a 6,000-or-so-word article which would further be
cut to perhaps 3,000 words or less. "You know, when people
read one of those things, they just don't realize the work that
goes into it. The lead, the organization, the choice of anecdotes
seem so obvious to them that they think there probably wasn't
any other way to tell the story. There are hundreds of ways to
tell any story, and getting the right one can be hell," Blank
says. So can covering the story. Though the piece Blank was
then working on was a cheerful one, he often comes home sick
to the stomach and heart from his more usual investigations of
disaster—whether the lone child dying of leukemia or 100,000
people perishing in a flood; sometimes it's weeks before he can
begin to think of reporting it as a job.

Obviously, a good part of the original content of the Digest
represents a highly sophisticated form of group journalism, and
today's writers accept it for what it is. Most of them, in fact, like
it. Covering the Italian earthquake last year, for example,
Roving Editor Gordon Gaskill had the help of his Italian wife
and Italian-speaking Senior Editor Francis Schell from the
Paris bureau. While other writers on the scene would take a
quick look, talk to a few people and go back to their hotel
rooms to pound out copy, Gaskill and his companions would
fan out in different directions in search of the telling anecdotes

or phrases that would make the Digest account seem fresh as much as six months later. Schell recalls spending four hours huddled in a tent in a hailstorm talking to refugees, an exercise he felt was amply rewarded by only two phrases. A soldier said that the roof of the concrete barracks in which he was lying "came down like a tombstone"; a woman telling of seeing whole potted plants come out of the rubble untouched, added, "If only they could have been children."

It's not hard to understand that the writer who has not only been on the scene himself but has probably been fed reams of quotes and facts by his research colleagues feels compelled to turn in a lengthy manuscript, lest he omit that single gem that can make a story sparkle. Hence, he comes almost to welcome the ministrations of the editor. Describing how he worked with the Digest's late William Hard, Jr.—incidentally, the best all-around editor I've encountered anywhere in a thirty-year career—Roving Editor James Stewart-Gordon says, "I'd write some 40,000 words to get 4,000. I'd do an outline that would go on for about eighteen pages in which I'd say all sorts of outrageous and funny things and then write a story of exactly eighteen pages. Bill would sit down and meld the two together. He'd pick things from the outline that I thought were too far out. For example, I did a wrestling story in which I said in the outline that promoters were so prosperous that they were smoking two cigars at once. He lit on that phrase and used it, saying, 'That's very descriptive.' He had an uncanny knack of keeping the color of the story."

James A. Michener, famous for his long, long novels, is even more grateful for Digest editing. Though Michener appears often in the Digest, he confesses in an introduction to *A Michener Miscellany* that, having no journalistic training, he could never learn to fashion a good Digest "lead" or to write concisely. As to leads, he says that "the editors have written them all. It is my custom when I see an article of mine in print to say, 'Damn! Why didn't I think of starting it that way?'" As to length, Michener reports, "The first article I submitted . . . gave the editors sixty-four pages of copy when they needed eight. I have maintained that proportion, more or less, through the years. I have been well treated by the cutters, for often they have made my inchoate reporting neat and my rambling thoughts concise. . . . I should add that Lewis [Michener's editor, Hobart Lewis] proved to be understanding in dealing with my weaknesses, although when I placed my first assignment on his desk, he cried, 'My God!' As late as the autumn of 1971 when I submitted an unusually long piece, he wrote in the margin: 'Michener still hasn't figured out whom he's writing for.' "

On the whole, it must be said that the lot of the regular writers for the Digest is not exactly a sorry one, despite the prose that falls into the wastebasket. Their income is as closely guarded a secret, and probably suffers from as much disparity, as the income of other Digesters. Estimating it is complicated by the fact that article fees vary—from a base of $2,400 to around $4,000—as do methods of payment for regular writers; some get low article rates and high retainers, others get high rates and low retainers, still others are on salary. The last figure I heard—Digester's won't fall for the Lucas trick—put the top writer's annual income at something between $40,000 and $50,000. This would mean that writers, on the whole, make considerably less than a good many editors at the Digest but no doubt as much or more than they could get elsewhere in the market. The one criticism that Norman Cousins, who is otherwise glowing in his praise for Digest editorial methods, has about the magazine is that it no longer pays writers enough. Though the base Digest rate has risen from the $1,400 with which DeWitt Wallace astonished George Kent in the 30's to today's $2,400 (only $1,500 for articles done just for foreign editions), the increase is no match for either the cost of living or the competition. Kent, for example, was being paid $300 to $400 by other major magazines against the Digest's $1,400; nowadays, many magazines pay $1,000 or more and some do even better than the Digest. By that standard, the Digest base rate today should be $4,500 or $5,000, especially when, as Cousins points out, many of these articles find their way into

editions of the Digest abroad with no additional recompense
to the writer.

If Digest writers aren't likely to get rich, there are other
compensations. They have what amounts to a free ticket to the
world and, despite some mutterings from the watchdog in
Pleasantville, it's generally first class. In moments when the hot
pursuit of facts is not feasible, Digest writers have been known
to relax with good food and wine, to try the gaming tables at
Monte Carlo or Macao, and even to test the proverbial writer's
spell over women. Despite tales I've heard, I'm a little skeptical
about the extent of this last diversion, owing to an experience
I had at *Parade.* A colleague there who was on the road a lot
met a writer from another magazine in the bar car of a train.
As the juice flowed, they began trading boasts about conquests
until it reached the putup or shutup stage. A hundred-dollar
bet was made to be paid to the first of them who, upon his
word as a gentleman, would say that he had enjoyed free
female companionship in bed on a writing trip; for the five
years I followed this wager no money exchanged hands. But,
just as they are better paid, Digest writers may have more
sexual attraction. One of them bragged to a Digest researcher
that, during a lengthy story-hunting stay in a foreign capital,
he had acquired a beautiful, young mistress to warm his
expense-account pad. "She used to be a prostitute," he said,
"but she wanted to move in with me, because she swore I was
the only man who ever gave her an orgasm." My informant, a
skeptical lady well versed in parrying the thrusts of amorous
and/or alcoholic writers, said, "You know, he couldn't understand why I laughed in his face."

Digest writers don't go entirely unnoticed by the rest of the
world, of course. Roving Editor John Hubbell, for example, was
honored in 1966 by the Sigma Delta Chi, the national journalis-
tic fraternity, for a book, *The Case of the Missing H-bomb.*
Washington Senior Editor John Barron also got the Sigma Delta
Chi award for a series of articles on excesses in the Internal
Revenue Service. Cornelius Ryan was pinned with the French
Legion of Honor for *The Longest Day*; Roving Editor Leslie

Velie won the American Bar Association Award for articles about the court system as it relates to juveniles. And so on and on. If they aren't Richard Harding Davises, Digest writers nevertheless are appreciated for their reporting on the American scene, and like the magazine itself, they can take quiet pride in the fact that stories they wrote may have saved a life, altered a political contest, informed a citizen or simply entertained millions of their fellow human beings for a bright moment.

Perhaps the best commentary on the writing life within the world of the Digest is that as few writers as editors or other employees willingly leave their posts until disease, age or death does them part. Woollcott's statement that the Digest has taken the pleasure out of writing should perhaps now be amended to say that it has put the pleasure into reporting. And if to some extent they are prophets without honor in their own country, it's a good bet that, as Steinbeck discovered, they are better known in most of the world's nooks and crannies than nearly any other writers of English.

XII

"Go Tell It on the Mountain"

Nowhere is the serendipity in the Reader's Digest's saga of success more evident or astonishing than in the development of its international operations. Only the imagination can grasp the complexity of events and personalities involved in bringing into being and running a business that publishes a monthly magazine in thirty-two countries and thirteen languages, manufactures and sells books, records, paintings, audio equipment, candy and other goodies by the million in almost as many lands. Unlike most other large international enterprises—the oil companies, say, with their black gold or IBM with its thinking machines— the Digest deals largely in the products most vulnerable to the stresses of varying languages and cultures: words and ideas. Yet it has managed to peddle these items so widely over the last forty years that today the magazine's circulation abroad stands at 11.5 million, and its entire foreign enterprise brings in about half the company's estimated $700 million gross. An achievement of this kind obviously takes brains, persistence, money— and the kind of luck, or genius, that seems to have graced nearly every move DeWitt Wallace has made in some eighty-seven years of living.

Even more than most human enterprises, a complicated international operation such as the Digest's depends upon finding people uniquely equipped for the venture. While many such characters have walked on and off the Digest stage since the first foreign edition was launched in Britain in 1938, none is more fascinating than Senior Editor Dennis McEvoy. The Digest's foreign drama in which he has played his large part could well be called McEvoy in Wonderland. In a way, it begins, as so many things at the Digest begin, with a Digest article.

The piece, entitled "70 Per Cent Is Not Passing," appeared in the November 1941 Digest and was written by Dennis's equally colorful father. The thesis of the article was set forth thusly: "Experience had taught me that merely learning the names of things might get me 70 per cent passing grades in school; but that out in the world a lawyer either wins his case or loses it, a doctor's patient either gets well or doesn't. In life nothing below 100 per cent is passing." J. P. McEvoy went on to report how he tried to teach his son this thesis by what must still be the most unusual education any boy has ever received. Instead of answering six-year-old Dennis's questions, the father gave him an encyclopedia; the summer after kindergarten, Dennis was boarded on a farm in France where he learned the language; after two years of U.S. military school, the boy was sent to "a Spartan school in Germany" to learn *that* language; at sixteen, Dennis went to work for a period as copy boy and then reporter on the *San Francisco Examiner*; the same year he went with his father to the Far East and was left alone at the YMCA in Tokyo to learn *that* language; still sixteen or so, Dennis returned alone to Chicago and got himself admitted to the University of Chicago from which he graduated. Already a fan of the father, DeWitt Wallace was intrigued with what such an education must have made of the son and would be aware of his probable abilities when and if they met.

But Dennis McEvoy's beginnings of a career took him far away from the Reader's Digest, except for an article he sold the magazine, "Japan's 'Patriotic' Gangsters," which appeared in January 1940 while he was a United Press correspondent and language student in Tokyo. This piece made Dennis persona non grata in the land of the rising sun, and he went on to serve as a *Chicago Times* correspondent and Office of Naval Intelligence agent in Southeast Asia, a *Times* and CBS reporter in Moscow during the fall of that capital, and finally a Marine Corps lieutenant with ONI in Washington. A chunky man with an open Irish face, young McEvoy had by then picked up a number of skills from his strange education. He could speak and read French, German, Japanese, Russian, Chinese and Spanish, some to perfection and all passably well; he was a karate expert; he could stand on his head and sing an aria from *Pagliacci* and stop his heart from beating for a minute or so at will; more important, he could give birth to outrageous ideas. One of these was that the all-American Reader's Digest would sell like raw fish in a defeated Japan.

With VE day signalling a probable end to the war, Lt. McEvoy travelled to Pleasantville to present his idea to a wisely skeptical Wallace. Why would the Japanese, after defeat in such a bitter struggle, accept an American magazine, Wallace wanted to know. "The Japanese are realists," McEvoy argued. "They'll want to know all about the democracy that beat them."

Wallace was persuaded enough by this answer to suggest that Dennis, still only twenty-six years old, go to Tokyo as a Digest correspondent as soon as the shooting stopped and investigate the possibilities. "Have you ever had any publishing experience?" he asked.

"No, sir, not even one day," McEvoy replied.

"Well, neither did Lila or I before we published the Reader's Digest. It is not all that complicated. All you need do is spend a few weeks around the shop before you go to Tokyo. Talk to the men who are running the various departments. Find out what they are doing and why. The rest is common sense and knowledge of the terrain, which you have," Wallace said.

Virtually the day after VJ day, Wallace interceded with Secretary of Defense James Forrestal to have McEvoy discharged and given priority transportation to Tokyo. In San Francisco on his way out, McEvoy received a wire from

Wallace: "May your trip be more momentous than Commander Perry's. Best regards. Wally."

Young as he was, McEvoy was already sophisticated enough to know what he didn't know. A gregarious man who meets people easily, he picked the brains of those more expert on matters of printing, government regulations, real estate, financing; among them, Major James Monahan, a reserve Air Force officer, who was later to become a Digest senior editor and arch enemy of the cigarette industry, and L. W. Chamberlain, then resident vice president of the National City Bank in Tokyo. By February 1946, McEvoy had managed to secure Supreme Commander Douglas MacArthur's permission to publish and had established enough feasibility to bring Dr. Barclay Acheson, Digest Director of International Editions, and production expert Kent Rhodes to Tokyo. After a two-week study of the situation, they told McEvoy to hire a Japanese staff and go ahead.

Jobs were hard to come by in shattered Tokyo, particularly for those who had shown any resistance to their country's militaristic spirit. Thus, McEvoy was able to hire as editor Bunshiro Suzuki, former editor of *Asahi*, one of Japan's two largest newspapers. Suzuki had been scarred for life when a sword wielding "patriotic gangster" attacked him in his *Asahi* offices for his anti-militarist stand. For an office manager, McEvoy reached back into a fantastic war experience which is worth recounting to show how all things seem to work together for the good of Reader's Digest.

In 1943, when McEvoy was with ONI in Washington, a plane bearing one Mateo Okini, a full captain in the Japanese Navy and chief of Japanese naval intelligence in China, crashed in the Chinese interior. Rendered unconscious, Captain Okini was taken prisoner before he could commit suicide, as the Japanese code required of a man in his position and with his knowledge. As a result, he became one of the most prized prisoners of the war in Asia. In the midst of a struggle among allies as to who should hold him, the Americans almost literally kidnapped Okini and flew him right to Washington where it became the task of McEvoy and another language officer, Lt. Don Gorham, to interrogate him.

Although he was polite about it all, Captain Okini would say nothing of consequence. All he wanted to do was kill himself, and elaborate precautions had to be taken to see that he didn't have the means. To make matters worse, he was gloomy over the loss of a leg as a result of the accident. The Americans began to think that they might get somewhere if they could at least cheer the prisoner up. So, against the better judgment of their superiors and at considerable risk to themselves if anything went wrong, they "sprang" their precious captive from confinement, took him to a private apartment where an authentic Japanese party had been organized, including special food, sake, music and Japanese waitresses flown down from New York to act as geisha girls. It worked. Touched by this kindness and even more by such appreciation of his own customs, Okini broke down and talked and forgot about doing away with himself.

Going back to Tokyo must, however, have been a greater act of courage than going to war for Okini. His very survival made him a kind of outcast, and the Digest job must have seemed providential. Okini chose to face the issue head-on in hopes of helping others with a similar fate and wrote a book, *I Am One of the Living Dead*, which turned into a best seller. He also worked for Japan's Wounded War Veterans Association. Thus, Okini became a kind of pivotal personality in that struggle going on within the Japanese soul to discard old values for new —a struggle in which the Digest's part was noted by none other than Supreme Commander MacArthur who wrote, "I am grateful for its assistance in this greatest reformation of a people ever attempted in history."

McEvoy's guess that Japanese curiosity about things American would overcome any reluctance to do business with the former enemy was right. The first press run of 120,000, selling for 3.5 yen, or 23 cents U.S., was sold out within hours to crowds lined up in the street. From then on, sales soared as fast as they could be met until circulation reached a peak of 1.4 million. But competitive Japanese publications revived as fast as Japanese industry, and a new pride in their own accomplishments and concern for their own problems cooled the public's super-heated interest in the United States. Circulation of the Japanese Reader's Digest dropped back to around 500,000 where it remains today—still a giant among serious monthly magazines in that country. Other aspects of the Digest business are doing well in Japan, too, according to Digest President John A. O'Hara, who was recently in charge of international operations. Two of them—an ingenious reproduction of the great masters of art and the Foreign Study League which sends Japanese groups to the United States—prosper more richly in Japan than anywhere else on earth.

The whole Japanese operation was given a solid foundation by one of those bits of serendipity. Since profits couldn't be repatriated then, McEvoy bought a piece of land across from the moat surrounding the Imperial Palace, and ultimately about a quarter of a million dollars went into construction of a modern office building designed by Antonin Raymond who had worked with Frank Lloyd Wright on the famous Imperial Hotel. The choice of architect is odd in view of a favorite McEvoy story. When Harry K. Thaw, the Pittsburgh millionaire who shot architect Stanford White in a love triangle, was released from captivity, he took a trip around the world, according to the story. Stopping in Tokyo, Thaw went into the odd-looking Imperial Hotel, clapped his hand to his head and cried, "My God, I shot the wrong architect!" In any case, the Digest building proved to be too small and graceful to compete economically in high-rising Tokyo. In the mid-60's it was replaced by the $30 million Palaceside Building, jointly owned by the Digest, the Japanese newspaper *Mainichi* and the Sanwa Bank.

With the occupation ending and the Japanese Digest well established, trouble-shooter McEvoy was given a new assignment in 1951: starting an edition in Spain. This would seem a piece of cake for a man who had overcome the physical obstacles of publishing in a war-devastated city and the psychological obstacles of selling American optimism to a defeated people whose language and culture were totally alien. But at the time Spain was even more challenging. Diplomatic relations were at the lowest ebb; Spain had been excluded from the United Nations, and a 1946 resolution by the United States, Great Britain and France had called for the ouster of dictator Franco. In addition to that, power forces in Spain were unalterably opposed to everything the Reader's Digest stands for. In a country 99 percent Catholic, church extremists looked upon the magazine as an advocate of muscular American Protestantism; in a dictatorship, the single Falange Party viewed any journal advocating democratic principles as a threat. In Spain, there would be no American Supreme Commander to open doors for McEvoy.

Being aware of all this, McEvoy began mending fences even before he left Tokyo, and ran into another instance of that amazing grace that marks the Digest story. As somewhat of a Digest oddity—a Catholic, more by birth than conviction—McEvoy, along with the French and Belgian ambassadors, served as a lay adviser to the Papal Nuncio in Japan. In this capacity, he had signed a request from a missionary priest in Hokkaido for money to buy a stained-glass window for his church. He had forgotten the incident by the time he got around to calling on the Spanish chargé d'affairs in Tokyo, Sr. Francisco (Paco) de Castillo, for advice. Paco, a friend who favored publication of the Digest in Spain, reminded McEvoy of the window and said that the grateful priest might be induced to write a letter of introduction to his old classmate and friend, Don Fernando Martin Sanchez y Julia, a "grey eminence" who, despite such paralysis from muscular dystrophy that he could move only his head, ran Catholic Action, the lay arm of the church in Spain and was known as one of the most powerful men in the country.

The letter proved almost as useful to McEvoy in Spain as an edict from MacArthur in Japan. Martin Sanchez arranged the necessary first step, an interview with Franco for Dr. Acheson, McEvoy and Dr. Eduardo Cardenas, editor of the Latin American Spanish editions. It was a tense time for the American trio, but Franco's somewhat vague comment on their project was encouraging, "As far as I'm concerned, there is no inconvenience." His minions took a different view. They submitted some twenty-eight demands as a condition of publishing. Among them: would the Digest guarantee not to publish *in any edition* any article critical of Spain or General Franco; would the Digest guarantee to refrain from publishing *in any edition* any article critical of the Catholic Church or its doctrine? This was, of course, unacceptable, and it took a year of negotiations before an agreement was reached in which the Digest promised to observe Spanish law which meant that it would not criticize, *in Spain*, the Spanish government or the Catholic Church.

The usual success followed. The first edition, appearing in October 1952 with a handwritten welcome from no less than Franco himself on the cover, sold 125,000 copies and circulation gradually rose to 250,000, the largest of any general-interest magazine in Spain. Continuing aid and advice from Martin Sanchez, a member of the Spanish Parliament, saved the magazine in the late 60's when he got what is known as "the Reader's Digest amendment" written into a law prohibiting foreigners from owning a newspaper or magazine in Spain. The amendment dated the prohibition from November 1952, and the Digest came out in October. An almost careless signature on behalf of an obscure missionary priest had paid rich dividends, indeed.

By the time the Spanish edition was established, the Digest had developed considerable sophistication in foreign operations. Not even Wallace remembers precisely the genesis of the decision to publish in Britain in 1938, calling it now "a logical extension of the magazine's desire to serve people." Its immediate success, however, was a factor in 1940 when, with Axis propaganda flooding Latin America, it was suggested that circulation of a Spanish language edition of the Digest would be a good counter move. A preliminary study indicated that there just weren't enough people south of the border with twenty-five cents to spare to make the project feasible. But Digest General

Manager Albert L. Cole kept turning it over in his mind and finally came up with the suggestion that the magazine be sold for ten cents a copy and supported by advertising—the first advertising the Digest had taken anywhere. Again instant success. Circulation in Argentina alone, for example, jumped from 25,000 to 75,000 within a year and reached 400,000 by February 1942. A Portugese edition was introduced into Brazil and quickly climbed to 300,000. Perhaps more important in the long run, advertising worked so well that it was added to the British magazine and became a pattern for all foreign editions.

In 1942, with Europe set aflame by war, the Office of War Information asked the Digest if OWI could have permission to translate and distribute the magazine in neutral Sweden. The Digest refused to be used as an arm of government but promised to look into publishing there itself. Dr. Acheson, who had just been appointed director of international editions, and Marvin Lowes, an American who had founded and run the British edition for three years, set off for Sweden. Off Newfoundland, their plane crashed and broke in two; twelve passengers forward perished, but Acheson and Lowes who had been in the rear smoking compartment survived. Flown back to the United States, they boarded the next flight for Sweden with the usual results: the first edition in March 1943 had to be reprinted twice to satisfy demands; by the end of the war, circulation was 235,000 in a country of only 6.5 million people.

Dr. Acheson, Lila Wallace's brother who had been trained as a Presbyterian minister and gained foreign experience with the Near East Foundation, was on his way to becoming Pleasant-ville's ambassador to the world. A balding, pipe-smoking type of man, Dr. Acheson, according to McEvoy, presented a front as seemingly unsophisticated as the publication he represented. He was full of homilies, and his favorite story was that of the Scotchman in hell who, boiling in oil and prodded by the "de'il's" pitchfork, cries out, "Oh, Lord, I dinna ken! I dinna ken!" The Lord thunders back, "Well, ye ken the noo!" Dr. Acheson never tried to be a linguist; like a proper ambassador, he used interpretators when necessary and was never abashed in the presence of the mighty, like Franco. "Dr. Acheson was an 'amateur' in publishing—like Mr. Wallace when he launched the Reader's Digest in 1922," says McEvoy. "Some amateurs! Most 'professionals' would have to get up very early indeed in the morning even to stay in the same race with them."

Dr. Acheson's chief attribute, in the view of McEvoy and others I've talked to, was his ability to size up people quickly, regardless of nationality. From the first, the Digest adopted a policy of staffing foreign editions with local people. In the early days, Americans were often used as managing directors to show the way—Paul Thompson, for example, started and ran both the French and German editions for a number of years until he was recalled to Pleasantville to become director of international editions. But, as of this writing, there is only one American managing director abroad—in Hong Kong. By the time of his death in 1957, Barclay Acheson had in place the almost elite corps of foreign Digesters, some of them now also dead or retired, who have run the business over the years.

His first invasion of the continent through Sweden is typical of the Acheson style—and luck. One of the earliest contacts he made in Stockholm was Count Folke Bernadotte whose wife, Estelle, had been born a Manville and raised in the stately parental home in—would you believe it?—Pleasantville, New York. Count Bernadotte, who later died a hero's death as UN mediator in Palestine in 1948, was so sold on the Digest that he agreed to become chairman of its Swedish board of directors. It was Dr. Acheson's habit always to start at the top, and when it was decided to publish in Italy in 1948, he knocked on the door of the largest Italian publishing firm, Mondadori. As related by Mario Ghisalberti, then working for Mondadori but now retired after a twenty-year Digest career, Dr. Acheson and Paul Thompson came seeking "advice"; they went away with an agreement for Mondadori to print and distribute the magazine and with Ghisalberti as editor.

Actually, according to Ghisalberti, Mondadori had craftily proposed him for the post, thinking he would keep it within their fold. After talking to Acheson & Co., Ghisalberti had other ideas; he would keep it independent. A good thing, too. With the average Italian magazine selling about 70,000 copies, he astonished Mondadori with an initial print order of 250,000 and then shocked them with a follow-up order for 80,000. The second print order was for 350,000 and so on up to an eventual 750,000. Ghisalberti's explanation of the reasons for this growth would probably do for the same phenomenon in the other countries of war-weary Europe. "Everything American was popular at that time," he says. "The Italians, trying to reconstruct their country after the devastation of war, were sympathetic to the main themes of self-help in Reader's Digest—the pioneer spirit."

It's well they were since, in the early years, no foreign editor was permitted by Pleasantville to run any article that had not first appeared in the United States edition of the Reader's Digest. DeWitt Wallace's main interest in going abroad was to spread the word, to "go tell it on the mountain" that the American values of free enterprise, democracy, self-reliance work; his quoted description of the Digest as a "window on the world" might more properly then have been phrased "a window on America for the world." Although Wallace would from time to time have one of the foreign editions monitored for him, his personal interest in them never seemed high. Writers whose work might be appearing in Digests everywhere in the world but the United States would, for example, be queried testily by Wallace as to why they weren't writing for the magazine anymore. Even when abroad, the Wallace interest in his own enterprise was muted, to say the least.

Until recently, the Wallaces were indefatigable travellers, leaving Pleasantville mysteriously for parts unknown once or twice a year and popping up almost anywhere on the globe. Perhaps knowing that their privacy would be relentlessly invaded by fawning attentions, they never informed Digesters of their plans. The one thing they seemed consistently interested in abroad was the physical facilities, possibly because Mrs. Wallace sent her own decorator around the world to make sure that Digest offices everywhere had the same touches of elegance as those in Pleasantville. In London, the Digest occupies suitably low-keyed offices tucked into a corner of the city's poshest location, Berkeley Square. In Paris editorial offices for both the French edition and Pleasantville's outpost, the European Editorial Office, are in a converted mansion on Boulevard Saint-Germain in the Left Bank sector. While being nearly perfect as to location and refinement, the antiquity of this particular building offers a few drawbacks in the conduct of modern business. A while ago members of EEO put together a spoofing report on what they called OOO—Office that Overcomes all Obstacles —which describes their physical situation thusly:

"A rule which, unfortunately, is being disregarded in this age of sexual license by most organizations, is still being strictly observed by the tradition-bound OOO: men and women work back to back. The male members of the staff face the garden, the women face the street. However, a notable concession to the pressures of the 20th century was made when OOO desegrated the bathroom. Here the two sexes mingle freely and many fruitful exchanges on story ideas have taken place while members of the staff merrily jostle for a place at the single wash tap.

"The organization's 11 offices have come down to OOO virtually unchanged since the days of Louis XIV, France's Sun King, although it is rumored that the elevators, ces parvenus, were introduced in 1800. Unfortunately, a coat of paint applied recently has taken away some of the original splendor. But there are some places in OOO where history mingles happily with present-day conveniences. Thus the ultra modern Xerox machine is flanked on one side by a marble washbasin dated 1712, and on the other by an exquisite bathtub of the same vintage. There is also a sign of perhaps extensive historical interest which reads: 'Laissez les W.C. dans l'etat ou vous souhaitrez les trouver en entrant.' The bathtub is now being used as a filing cabinet for outdated background files. This explains why at OOO the commonly used French expression 'étre dans le bain' does not mean 'being with it' but rather 'being outdated and discarded.' Time and again visitors are baffled by this example of OOO's quick wit and keen sense of observation. Another feather in OOO's cap.

"When winter comes and covers the graceful building with a white mantle of snow, eleven little electric heaters at OOO purr away bringing the temperature up to a luxurious 2° C (35° F). However, because one heater recently burnt a hole in the chief's door, there is some question of replacing the heaters with plaid rugs and mittens for all."

Despite such privations, Parisian editorial people have fought many a battle to remain in the heart of their beloved city rather than move to more economical and efficient offices on the outskirts with the rest of the operation. Perhaps because the home office has functioned so successfully so far from Manhattan, this search for real estate or rentals in cheaper, less desirable neighborhoods in foreign cities became something of a policy during an economy move in the early 70's. Hong Kong operations, for example, were transferred from downtown Victoria near the swank Mandarin Hotel to an area of warehouses so bleak that there's scarcely a noodle shop where employees can find sustenance. In Mexico City, Pablo Morales, longtime editor of Latin American Spanish editions, president of the press club, friend of ex-President Eccheveria, left the Digest rather than move from the sumptuous villa he had turned into editorial offices. Morales's motives were more than sybaritic; he argued that moving into dingier quarters with the business department meant the end of editorial independence. The intensity of some of the battles about real estate abroad only serves to underscore Mrs. Wallace's contention that surroundings do make a difference in the way people work.

A true pioneer in creating unusual surroundings was the Digest's Australian company. In a drab lower-middle-class suburb of Sydney, it built an edifice that can be described only as looking like an Aztec ruin. Within, however, there is a beautifully landscaped roof garden onto which the executive offices open. Because this garden is situated directly above the computers, a number of Australian staffers got a pool going—Australians will bet on anything—as to when the roots of thriving trees and vines would finally reach down into the delicate electronic machinery and bring the whole operation to a halt.

When the Wallaces went to Sydney, perhaps the remotest out-post of the Digest world, they wanted to see this wonder, thus giving rise to another version of a story that has been told in almost identical detail of their visits elsewhere in the world.

One Monday morning at precisely nine o'clock, a man and woman walked into the offices of the Australian Reader's Digest. The man asked the receptionist, "Is John Grant Cooper here?"

Then managing director of the Australian company, Cooper was a man of imposing mien and some pretention. The way he was viewed by his staff is indicated by their story that he had a small balcony put on the front of the building so that he could address assembled multitudes. Thus, the receptionist asked warily, "Who shall I say wants him?"

"Tell him we're the Wallaces."

The girl took a couple of leisurely sips of her morning tea, phoned Cooper's secretary and said, "There's an elderly couple down here named Wallace who want to see Mr. Cooper."

"Find out what they want," the secretary said.

Turning back to the Wallaces, the receptionist asked, "May we tell Mr. Cooper what your business is?"

"We're just visiting offices of the Digest."

When the receptionist relayed this to Cooper's secretary, a girl was sent down to conduct the visitors on a tour of the building. The Wallaces meekly followed her, and a very surprised and chagrined Cooper discovered that they were in the building only by bumping into them in the hall.

It's possible that the spirit of the Wallace view of the world was captured unconsciously by the same amateur cartoonist who had a vision of the back sides of the Pegasuses on the cupola in Pleasantville. His drawing showed a couple viewing Mount Vesuvius. The woman was saying to the man, "Wouldn't that look lovely back of the Guest House? Don't you think we ought to move it?"

Despite the Wallace firmness that foreign Digests use only made-in-America material, it was, of course, recognized at once that certain articles in any given edition of the United States magazine would make no sense at all to foreigners—a local school board squabble in countries where education is rigidly controlled by central government, birth control in countries dominated by Catholicism, baseball everywhere but Japan. To fill out their tables of contents, editors were urged to go back through twenty years of Digests and pluck those pieces that actually were "of lasting interest." This policy determined the name of the first foreign-language edition— *Selecciones* (Selections) *del Reader's Digest*—which was followed in all subsequent such editions. In Stockholm, Dr. Acheson ran into one of the first of the many translation quirks that were to plague the magazine over the years. The Teutonic languages offer no satisfactory equivalent of "selections"; thus, the Swedish edition became *Det Basta* (the Best) *ur Reader's Digest*; the German *Dat Beste*; the Dutch *Het Beste*. This bit of truth in packaging, oddly, was never applied to English-language editions which appear everywhere as the Reader's Digest.

By the mid-60's, restricting foreign editions to material that had first appeared in the United States would no longer work. For one thing, the barrel was empty; editors had reached back to grab everything remotely usable from ancient Digests. For another, that wave of interest in all things American had subsided across a reviving world. Something had to be done, so Paul Palmer, a Wallace lieutenant who could be trusted in the area of both philosophy and technique, stepped down from executive editor to senior editor and moved to Paris to supervise creation of the first original articles primarily for foreign use. The demotion, if it was that, worked no apparent hardship on Palmer, a handsome and elegant man whose greatest public moment must have been appearing before millions of television viewers in black tie as judge of the best in show at the famed Westminster Kennel Club dog show, whose refinement of taste was displayed in a cookbook he compiled admittedly from the recipes of his five wives and whose predilection for order over democratic chaos was displayed by his decision to live out his retirement in a tidy European capital. Palmer's approach to the Digest problem was to import sure-fire Digest writers to Europe, give them research and translation assistance and assign them to subjects that would "travel"—that is, something like international soccer, the wonders of the Matterhorn, or whatever might be of at least mild Europe-wide interest.

Though better than nothing, the Palmer program did not satisfy the thirst of both local editors and their readers for articles about events and personalities in their own countries— nor the absolute need for enough articles of any kind to fill up the magazines. So the inventive Digest came up with another device new to journalism: the adaptation. If the subject of a United States article such as the training of airline hostesses was appealing in a given country, the local editor could assign a writer to "adapt" it. He would follow the original as closely as possible as to structure and point of view, even picking up words and phrases where relevant, but supply local facts, names, quotes, references. This not only made available many otherwise useless United States articles but proved an effective training ground for foreign writers unused to the American system of journalism. It also resulted in the next logical step: Foreign editors, running out of material to adapt, were permitted to recruit writers and assign articles on subjects of their own choosing. Today the Reader's Digest buys more articles for use abroad than it does in the United States.

An idea of the variety of Digests around the world can be gained by a quick look at the contents on different covers (all Digests are the same size, use the same device of listing articles on the cover) for any given month. My own inspection of just a few at the time of writing showed that in one month the Australian edition used three of the titles in the current United States edition, the Canadian five, the British and French only two. Canada had seven articles of local interest that month, not counting departments, Britain and France six each, and Australia four. It would appear that Wallace's desire to have his little giant speak with a single, uplifting voice had been surrendered to the exigencies of the times, but this isn't necessarily so.

As adaptable as its articles, Pleasantville set up a system to make certain that whatever the subject, whoever the writer, wherever the events took place, any article in any edition of the Digest would meet the same technical requirements as to length, structure, readability and have the same philosophical point of view as those in the United States. The essence of the system is simple: *all* purchases of articles for foreign use must be approved by Pleasantville, and *all* articles must go through Pleasantville editing by a special "murderer's row" established for the purpose. In practice, this is costly and somewhat cumbersome since, no matter what language an article is written in, it must be translated into good English for review and editing in Pleasantville and then retranslated for publication. But it does achieve the Digest purpose: though the tongue be different, the tone of voice is very much the same.

The tongue does, however, get twisted from time to time. Never easy, translation is particularly difficult between English and Japanese and vice versa. Both Chinese and Japanese have pictorial languages, using ideographs instead of words, but there the resemblance stops. A straightforward Digest article in English can be translated into straightforward Chinese; Japanese, on the other hand, has all sorts of marks for pronunciation, and a kind of inverted Germanic grammar that defies direct translation. Even at best, a Japanese text is likely to print out a third longer than English. Discussing this difficulty, McEvoy says, "For instance, the phrase, 'Why not?' in English could be nine words in Japanese: *Do shite sono koto de wa arimasen desho ka?* We would change it to 'Of course!'—which is likewise two words in Japanese: *Morchiron da.*" Such a switch is not always possible, and some things don't translate at all. As the famous Joe series travelled around the world, the character whose body was talking took on an equivalent popular name in other lands—Juan in Latin America, John in Britain, Peter in Germany, Lao Chou in China. In Japan, however, he was merely "I am . . . ," as in *Watakushi wa kokoru,* or "I am a Heart."

Even in the Latin languages of the West, translators can have a hard time dealing with the slang or fractured English that sometimes finds its way into the Digest in the guise of color or

authenticity. A classic case was the book condensation of the
late Billy Rose's *Wine, Women and Words*. The French edition
wanted to use it, but the translators gave up on Rose's Broad-
wayese, beginning with the title itself. Pierre Denoyer, then
editor of the Digest's French edition, went to the one man in
France whose experience, he knew, spanned both worlds and
languages, Maurice Chevalier. Though it was out of his usual
line, the great French actor and entertainer was intrigued. He
managed to turn the title into *Champagne, Danseuses et Stylo-
graphe*. Under his hand, a phrase like "it was a cinch bet" became *"ce'etait du nougat"*—"it was candy." He did, in fact, such
a good job that the Translator's Club of Paris gave him a
luncheon and an honorary membership.

Whatever the problems of translation, they seem minor compared to the logistics of running the whole business in so many
parts of the world. Just for the record, the Digest lists the
following editions in which it is possible to buy advertising:
Asian, Australian, Belgian-Flemish, Belgian-French, British,
Chinese, Danish, Dutch, Finnish, French, German, Iberian,
Indian, Italian, Japanese, Argentine, Brazilian, Central American, Chilean, Columbian, Mexican, Peruvian, Puerto-Rican,
Uruguay-Paraguay-Bolivian, United States, Spanish, Vene-
zuelan, Portugese, New Zealand, Norwegian, Overseas Military,
South African, Swedish, Swiss-French, Swiss-German, Canadian-
French. The very first Digest advertising effort was based on
the concept of selling international ads in a continent-wide
edition, but it was soon found that the advertising mother lode
lay in local ads. The Latin American edition was broken up to
get at this, and the other editions are, of course, autonomous in
seeking ads for their own markets, as they are in nearly every
other way.

Still, it might be supposed—as, indeed, I did suppose all the
while I was at the Digest—that the company would take advantage of its international outlets by making a standardized
product like an album of Strauss waltzes in the most favorable
place and shipping it around for distribution. Not so. According
to President O'Hara, the Digest avoids, if possible, shipping

anything across borders, except ideas. If one edition likes another's idea of selling Strauss waltzes, it hires its own orchestra, cuts its own records or makes its own tapes, prints its own jackets—the works. One reason is that there are annoying import restrictions on many items; a bigger one is that shipping problems, docking problems, labor problems generally end up making it more expensive to ship any item than to do the whole thing over again in the country of distribution. When the Argentine edition of the magazine was being printed in Florida, O'Hara recalled, it never came out on time because the Digest lost control of it as soon as it was loaded on a ship that might stop for bananas one place, coffee another; a whole shipment of pre-sold encyclopedias sank enroute from Spain to Mexico. To solve the Argentine problem, the Digest moved its printing of that edition to Brazil. And, just to make your head spin a little and prove that the Digest isn't always consistent, the Brazilian edition is printed in Portugal!

Considering all the swings of history in thirty years and the various political regimes with which the Digest has worked around the world, it is amazing that the magazine has run into little significant trouble with foreign governments. The major exception is Cuba. When Fidel Castro took over that island country, the Digest's business offices for all of Latin America and an expensive, new press were located in Havana. Digest personnel had almost literally to flee for their lives, abandoning $1.6 million in plant and equipment, and relocate in Mexico City. As in other aspects of its business, however, the Digest is quick to abandon an unprofitable foreign situation. Any number of things can cause this: political unrest, inflation, intolerable restraints on commerce. In recent years, the Digest closed down its companies in Brazil, Argentina and Venezuela. Magazines are still shipped into these countries for newsstand sale, and oddly the Brazilian circulation which had dipped to 95,000 before the local company was disbanded is now ranging between 175,000 and 200,000.

One difficult situation from which the Digest apparently will not retreat is ironically in the nation's closest neighbor to the north, Canada. For years Canadian nationalists have been hectoring foreign publications such as Reader's Digest and *Time* with measures just short of actual expulsion. Most recently, it's a provision of the income tax law that stipulates foreign-controlled publications must be 75 percent Canadian owned to qualify for tax deductions for advertising costs. To get around this, the Digest is spinning off the magazine into a new company, Reader's Digest Magazines, Ltd., that will in turn be owned by Reader's Digest Foundation of Canada that will in its turn have 75 percent Canadian ownership. The Foundation will use its money to improve journalism in Canada, a service the magazine may need since another part of the act stipulates that the Canadian edition of a foreign-controlled publication must have contents that are 80 percent different from its parent publication. Already the editorial staff in Montreal has been increased by two thirds, and Canadian writers are being put under contract. President O'Hara is certain that the Digest will stay in Canada—the other parts of the business, unaffected, remain within Reader's Digest Association (Canada) Ltd., 67.3 percent of which is owned by Pleasantville—but concedes the battle to do so will be costly for a while.

The Digest's willingness to pick up its marbles anywhere when it isn't making money should be proof, if proof is needed, that its international operations are not somehow part of the United States government's propaganda or intelligence apparatus. Still, there will always be those, particularly from behind the iron curtain, who can never be convinced. I ran into one such on a visit to Mexico City. The Digest's then Latin American editor, Pablo Morales, and I were having a drink in the press club when the local Tass man came in. Informing me in a whisper that the Russian was known to be a low-level KGB agent, Pablo invited him over. If he wasn't low level, he ought to be. Within minutes he was quizzing me.

"Where do you live?"

"In Connecticut."

"Oh, yes, I know it well. I went once to Yale. But I thought you work for Reader's Digest?"

"Yes, I drive to Pleasantville."

"Ah, headquarters. And why are you here?"

"On business."

"Oh, on business, yes. And do you have many Americans here in your Mexico City office?"

At that point Pablo and I decided it was time to go off for lunch. But, despite official skepticism about its motives, the Digest has from time to time sent emissaries to Communist countries such as Yugoslavia to investigate the possibilities of publishing, and at one point there were high-level talks aimed at getting Russia to accept circulation of the Digest in return for circulation of its Russian imitator, *Sputnik*, here. Nothing has come of these ventures, partly at least because there's no money to be had from them.

Meanwhile, the Digest is content with its reception in its own condensed world. Even though they were solicited, the tributes from world leaders published in the magazine's fiftieth anniversary issue of February 1972 were impressive. Included were: President Nixon, Prime Minister Edward Heath of Great Britain, Prime Minister Eisaku Sato of Japan, Chancellor Willy Brandt of West Germany, Prime Minister Jacques Chaban-Delmas of France, Prime Minister William McMahon of Australia, Prime Minister Golda Meir of Israel, President Ferdinand Marcos of the Philippines, King Hussein I of Jordan and Juan Carlos, now King of Spain. More flattering than these may have been the unsolicited mention in London's *Daily Sketch* that Juan Carlos' favorite reading was the Reader's Digest. The fact that the *Sketch* went on to say that the King is not a "heavy intellectual" was of little concern to Pleasantville. When you get right down to it, how many intellectuals are there anywhere?

XIII

You Can't Take It With You

When most Americans think of philanthropy, the names that are likely to spring to mind are Carnegie and Rockefeller and possibly Ford. Another name that might belong to this list, if the nature and extent of their gifts were better known, is Wallace. Almost since the day their little magazine started showing a profit, DeWitt Wallace and Lila Acheson Wallace have been as busy giving away their money as making it. A few years ago, Wallace was quoted as saying that he and his wife together were annually dispersing to people and causes in which they believed between 90 and 114 percent of their income, and this presumably does not include the charitable contributions of the corporation, Reader's Digest Association, Inc., and the foundation, Reader's Digest Foundation, of which they are sole owners. Since, with some exceptions, the Wallaces operate their giving program as guardedly as their business, only the wildest guesses can be made as to the total amount of money they've managed to distribute in more than fifty years. An addition of the figures that have somehow leaked out yields a total of more than $88 million but common sense would put the true figure well in excess of $100 million.

The motives of America's large givers have always been suspect. Carnegie was flayed unmercifully by the press for going around giving libraries while starving his workers into strikes, and when Richard B. Mellon's benefactions made possible the building of Pittsburgh's East Liberty Presbyterian Church, it was promptly dubbed "Mellon's fire escape." Perhaps conscious of this, the Wallaces have been less reticent about the philosophy behind their giving than the figures. "My wife and I discovered many years ago that there are more satisfying uses for money than the accumulation of it," says Wallace. For once briefer than her husband, the old master of condensation, Lila Wallace likes to cite her favorite will: "Being of sound mind and body, I spent it all."

Terse as these words are they say a lot about the Wallace giving. Having no children, they are free of the classic motive for accumulation, building a family dynasty. And, clearly, as in the case of others with incomes the size of the Wallaces's, most of what they didn't give away would go to the government in taxes. Keeping as much of their excess money out of the hands of government as they can and directing it toward their own causes harmonizes with that tonic chord of individualism that rings through half a century of Digests. Beyond that, as Mrs. Wallace's rather flip comment suggests, the Wallaces seem truly to enjoy giving; it is the only real hobby they have. A look at the pattern of Wallace giving suggests that they have been far more interested in watching their money work, in controlling the way it works, while they live than in building monuments or "fire escapes" even though there are by now a number of buildings and institutions around the world bearing the Wallace name.

The upfront part of the Wallace giving is, of course, the money distributed by the company itself and the Reader's Digest Foundation, created as early as 1938 from a block of stock they set aside for the purpose. While specifics of these grants are no more available than company profit figures, Digest spokesmen cite the record published in the magazine's fiftieth anniversary issue, February 1972, as indicative of the amount and spread of this giving. In a box entitled "A Summary of

Digest Philanthropies Over the Ten Years 1962 Through 1971," a total of $19,677,000 is given, broken down as follows: education and youth, $8,897,000; humanities, $2,896,000; medicine, $2,436,000; religion, $2,424,000; civics, $1,475,000; arts, $1,157,000; all else, $392,000. A note explains that the total amount was dispersed almost equally by the corporation and the foundation and that the annual totals were almost equal, too, or about $2 million a year. A final line identifies all this as "a corporate responsibility: helping to strengthen U.S.A."

While a number of these corporate gifts represent the standard support of local community chests, hospitals and the like, many are unusual. Among these was a 32,000-square-foot park on Lenox Avenue between 139th and 140th streets in Harlem. At the dedication on December 5, 1971, Digest Chairman Hobart Lewis said that "a small friendly pocket-sized magazine" gives a "small friendly pocket-sized park" to citizens of New York. But the most extraordinary experiment in corporate giving was launched in the mid-60's when about a third of the Digest's employees received half a million dollars in individual amounts ranging from $450 to $4,000 to distribute to their own favorite charities. Each employee was allowed to make up to six gifts, the only stipulation being that the recipient qualify for federal income tax deductions. The result was a number of gifts to small organizations of which no corporate board could be aware —my wife and I, for example, gave part of ours to a tiny local art center—but a breakdown of employee gifts for 1966 was predictable: $178,288 to colleges, $71,024 to churches and $4,475 to race relations programs.

As usual in any matter of giving, somebody didn't like it. In this case, it was a Mrs. Carl H. Pforgheimer, Jr., president of the Westchester Council of Social Agencies, who was quoted by the *New York Times* as saying, "We would much prefer to see a corporation make its gifts to health, welfare and recreation organizations through the Westchester County United Fund." This despite the fact that the Digest did give $25,000 to the fund. In the end, though, it wasn't such criticism that caused the program to be dropped a few years ago. In an effort to make it more fair within the company, the fund was distributed in smaller and smaller amounts to more and more people; this brought on such a massive amount of clerical work in keeping track of the donations that the whole project became untenable.

The Wallace private donations concededly far surpass anything the company has done. Beyond some headline-making bequests, little was known about them until the "Foundation Center Source Book 1975-76" was distributed by Columbia University Press. In this huge compendium of where the money is are several pages devoted to something called the DeWitt Wallace Fund, Inc.; address: High Winds, Mt. Kisco; directors: DeWitt Wallace, chairman, president and treasurer, Lila Acheson Wallace, vice president, W. B. McHenry (the Digest's attorney), secretary. Incorporated in 1965, the fund listed assets of $18,303,702. Its purpose: "Support primarily for independent schools and activities fostering qualities of leadership and character in young people, including scholarships, summer camps, experiences abroad, speaking contests and explorations, projects promoting an understanding of the history and economy of the United States, and special medical and educational projects."

In true Wallace fashion, the money was dropped as gently as a nationwide snowstorm, drifting a little here and there but mostly leaving a thin white blanket. For the year ending December 31, 1974, the Source Book reports expenditures of $1,859,384, including $1,782,665 for 128 grants. Most of these, as stated in the purpose, were to educational institutions or youth organizations. The largest was $291,667 to something called the Wooster School Corporation of Danbury, Connecticut, for scholarships; the smallest—showing that the Wallace eye for detail transcends business—was $44 to the Berkshire Farm School for Boys in Canaan, New York. Gifts to YMCAs and YWCAs were scattered from Bangor, Maine, to the Harlem Branch in New York, to Greater Little Rock, Arkansas, to Great Falls, Montana. The variety of organizations receiving funds is illustrated by a few: the Darien (Connecticut) Book Aid, $300; the National Audubon Society, $5,000; the American Field Service, $20,000; Young Life Campaign, $40,000.

Despite their spread, Wallace gifts clearly favor projects and organizations that hew to the Digest's ideological line. There's a marked preference for the Protestant form of "muscular Christianity," for institutions promoting free enterprise and patriotism. And the proliferation of educational grants from the DeWitt Wallace Fund, Inc., will come as no surprise to those aware of Wallace's major charitable interest over the years—Macalester College in St. Paul, Minnesota. Wallace's serious financial interest in the college his father headed, the college he dropped out of, began in 1939. His motivation is simple and acknowledged: making up for his youthful rebellion against the lifelong passion for formal education that caused Dr. James Wallace to struggle so hard to keep Macalester afloat. In the authorized book on the Digest, James Playsted Wood puts it this way: "He was shocked when in 1956 he read the story of his father's long and hard effort and came to sharp realization of 'the suffering, acute and prolonged'—the words are his—that it entailed. It was evidently at this point that he determined to do everything more that he could to bring his father's dream to full fruition."

The extent of Wallace's support for Macalester is again uncertain; one published figure puts it at $40 million. What is certain is that his gifts have turned it into a well-equipped, first-class institution. And none of the students or graduates, among them Vice President Walter Mondale, can be unaware of the boost their institution got from Wallace, father and son. There is, for example, a James Wallace Professorship of History, a James Wallace Professorship of Religion, a James Wallace Professorship of Political Science, a Barclay Acheson (Lila Wallace's brother) Professorship of International Studies, a Janet Wallace (DeWitt Wallace's mother) Fine Arts Center and a Lila Wallace Court. Unfortunately and probably painfully for both parties ,the Wallace interest in Macalester came to an end in the late 60's amid many rumors as to why. Wallace was certainly dismayed at evidence that Macalester students were as aroused and disrespectful of Digest values as their fellows elsewhere in that pro-civil rights, anti-Vietnam war era; one student, for example, turned the flag upside down in the presence of a Wallace representative, a calculated insult in view of the Digest's flag promotion. A more likely reason for the break, however, is that, according to a knowledgeable informant, Wallace got tired of making up the deficits for what he regarded at the time as mismanagement of the institution. Although Wallace gifts to Macalester have recently resumed, it is unlikely that the relationship will ever be quite the same again.

In addition to putting his money where his heart is, Wallace reveals some of the Scottish skepticism that has made him such a shrewd businessman in the way he often does it. Most Wallace donations are in the form of "matching funds"—that is, if your church or school or whatever needs $20,000, Wallace can easily be persuaded to give $10,000, provided that the organization in question can raise the balance from other sources. Thus, the Wallace gift becomes energizing, seed money; by the time it's given, the matching efforts virtually assure the existence of a lively, active organization.

In an interesting parallel to their personalities, Lila Acheson Wallace's considerable giving has been far more open than her husband's. A woman who, even in her eighties, remains flirtatiously feminine, wears the brilliant colors her husband likes, drinks martinis and dances, Lila Wallace is given to the grand, impulsive gesture that may be the ultimate pleasure of the truly wealthy. There's a story that at one fund-raising luncheon, she hauled her check book out of her purse and wrote a check for a cool million on the spot. Whether apocryphal or not, the story catches her spirit as exhibited in a true account by C. R. (Bob) Devine, Digest vice president and director of public affairs, who often helps Mrs. Wallace on her philanthropic projects.

Told to look around on a trip to Turkey to see if there was a place where Mrs. Wallace could invest some funds in memory of her brother, Barclay Acheson, who had spent his younger years in Middle East relief work, Devine interviewed some forty-four people in four days. The consensus he got from them and brought back to Mrs. Wallace was that she should help, if she could, on a campaign just getting underway to construct a five-story wing on the American hospital in Istanbul. Devine proposed that Mrs. Wallace supply money for building and furnishing one of the operating theaters in the wing. "She looked at me with a little twinkle in her eye and said, 'How much would a whole wing cost?' " Devine relates. "I told her that it was a lot of money, and she said, 'What's the matter— don't you want to build it?' I said, 'Well, it's your money.' She said, 'Go build it then,' " The wing was built, and it was a lot of money—$6 million.

By then, however, Mrs. Wallace was used to giving a lot of money. She had already given $3 million to build the World of Birds in the Bronx Zoo; $2 million to her alma mater, the University of Oregon; $1 million to the Bronx Botanical Gardens; $1 million to Northern Westchester Hospital; $1 million to save Egyptian art works from flood at Abu Simbel; $5 million to the Metropolitan Museum of Art. An evident underlying theme to Lila Wallace's philanthropy is the beautification of public places, a form of giving that by its nature can't be hidden. Her work in refurbishing the Great Hall of the Metropolitan Museum in New York, for example, evoked a feature story in the *New York Times* by Grace Glueck. After pointing out that Mrs. Wallace had donated Digest stock in an amount to provide an income of $100,000 a year for maintenance, including fresh flowers, Mrs. Glueck quotes Mrs. Wallace as explaining: "That lovely beautiful room had become such a mess. About five years ago I asked if I could put flower arrangements there on a weekly basis. It gave the hall a little life, but I still wanted to clean it up—it had got so commercial. When Mr. Hoving (Museum Director Thomas Hoving) wrote that they were going to fix the steps, which I'd always thought were horrible, I decided to help re-do the whole thing."

Lila Wallace's concern for beauty led to the charity which for her rivals Macalester, if not in money, at least in interest— the restoration of Boscobel, an eighteenth century country home on the Hudson River. Built by States Morris Dyckman in the style of the famous Robert Adam, Boscobel, which is a corruption of the Italian *bosco bello*, beautiful woods, fell into such disrepair after the last of the family died that it was sold to a wrecker for thirty-five dollars. At this point, Mrs. Wallace stepped in, had the house moved piece by piece from its original site, which had become a public park, and restored it on a site overlooking the Hudson between Garrison and Cold Spring, New York. In the end, the venture cost $8 million. Now open to the public with a sound and light show on summer evenings, Boscobel is, as former New York Governor Averill Harriman said, "a unique and unsurpassed triumph of the early American builder's art."

Perhaps not to be outdone by his wife in illuminating history, DeWitt Wallace announced about the time of this writing a gift of $4 million to Colonial Williamsburg, a favorite vacationing spot of the Wallaces. The first major donation to Williamsburg outside of those from the Rockefeller family, the money will be used to construct the DeWitt Wallace Theater in which the film, "Williamsburg: Story of a Patriot," will be shown to visitors. Despite the emphasis on patriotism and history, the gift remains uncharacteristic of Wallace who is fond of quoting Horace Mann as a key to his interests: "To make money immortal, invest it in men." When it comes to this investment in men, what might be called his living projects, Wallace tends to put a lot more than money into the effort. For a man with supposedly only the magazine on his mind, he often devotes an extraordinary amount of time and attention to charitable ventures, but then, as in the interesting case of the World Press Institute, it is often hard to tell where the concern of Wallace, the editor, stops and Wallace, the giver, begins.

If the Digest is, as sometimes described by Wallace himself, "a window on the world" for readers, it serves as handily to let the Wallaces themselves see new ideas. One such came along in the February 1958 issue when Clarence Hall wrote about a young soldier, just turned student at Rutgers University, named Harry Morgan who had more or less on his own started something called Friendship Ambassadors, a program through which he would bring young people from abroad and give them a down-to-earth tour of the United States so that they could see for themselves what the country was all about. It can be imagined that the story was especially interesting to Wallace, the salesman of America. Significantly, Wallace generally gave foreign Digesters visiting headquarters time and ample expenses to see as much of the United States as possible. In any case, he dropped a congratulatory note to young Morgan who at the time considered it routine.

Much more important to Morgan was that the Digest article brought mail from all over the country, including gifts of some $1,000 which could provide a basis for his program that summer. It also brought a phone call from a man named Ralph Smith in Kansas City. Smith wanted to meet Harry the next Saturday at the Waldorf Astoria in New York. "My cousin, Herbert Hoover, lives there. If I'm not in my room, I'll be in Hoover's suite," he told Harry. An impressed and hopeful Harry was in New York hours early, finally met Smith on the dot of the appointed hour in the Waldorf lobby. A hard-talking, six-foot Kansan in his seventies, Smith turned out to be "a man who kept Reader's Digest next to the Bible" and who had helped others he'd read about in the magazine—a whole dormitory for "the little professor of Piney Woods," for example. Smith wanted to know what Harry would do in the coming summer if he had the money. "Get a station wagon and take a group of visitors all over our country—to our national parks and such," Harry said. Expecting a lot more from a man so well heeled, Harry was surprised when Smith offered only to lend him a second-hand station wagon from his ranch—and pay his way to Kansas City by bus to pick it up. But beggars can't be choosers, and so Harry went; during a long talk in the palatial Smith home, Smith offered to "loan" Harry $1,500 against the $3,000 air fare to bring the young visitors from Europe.

Back at Rutgers with the station wagon, Harry got another call—this one from Eddie Eagan, the boxing commissioner, who had also read the Digest story. Harry was invited to the Eagan home in Rye, New York, for a weekend during which Mrs. Eagen offered to pay the transportation, allowing him to forget the Smith loan. But Smith wasn't to be denied; throughout the whole trip, he kept in touch with the group, buying them a steak dinner in Chicago's Palmer House, arranging for the foreman of one of his California enterprises to "loan" Harry $1,200, talking long distance to Harry every evening. Smith would ask Harry what they had for dinner. If Harry said steak, he'd respond, "You're spoiling those people—they'll think America's streets are paved with gold. Get them weanies and beans." When Harry would report that they did have weanies and beans, Smith would accuse him of "starving those people." When they reached Kansas City on the way back East, Smith confessed to how much pleasure he'd taken in following them on the map and added: "You know that $1,200 I advanced you in California—it's no loan, keep it."

Exit Smith, enter Wallace. The next summer, at the suggestion of a fellow Rutgers student from Italy, Dorio Mutti, Harry decided to organize a trip for foreign students already in this country instead of spending so much money importing them from abroad. Once again the Eagens were interested backers, and at a party in their home Harry met DeWitt Wallace for the first time. "We talked about three minutes," Harry recalls. "I thought he was just the editor of Reader's Digest. I didn't know he owned the joint." When Harry and the students returned from this trip, he called the *New York Times*, and they did a feature story on the experience. Days later at Rutgers, Harry got a call from DeWitt Wallace. The Digest editor seemed hurt that another publication would get Harry's story but suggested lunch at New York's Pinnacle Club. It was the beginning of a curious relationship during which the impecunious Rutgers student lunched in luxury almost weekly with the Digest's founder. Another story by Clarence Hall was planned for which Harry got $2,500, happily a little more than enough to cover his college debts just before he graduated. Then his future would be up in the air.

Wallace, meanwhile, became more than a little intrigued by the public reaction to the second Morgan story. Letters were flowing into Pleasantville in such quantity that they were shipped down in mailbags to Rutgers where Harry's fraternity brothers would help him open them and count the money. As it piled up, Wallace wanted a daily accounting from Harry and advised him to send some note of thanks to the contributors. He was astounded when he learned that most of it—some $20,000—arrived in cash in envelopes with no return address, a fact he quite rightly took as a tribute to people's faith that the Digest would put the money to good use. Obviously, Morgan was a drawing card.

Wallace suggested that Harry try a lecture at Macalester College; he would pay expenses and $300. When Harry returned enthusiastic about the college, especially its marked internationalism, Wallace said, "I have some influence out there. How would you like to make it the base for developing Friendship Ambassadors?" Harry liked the idea, but there was the matter of salary. He consulted Hall who suggested asking for $12,000 a year. Wallace's response was that it would be more than a lot of professors were making; how about $6,000? Harry phoned Hall, "Well, you were 50 percent off." "Oh, he gave you $18,000?" "No, six." Nevertheless, Harry took the job to see what might come of it.

Instead of Friendship Ambassadors, Harry proposed something he called the World Press Institute—a program that would import a dozen or so working editors or reporters from various countries, headquarter them at Macalester but take them to important places and events all over the United States, have them file stories back to their publications on what they were seeing and doing. Wallace liked the idea, and Harry expected the Digest to pick up the tab. Not so. "You go out and see what you can raise," Wallace told him. The Digest was, in fact, the last to come in on a blue ribbon coalition including such names as IBM, RCA, GM, Exxon that Harry finally put together. The Wallace instinct about Morgan paid off—almost too well. The publicity Morgan generated in raising funds brought him a much more lucrative job offer and, being new and thousands of miles from Pleasantville, he asked Wallace for a raise. Harry was admonished that, since even second stringers at the Digest make amazing salaries, he could put working anywhere else out of his mind if he was interested in money. A small raise did, however, follow this discouraging note, and Harry settled down to put WPI so solidly on its feet that it still thrives after fifteen years.

Once WPI was organized, Harry came east to Pleasantville to seek new opportunity, but he soon left the Digest to return to a variation of his first love, Friendship Ambassadors, which now sends American groups out to see the world and which, of course, has some Digest funding. An incident between the time Harry left his Digest job and got his new venture going reveals the Wallace concern for individuals. Inviting himself to Harry's New York apartment, Wallace came right to the point, "When did you get your last paycheck?" "Last month." "From whom?" "Well, you gave me some money when I left, and I put it in the bank and pay myself every month." During this exchange, Wallace wandered around the apartment, peeking into closet doors, opening the refrigerator. "Well," he said, "I see you are well stocked up with food, so you're all set. Now let's talk about another article."

The Wallace quiet generosity to employees, former employees, friends and family is something that can't, and shouldn't, be published in detail. Typical is the story related to me by one editor whose wife fell gravely ill. The day after he had taken her to the hospital, he came to the office to find a handwritten note from Wallace offering him any financial assistance he might need. When the editor declined such help, fresh flowers and personal notes from the Wallaces arrived daily in his wife's hospital room. But not even a Wallace could meet every personal emergency that comes to his attention, let alone those that don't, from the thousands of people who surround him. It's enough to say that his efforts in this regard are legendary and that, taken together with his more institutionalized giving, they demonstrate that he has tried to live up to the promise of his youthful letter to Mt. Hermon School in which he said that he wanted to "do as much good in the world as possible."

In fact, the Wallace joint philanthropies have probably

played almost as much of a part in the many rewards they have received as the magazine they publish. These awards, culminating in Medals of Freedom bestowed upon them by President Nixon on January 28, 1972, are too numerous to list. But a most unusual one came along in 1970 when Canadian born Lila Acheson Wallace became the first woman to receive the Golden Door Award from the American Council for Nationalities Service, an annual award to citizens of foreign birth who have made outstanding contributions to American life. The citation said in part: "Major gifts, combined with personal involvement —to such organizations as the University of Oregon, the YWCA, the Metropolitan Museum of Art, the Metropolitan Opera, the Julliard School—the restoration of Boscobel, her imaginative pursuit of beauty, are among the notable contributions she has made in furtherance of the arts, education and social betterment."

The Digest has been accused from time to time of promulgating too solemnly a number of trite aphorisms. But one that the Wallaces have obviously taken to heart themselves is that old saying that "you can't take it with you." Having done this, though, they raise interesting questions for the future. The Wallace giving is not only a witness to their generosity but an outspoken witness to the unknown profits their company earns —to give a lot of money you have to make a lot of money. How will these profits be dispersed when the Wallaces are gone? The legal machinery seems to be in place to go on channelling them into some sort of good works, but somebody has to run it. Will they be animated by the same spirit, seek the same goals? Sure answers to these questions, as to most questions about the Digest's future, are impossible; nevertheless, they make for intriguing contemplation.

XIV

The Bottom Line

What's going to happen to the Reader's Digest when in the course of nature the man who founded it, has run it with such a sharp eye for detail for fifty-five years and still, with his wife, owns all the voting stock, is no longer there? This is one question that evokes evasive answers in Pleasantville. Oh, they know, some claim, but they can't say. In any case, and understandably, nobody likes to think about it. The Reader's Digest has for so long been DeWitt Wallace and vice versa that the publication, and even the place, are unthinkable without him.

In Pleasantville, it's easy to postpone such thinking; Wallace seems durable as rock. Although he's having a little trouble with his eyes and hearing in his late eighties, he still takes steps at a run, still exhibits the same keen interest in details of every aspect of the business. Significantly, his father and a brother survived beyond ninety. The situation reminds me of the time when writer Noel Busch went to Spain to do a piece on Prince Juan Carlos, then thought to be Franco's successor. I asked Busch whether he was sure that the kind of article he wrote would stand up long enough to be published in view of the fact that Franco was in his eighties and ailing. "Well, you've heard the thing about absolute power," Busch said. "My variation on it is that wealth preserves and absolute wealth preserves absolutely." In that event, Busch was right—it was a number of years before his predictions about Juan Carlos became true.

The Franco analogy has other merits for consideration of the Digest case. It's almost axiomatic that a strong personal leadership of any human institution, especially when it is based on benevolence, tends to leave a vacuum in leadership behind. Whether in the Kremlin or the office of Time Inc., the passing of the leader generally brings on a struggle for power. This could happen in Pleasantville, too. But it is only possible at this point to make some guesses, hopefully more or less educated, about the future—and to express some hopes.

One significant fact is that Wallace has now personally survived the first "take-over" generation, and it may be just as well. When in the 60's, Hobart D. Lewis, twenty years younger than Wallace, was moved rapidly through the paces of editor-in-chief, president, chairman, while the Wallaces faded to the anomalous title of "co-founders," it was thought that the lines of succession were clear. A handsome and polished man, Lewis looked like everybody's idea of chief executive. But, in fact, Lewis turned out to be more like any strong leader's ideal of the perfect second man. Even at the time of his appointment as nominal head of the organization, *New York Times* writer Richard Phalon speculated shrewdly that Wallace would "nonetheless remain as chief executive officer." Lewis expressed his deference to Wallace in nearly every public utterance, notably the interview with BBC in which, after outlining the Wallace philosophy, he said that "each one of us who has been here over the years has acquired that outlook on life, agrees with it enthusiastically and communicates that in memoranda and conversation and in just the articles we accept and those we reject. . . ."

Lewis's job can't have been easy. Despite all his titles, he presided over a board of directors, none of whom, including him, owned or controlled any voting stock in the corporation. It must have been a little like one of those shadow Junior Achievement boards or the day a high-school class takes over city hall. To dress up the corporate front, the Digest a while back appointed two aging outside directors—Harold H. Helm, a retired banker, and Laurence S. Rockefeller, whose many splendored activities are hard to define. Among these was authoring, or having authored, an article for the Digest on the "simple life" which he sometimes demonstrated by arriving for board meetings in his own helicopter. But to us on the sidelines such shenanigans merely deepened the feeling that there was something unreal about this corporate charade in an organization where all important, and some not so important, decisions were still made by one man. Two examples of many: the president and executive vice president fired a certain executive who thereupon went to Wallace and was restored to his post; the editor-in-chief in his own handwriting flatly rejected an article which another editor sent to Wallace, albeit *minus* the editor-in-chief's damning note, and got permission to use it.

Such instances might account for the fact that, during a large part of his regime, Lewis seemed to be elsewhere. Another factor in this, of course, was his friendship with President Nixon, a relationship so close that Lewis's Bedford home was one of the few private residences that Nixon visited while in office and that, according to an undenied story in the *Washington Post*, Lewis raised $100,000 in cash from a midwestern golfing partner for Nixon and then, at the request of Nixon's secretary, Rose Mary Woods, personally picked it up from the White House safe and later borrowed it for his own personal use. Lewis started breaking with the White House over the famous "Christmas bombing" and later was chief orchestrator of the Teddy White book outlining Nixon's betrayal of trust in the Watergate affair. Queried as to whether he would contribute to a Nixon defense fund, Lewis was quoted as saying that he had to pay his own taxes. According to Billy Graham, a friend to both Nixon and Lewis, who was his editor, the Lewis attitudes toward Nixon should be easy to understand.

"The Wallaces, Al Cole, Lewis all fell into the same trap I did," Graham told me. "All the time I had any association with

Nixon, he was a perfect gentleman. For example, he never used foul language, and I never saw him drinking. Lewis told me the same thing." Graham thinks that there was a change in the Nixon character owing to the strain of Watergate revelations and the taking of sleeping pills to ease it. At one point a White House doctor called Graham, told him he thought that the President might commit suicide and asked Graham to do something. Graham, who had always been able to get through to the President by phone, was turned away by the White House switchboard. Graham said that he later learned that Nixon had issued orders that there be no further contact with the evangelist, lest Graham be tainted by Watergate. "He had one characteristic—absolute loyalty to his friends," Graham claims. "Trying to save them—people like John Mitchell—he destroyed himself. I can understand the Reader's Digest position. To the editors, it was incredible until it came out, and then it just sickened them, like it did me."

Even when on the premises, Lewis had a habit of shelving letters, memos, verbal propositions. Perhaps it was the cautious reaction of a man with a long shadow leaning over his shoulder, or perhaps it was a personal characteristic. As it's been said of Franklin D. Roosevelt, Lewis was so affable and receptive in personal confrontation that people could never understand why nothing ever happened later to the matter in hand. One executive who worked closely with him told me bitterly, "He never argued with you; he just wouldn't make a decision." Still, at the end of a decade when Lewis reached the supposedly mandatory retirement age of sixty-five, it was announced that he had been asked to stay on indefinitely, presumably by Wallace. Then suddenly last year, he was divested of his posts as editor-in-chief and chief executive officer, also presumably by Wallace, and vanished from Pleasantville to offices in the Pan Am building; early this year he was firmly retired by the appointment of a new chairman, Kent Rhodes. A Digest writer with whom I was discussing Lewis said that he had never, in all those ten years or so, received a reply to any letter he had written to the editor-in-chief. He pretty well summed up the fate of the first "take-over" generation when he said, "I always thought that HL didn't exist, and now he doesn't."

Nevertheless, there was one factor in the Lewis appointment that deserves a very close look. Since he had come up through editorial, it was felt that making Lewis the figurehead clearly signalled Wallace's intention of having the company controlled by and in the interests of magazine editorial. Some of us weren't too sure. It wasn't encouraging that the same perceptive *Times* writer, who guessed that Wallace would still be running things, quoted a "source" to the effect that Lewis "understands the business world. He speaks the language." Although he had spent most of his Digest career in editorial, Lewis had come to Pleasantville from a Philadelphia advertising agency to write promotional copy. As president of the company, his enthusiasm for business was marked—and somewhat naive. At one Guest House luncheon for the representatives of a mattress company, he reportedly was discovered by his arriving guests stretched out on a sample of their product. On another occasion, Lewis brought on the biggest public ruckus the Digest has endured in years by plainly favoring business over editorial.

It was the famous Samm Sinclair Baker case, and it was so startling that it rated long entries in the press sections of both *Time* and *Newsweek*, the one called "Indigestion at the *Digest*," and the other simply "Undigestible." What wouldn't go down was a book that Baker, a former advertising man himself, had written about the advertising industry for Funk & Wagnalls, then a Digest subsidiary, and entitled, *The Permissable Lie*. Five thousand copies of the book had already been printed before the Digest suspended publication. Although the Digest offered to let Baker keep his advance and give him the books, along with the plates, he would have to expunge the publisher's name before using them. While Funk & Wagnalls editors said that the book was a mild call for the advertising business to "clean up from inside," Lewis said, "The decision not to publish Baker was essentially mine. It's our prerogative to publish what we want. We simply don't want to sponsor Mr. Baker's message. We have criticized some advertising practices in the magazine, but it's not our policy to criticize an entire industry." Another reporter quoted Lewis as saying that "advertising is good for business and business is good for the country."

If there is an echo in that statement of "Engine Charlie" Wilson's famous line about General Motors, it's probably intentional. The Digest has always been heavily on the side of business. Indeed, there is evidence that, in creating his little magazine, Wallace was at least as much of a businessman as an editor—and maybe more so. His own background had been in the business end of publishing and in the promotional end of business at Westinghouse. Editorially, the Digest was far from a new concept. In his history of the American magazine, John Tebbel makes this clear. One of the first—*The American Magazine and Historical Chronicle; for All the British Plantations*—which appeared in March 1743, he describes as "a kind of Reader's Digest of several British magazines, with articles from the leading British periodicals abridged to provide a cross section of what was being talked about in London and Edinburgh"; a hundred years later, in 1844, *Littell's Living Age* became, in Tebbel's words, "a kind of literary Reader's Digest, offering American readers a selection from leading British periodicals . . ." Whether Wallace knew about these predecessors and others or not, it is fairly obvious that his innovation lay more in the realm of packaging than in creating some new editorial device. For some fourteen years, Wallace wrapped up a plentiful product, the editorial content of virtually all American journals, in a tidy, handy form for his customers; significantly, the Digest often still refers to itself as "a service to readers" rather than a magazine. If, in the early days, Wallace had suffered the classic editorial symptoms—a reverence for "the word" per se, a desire to inflict his own views upon the world— it is likely that he would have gone the normal route and started a magazine of original material which, given recent history, might now be defunct. By the time Wallace did get around to creating original material, he was already sitting atop a wildly successful business and, therefore, insulated from much of the American experience—the Reader's Digest raked in money steadily all through the Depression, for example, when ordinary men were standing on breadlines and less fortunate capitalists were jumping out of windows—and quite naturally convinced that money, instead of being the "root of all evil," was the logical reward of virtue.

My most vivid impression upon arriving at the Digest was that the tension normally existing between the editorial, or creative, side and the business side of most publishing enterprises was almost totally absent. This tension was most dramatically and publicly conveyed, whether it was a reality in practice or not, by *New Yorker* Editor Harold Ross's injunction that no advertising representative of the company even set foot on the editorial floor. Convinced of its own purity, *The New Yorker* twitted the Digest back in 1955 when the latter began taking ads: " 'The same unprejudiced and uninfluenced reports of the world we live in will be found in these pages each month,' says the *Digest,* acting like a boy entering a pool hall for the first time to discover sin and rise above it. Well, the tarnished old *New Yorker,* whose very first issue was loaded with ads (there must have been at least a hundred dollars' worth), now after all these years welcomes the Digest to the wicked fold, where all is fun and frolic."

It must honestly be reported that, in the years since, a good deal of fun and frolic at the Digest has gone on in a mingling of editorial and business. Editors have often been drafted as hosts, and even tour guides, at fiestas held for advertisers on the grounds, treated to weekends at the hunting and fishing lodges of wealthy businessmen; editors and writers are regularly sent out throughout the country, even the world, to speak at gatherings of advertisers; editorial talent is called upon to make advertisements read like the rest of the magazine, although they are clearly labelled as advertisements. One such enterprise was sufficiently unusual in the trade to provoke comment from *Time.* In 1975, the Digest sold a $1.2 million series of 12 ads, created by the editors and dealing with the American economic system, to a group of 150 corporate executives called the Business Roundtable. Of this, *Time* said:

"The *Digest* launched the idea in the fall of 1973. Said Richard McLoughlin, director of magazine operations: 'We thought that all kinds of people were taking potshots at American business and that the American economic system needs to be explained.' The series promises to provide a 'better understanding of our business system, warts and all.' The first installment, entitled, 'Whatever Happened to the Nickel Candy Bar?' glosses over the current recession but sums up instead the importance of high efficiency in industrial production: 'You have, we have, in our hands, in ourselves, the means to produce not just cars and books and songs and bread, but an entire way of life and economic environment second to none.'

"That statement is rather typical of much *Digest* prose and opinion. However, if the prosperous magazine (circ. 18.8 million) wanted to convey its views on economics to its readers, why do it in ads paid for by very interested parties? *Digest* Managing Editor Edward T. Thompson [now editor-in-chief] sought to explain: 'It is not reasonable to run an article on American business every month. We wouldn't run that many all in a row.' "

If the Digest's marriage with business meets little editorial resistance, the reasons are fairly plain. One is that a good many Digest editors, having never worked anywhere else, are not even aware that the situation may be unusual. Another is that Digest editors bear little resemblance to the "ink-stained wretches" of legend; their high salaries, along with bonuses, profit sharing and in some cases stock ownership, give them a very personal interest in the success of a high-profit private enterprise. Still another is that, there being no Newspaper Guild or other editorial union in Pleasantville, Digest editors have little option but to go along with management opinion or resign. Thus, unfortunately from my point of view, the corrective that works in so many other publications where writers write, and editors approve, views abhorrent to management and its sponsors (being good businessmen, most successful publishers, to my knowledge and experience, share in varying degrees the Wallace view of the world) is not generally operative at the Reader's Digest.

As indicated in other chapters, the only real corrective at the Digest has been the almost unfathomable Wallace mind. The instinct, or short attention span, that he apparently shares with millions of people seems to have transferred itself to his own enthusiasms whether they be business, the flag, Nixon or the Vietnam war. He seems to sense when enough is enough. For example, in the fall of 1972 when the Digest threatened to be overloaded with articles that were directly or indirectly pro-Republican, Wallace, though a large campaign contributor to that party, personally ordered a reduction in their number. And, while the Digest was beating the drums for victory in Vietnam long after everybody else had muffled them, Wallace suggested reprinting an anti-war article by Clark Clifford; alas and alack, Lewis apparently persuaded him to change his mind. It was in such situations where the editor in Wallace, the protective feeling that even overdoing his own point of view might alienate readers, prevailed in his mind over all other considerations. Perhaps Norman Cousins best captured the Wallace quality that keeps him from going overboard to the point of offending those who disagree with him when he told me, "Wally is conservative in the sense of Emersonian virtues like self-reliance. Unlike many right-wingers, he is neither mean nor cynical; he is never against people." And, being Emersonian, Wallace may well have taken to heart that philosopher's statement that "a foolish consistency is the hobgoblin of little minds." Baffling as it is, the Wallace genius has kept a successful balance in the Digest, a driver with all reins in hand, he's kept editorial and business pulling together like a team in stride.

As in all teams, however, there has to be a lead horse, and until Wallace drops the reins, it will be hard to tell which one it is. Does it matter? Listen again to Norman Cousins whose educated explanation for Digest success is that it is the best edited magazine in America: "The Reader's Digest has a good future if it can keep its editorial mystique, but the chances are that, when Wally is gone, the bottom line boys (men concerned only, or chiefly, with income and profit) who don't understand it will prevail." Cousin's prediction is probably based on the sad history of other magazines in recent years, but whether he knows it or not, it would gain considerable support from what's been going on inside the Digest during Wallace's effort to divest himself gradually of some responsibility.

Editing the magazine itself being Wallace's first love, it is, in a sense, the last to go; even at this writing, he is on the phone daily with his editors, dealing with problems running from individual articles to the fate of the individuals themselves. The question that the long Wallace dominance of editorial raises for the future is whether he will leave behind him on murderer's row anything more than a corps of first-rate second-guessers. Although Wallace has showed unusual interest in the business side for an editor, he has, beginning with the forceful Al Cole, permitted business a great deal more autonomy. As a result, in this observer's eye, the business people, like the camel the Arab took into his tent, have very nearly taken over the place.

In this connection, it is interesting to note that on the Digest board of twelve directors, as listed by Dun & Bradstreet in 1976, there were only three editorial people, aside from Wallace himself—Lewis, Condensed Books Editor John T. Beaudouin and Thompson. More interesting still is the selection in the late fall of that year of production man Kent Rhodes as chairman, and all-around businessman John O'Hara as president. In the same action, three new board members, all from the business department, were elected, one evidently replacing Lewis and reducing editorial representation to two. One of these, Thompson, with only the rather holy title of editor-in-chief so far, is also a member of the select executive committee, but it seems likely that he could be in for some lonely battles if his colleagues decided, say, that it is costing too much to run the magazine. (By its nature, editorial is always a cost figure with no sure means of whether it pays off or not. Who's to say, for instance, whether the Digest's huge circulation is a result of the successful sweepstakes method of selling or the pull of its articles? By now, it's close to a chicken-and-egg question.)

The exact arrangements for the passage of power—that is, money and/or stock—from the Wallaces to some other entity are at this writing another Digest secret. Chairman Rhodes and Vice President Richard Waters, who say they are aware of them, will only issue assurances that Digesters everywhere will find them satisfactory. But one thing all Digest executives with whom I talked agreed upon is true, if they have anything to do with it, the company will remain private according to the expressed wishes of DeWitt Wallace. "The only reason for going public would be to raise money," says finance man Waters, "and so far we haven't had to do that."

In all likelihood, then, the major Wallace legacy—which is the Reader's Digest—will fall into the directing hands of some or all of the current officers of the company. Since Rhodes is only a year from retirement age, the key figures would appear to be O'Hara, Waters* and Thompson. Barring unforeseen events, their chances are very good of being at last the "take-over" generation. Waters is only fifty, and O'Hara and Thompson are both forty-eight. In sharing relative youth, these three

* As this book was going to press, executive vice president Waters suddenly and surprisingly resigned from the Reader's Digest, indicating that the third generation power struggle may already be underway. If nothing else, the Waters resignation, following a trend begun a few years ago when President Hitesman and a few other vice presidents resigned with fifteen or twenty more years to go before retirement, demonstrates a marked decline in the Pleasantville *esprit de corps*. Virtually none of the first generation executives left the place until separated by death or forced retirement, and many of those have since hung around as consultants. Whether the recent rash of resignations is owing to a decline in loyalty or to the widespread dissemenation of *automatic* benefits that make resignation feasible would be hard to say. In the old days, a man had to negotiate retirement before his time directly with Wallace. One first generation executive I know waited out several unhappy and unproductive years until the very day he was entitled to retire simply because, as he admitted, he was afraid to approach Wallace for any other arrangement. Today, however, since the distribution of stock, high Digest executives who have been there any length of time can go off into the sunset trailing clouds of gold, whether or not Wallace approves. From the Pleasantville point of view, of course, this could be seen as good: there is, at last, regular movement within a long stagnant organization.

share another important attribute: They're all members of the third generation. As such, they have not had the intimate daily association on the job, as well as the poker-playing social relationship, with Wallace that inspired the sort of "loyalty" that made men of an earlier generation reluctant to talk with me. Indeed, the very fact that the present management was so willing to cooperate in the writing of this most unauthorized and unofficial book is strong indication that these men are looking outward into the world and onward into the future; it also indicates the beginning of a healthy and necessary independence. Moreover, they've all had the advantage of observing the problems and mistakes of the second generation. On the whole, it looks to be a good team for a new ball game, but the question remains: Who will call the signals and what will they be? Again, at this writing, I can furnish only material for guessing.

As previously described, Waters is almost the classic financial man. A graduate of Hobart College with a master's degree from Harvard Graduate School of Business Administration, Waters had experience with accounting firms in Massachusetts and New York before coming to the Digest in 1955. He's a director of some eight outside businesses and charitable organizations; at the Digest he is executive vice president and chief financial officer. While Waters' responsibilities have gone far beyond merely counting the money, he's the kind who still involves himself in everything from a million-dollar purchase to the lunch check of an editor who mistakenly took a guest to a restaurant when the Guest House was free. Like most guardians of the vaults, Waters is probably unloved but requited with enormous power in an organization where financial details are its most highly guarded secret.

O'Hara is as Irish looking as his name. A solid block of humming energy, with black hair and brows and an addiction to large cigars, O'Hara's had a finger in every business operation of the company, almost everywhere. Since joining the Digest in Britain in 1961, he has served in various capacities in Stuttgart, Canada, Australia and Latin America. Most recently, in Pleasantville, he has doubled as head of the Books and Recorded Music Division and director of international operations. Though amiable on the surface, O'Hara has a reputation for being ruthless when it comes to seeing that the figures on the bottom line are large ones.

The fact that O'Hara is not a native American would seem to be the natural evolution for an international company. O'Hara denies this. His ascendancy will not mean that the Digest may start drawing on foreign nationals to fill out its executive ranks. His own career, he claims, has been based largely on a rather rare willingness and ability to keep on the move. Finding able executives in foreign countries, where the talent pool is smaller, is too difficult at best without siphoning them off to Pleasantville, according to O'Hara. In any case, many, if not most, of them do better in terms of money and status at home than their counterparts in the United States, he says. Nevertheless, the O'Hara appointment is a sharp departure in view of the rather chauvinistic Americanism that the Digest has shown in the past and may represent an almost unconscious change in attitude of far-reaching consequences.

How far-reaching will depend on whether it is also a sharp departure from the concept of subordinating company policy to the needs and perceptions of magazine editorial. If little things mean a lot, as they sometimes do at the Digest, the fact that the newly appointed president, O'Hara, was not content with office facilities deemed suitable by Hitesman, Lewis and Rhodes but insisted on having an office exactly the size of Thompson's, created for him at considerable displacement of editors along the prestigious front corridor of the main building is ominous. But, perhaps because Wallace's passion for the magazine is so well known, executives like Rhodes, Waters, O'Hara, all pay lip service to it—consider Rhodes's choice of the word "mother." They could also have in mind, as they say, that golden list of subscribers upon which all other aspects of the business feed. Regardless of the reason, some go so far as to unselfishly proclaim that an editor should always be the company's top executive.

This could still well happen. Thompson is so new to the highest executive ranks that his chair is barely warm. A scenario upon which a number of Digesters agree is that, when Rhodes retires, Thompson might well be vaulted over all other heads to become chairman and something like chief executive officer. A look, therefore, at Thompson and his probable policies may be the best look we can now get at the Digest of the future, or at least what the public will see of it.

The most notable thing about Thompson may be the most revealing: as the third editor of the Digest in almost sixty years, he is the first "professional"—which is to say, a man who chose to follow the profession of journalism as such before finding his way to the Digest. This not only distinguishes him from his predecessors but from quite a few of his colleagues whose only experience of life and editing had been in Pleasantville. Even his journalistic background sets him interestingly apart from those on the staff who have climbed the same ladder. He didn't start out to be an editor. After graduating from Massachusetts Institute of Technology with a degree in chemical engineering, Thompson was a petroleum engineer for four years before going on to journalism, perhaps as a result of an inherited bent—his father, Edward K. Thompson, now editor of *The Smithsonian* was a longtime editor of *Life*. First an editor of *Chemical Engineering* and then co-managing editor of *Chemical Week,* Thompson joined *Fortune* as a writer in 1956, broadening his interests to the coverage of subjects ranging from rocketry to the entertainment business. He came to the Digest in 1960.

With such a background, having experienced a variety of editorial situations, Thompson is less likely to take the mystical view of Digest editorial processes that has so long prevailed. When I talked to him, he had already committed a heresy: he was instituting editorial meetings in which even junior members of the staff would be included. One purpose of these will be to come up with at least one article an issue that, according to Thompson, readers will be surprised to find in the Digest. He cited as a possible example of this the debate-in-print in the

October 1976 issue between Ford and Carter. An absolutely even-handed exchange, it was an important departure from the October issue of four years before where the name of Senator McGovern appeared only in damning references within other articles favorable to Nixon policies. The Digest's piece had to be done, incidentally, long before television debates were even mentioned; in fact, Ronald Reagan was interviewed also, in case he won the nomination. That a touch of Digest serendipity has graced Thompson was evident when the candidates' talk about taxes in the Digest made front-page news all over the country since it was by then the hottest issue.

Personally, Thompson in some ways resembles DeWitt Wallace—tall, blond, lean appearing, soft of voice and direct of speech. He doesn't, however, appear to suffer from his mentor's shyness and is, therefore, more approachable. Nor is he formal and indecisive like Lewis. The same man who complained that he could get no decisions from Lewis says of Thompson, "At least, he comes right out and tells you what he thinks, whether you like it or not." It's too early yet, of course, for anybody to know much of what Thompson thinks since his initials aren't yet the very last imprimatur on Digest copy. But, from what I gathered in his talk with me, I doubt that, despite an occasional shocker, readers who already "have faith in Reader's Digest" have much to worry about.

"I think we will continue to have a strong point of view," Thompson told me. "I think we will remain basically conservative, but not right wing—somewhere to the right of center. In holding to our point of view, we will also publish wholely neutral articles on certain subjects." With a journalistic background notably oriented toward business, Thompson didn't share my concern about a business bias in the Digest—nor, internally, business control of the company. He cited a fairly specific example to show that, in his words, "If somebody has to bend, it's the advertisers." A two-part article on poison gases in cigarettes (the Digest has never taken cigarette advertising) was scheduled for last October and November, but for reasons beyond the magazine's control the second part had to be rescheduled for December. Unhappily, Zippo, which buys only two large ads (fire is all right but smoke is bad) a season—in June for Father's Day and in December for Christmas—won't advertise in an issue with an anti-smoking article (you've got to do *something* with fire). When Thompson was asked if the poison gases article *had* to run in December, he said yes, and Zippo had to go.

Perhaps the most interesting Thompson innovation is what some might call a kind of retrogression. He wants to return the Digest more nearly to its original mission of being a "service to readers" by reprinting more articles from other sources. Thompson's aim is to reduce the original content of the magazine from the present 75 to 80 percent to 50 percent or less. This news will come as a blow to free-lance writers, as it already has to a number of roving editors and staff writers over seventy for whom Thompson arranged retirement. This last move could prove a blessing to readers, however, according to one believable anecdote I heard. One of these ancient writers was attending an editorial luncheon when the subject of initiating a series of articles on sex came up. The host, a very high-ranking editor, turned to the writer who was only a few years older than himself and said, "That's a swell idea. You could handle it, couldn't you?" The writer, a man who was evidently proof of the old adage that snow on the roof means that the fire is out in the cellar, smiled benignly and replied, "Oh, yes. Yes, of course. I remember sex."

Lending some credence to my suppositions about the O'Hara appointment, Thompson seems determined to make more use editorially of the Digest's unique international operations. He feels that the United States edition of the magazine has perhaps turned inward too much recently and, as one step toward making it more truly a "window on the world," he is urging United States issue editors to run more of the articles written for the Digest abroad. Thompson is also urging foreign editors to abandon the concept that the Digest, being American owned, is somehow a "guest in the country" and to develop harder-hitting articles on local issues along United States lines.

"I'd rather see our German editor use one tremendous piece on, say, German labor unions than a dozen articles on coo-coo clocks in the Black Forest," he says. To make more of a team out of editors from around the world Thompson is, for the first time in Digest history, holding regular regional and international meetings of editors.

From my point of view, this new spirit of internationalism at the Digest is one of the most encouraging developments in sight. It is, after all, the only publication in the history of the world that has gained such a firm foothold in so many different lands. It can't help but promote mutual understanding to have 100 million readers of so many languages and cultures absorbing the same facts—articles on nature, science, medicine, travel, history and the like are generally used everywhere—responding to the same dramas that confirm our mutual humanity and often laughing at the same jokes. And, although the Digest probably shares this with other international enterprises, there's no telling where the personal influence of thousands of Digesters around the world, their families and their friends, stops. I recall one story that is illustrative of how this works. Some years back, a British editor and a Japanese editor were quartered in the Guest House at Pleasantville together for about a week. The Englishman, who had fought in the Pacific and still hated his enemy, was displeased, not to say apprehensive. It didn't help that the Japanese, a survivor of the horrible firebombing of Tokyo, was neither apologetic about the history of his people nor especially in love with *his* former enemies. Returning from a party one night, the Englishman found the Guest House dark except for a small light burning above one of the Impressionist paintings in the living room where the Japanese sat silently contemplating the beauty of this work of art. A man so sensitive might be worth talking to, the Englishman thought; before the week was out, they were, if not friends, men who realized that they had a great deal in common through their mutual problems and pleasures in serving the Reader's Digest.

No matter how the command in Pleasantville is structured

after he's gone, Wallace has almost assured a continuation of his policies by what might be called the caution of success. Nobody in his right mind fools around with something that works. Not long ago the *New York Times Magazine* adapted an article, "Why nothing works the way it's supposed to," from Dr. John Gall's book, *Systemantics*. After a bitterly humorous look at the mysterious failures in organizations not unlike the Reader's Digest, the author concludes: "Although many of the world's frustrations are rooted in the malfunctions of complex systems, it is important to remember, finally, that *Some complex systems actually function*. This statement is not an axiom. It is an observation of a natural phenomenon. . . . We accept it here as *given*, and offer humble thanks. The correct attitude of thankfulness leads naturally to a final law of Systemantics: *If a system is working, leave it alone.*"

I have no doubt that the people of Pleasantville stumbled upon this truism long before Dr. Gall spelled it out for them. Indeed, the danger, as I see it, is not that the Digest will change but that, without the corrective of the intuitive Wallace genius, it may not change enough. Many things that crept into Digest procedures because Wallace once found them useful have, like the infamous laundry list, gone unchallenged for a variety of reasons, the chief being that whatever Wallace said or did is right. It's hard to argue otherwise, and yet I think that some of the criticism of the Digest over the years is well founded and would hope that younger ears in Pleasantville might hear it.

For example, the charge that the practice of planting original Digest articles in other magazines smacks of deceit seems to me well founded. However good the intention of all parties, the public can be, and probably is, misled; indeed, even tyro Digest editors are led astray. A favorite game on the editorial staff in Pleasantville used to be watching how a new editor would treat a Digest plant when he came across it in a magazine he was covering. Often, before he learned the names of regular Digest contributors and grew suspicious, he would grade a plant "Unusable—can't imagine such a piece appearing in

RD," or words to that effect. Professionals in the field of journalism outside the Digest are also confused. When I was briefly teaching a college journalism course, I found that the recommended textbook offered a Digest plant as the perfect example of how to write for a Sunday supplement—a fairly serious misrepresentation to a student in that no Sunday supplement would be likely to give its writers the time, research facilities and money to produce a piece of the quality in question.

Since the Digest now openly uses original material, it is almost incomprehensible why it would go on indulging in the fiction of being more of a reprint magazine than it is at the high risk of making a mockery of its otherwise extensive, expensive and admirable efforts to pin down every fact. It is improbable that Digest "planting" any longer is a significant factor in the support of other magazines, but if it is, the procedure remains highly questionable. Although, as reported, it seldom happens in fact, the planting system still does give the Digest the option of disguising its own opinion in the form of a supposed reprint from another magazine which may be the spokesman for, say, a profession, a veterans group, a service club. When, and if, this happens both the audience of the magazine first using the piece and the vast Reader's Digest audience are actually being duped.

Another Digest practice along the same lines, common to many magazines but raised to a higher power by Pleasantville, as is everything else, is ghosting. An increasingly sophisticated reading public has certainly by now been conditioned to the fact that people in non-literary forms of endeavor need help in putting their thoughts on paper. It would, therefore, seem unlikely that it could hurt the world's biggest magazine to employ the old "as told to" device or some other method of embodying its ghosts, holy or otherwise. Not doing so is, once again, an obvious form of deception that just doesn't go with the general moral tone of the magazine. If there is an excuse for ghosting without attribution, it would probably have to be that the Digest is only following "accepted practice," an excuse that has appeared too often in our courts lately; if there is a reason for it, it must be that the Digest doesn't really want its readers to know that, like the people of Britain in World War II, they owe "so much to so few," that the wide spectrum of opinion they are supposed to be getting is, in fact, a single beam focussed from Pleasantville.

Indeed, the Digest's handling of opinion in general may well be its most vulnerable spot. Much of the rage aroused by its articles on the World Council of Churches, for example, was clearly justified. All else aside, the technical effort of trying to reduce a subject of such depth and complexity into the Digest's brief, to-the-point format almost guarantees distortion. Few would question the right of DeWitt Wallace, or any of his editors or successors, to have and to print their own view of the World Council of Churches, or anything else—it's axiomatic that a publication without the salt of conviction is without savor. But it can be argued that the Digest does have an obligation to its readers to present such material as its own opinion rather than as a purported objective report. Whether it has also an obligation, as some argued, to allow readers to argue back in the form of published letters, it would certainly be a courtesy that is extended by almost every other purveyor of opinion.

In the presentation of opinion, as in so many other ways, the Digest seems almost a victim of its own experience. From the very beginning, Wallace had a strong point of view which he expressed indirectly through the kind of material he selected from other magazines. There was then, of course, no reason to label opinion as his own since it really wasn't except by selection; moreover, since everything the Digest published had appeared in its entirety elsewhere, the author's full report was presumably on the public record. When original material came along—a great deal more of which was placed elsewhere in the early days—it was simply handled in the same way. And no wonder. By then, the magazine was such a success that Wallace himself must have been amazed and unsure about tinkering with a proven formula. Since none of these practices seemed to make any difference to readers, why worry about them? It's still a good question. But to that must be added another question: Have readers gone along with these various forms of deception because they don't care or because they don't know?

Still another criticism merits serious consideration in terms of the Digest's future—Norman Cousins's statement that the magazine does not pay adequate author's fees. The rebuttal to this in Pleasantville is that the Digest still pays as much, if not more, than the competition. This is true as far as it goes. What the Digest overlooks, inadvertently or deliberately, is that it *has no competition in print.* The only other medium reaching audiences of the size and variety of the Digest's is television. As of now, the Digest is really in a struggle with television for both public attention and the advertising dollar. To me this is fascinating since I've long thought that what Wallace really invented was not a magazine in the conventional sense but a print version of the little home screen long before anybody knew such a thing would be on the market. The art of condensation as practiced in Pleasantville is not so much an editing process as a conversion process; like the people who adapt the printed word to the movie or television screen, Digest editors turn books, articles, jokes and the like that people don't have the interest, education or attention span to absorb into a more easily assimilated product. Nothing at all wrong with this, but if my assumption has any merit, the Digest ought to think seriously about the fact that its competition, television, is willing to pay for "stars"—a million a year for a Barbara Walters, for example, and many salaries in the $100,000 plus range for lesser anchor men and women. In the days when the Digest's competition was print—the other magazines—Wallace simply raked in the stars of that time—the J. P. McEvoys, William Hards, Max Eastmans—by paying them top dollar.

It's in this area where the struggle between the editorial, or creative, side of the enterprise and the "bottom line" boys begins to matter. In my day in Pleasantville, editors and writers were sometimes referred to contemptuously as "Wally's trained

seals" by the business people, and there was known to be
resentment at the generous amounts Wallace would distribute
to people whose contributions were difficult to assess. And the
fact that the business people have learned to manufacture best-
selling books to order or bump circulation almost at will with
bigger and better sweepstakes hasn't made it any easier. The
danger is forgetting that there is, as Cousins said, a "mystique"
to editorial work that can't be put on graphs. The history of
publishing gives ample testimony to the fact that success comes
from the gambles taken by brilliant editors and failure often
follows the pursuit of too cautious business practices.

Like a snowball rolling downhill, the Digest has grown so
fat in fifty years that it would take a long time before it began
melting in the heat of reader disaffection. For example, there is
evidence that the educated young have begun to eschew its
simplistic optimism. One item: the dean of one of America's
most prestigious journalism schools wrote me that neither he
nor, as far as he knew, any of his faculty or students even read
the world's largest magazine, much less study it. But it could
take a dozen years or more before such an attitude is felt in
Pleasantville, both in a decline of talent seeking work and of
readership among their contemporaries. Meanwhile, the kind
of expert management in line to take over the Digest can certainly keep it going with ever shrewder sales techniques and
sound financial policy. It will only be if and when people begin
to realize that the light has gone out of the lumbering giant's
eye that the enterprise will falter.

In a television interview before the opening of his new
version of *King Kong*, movie producer Dino DeLaurentiis went
right to the heart of what I've been trying to say about the
Reader's Digest without Wallace. DeLaurentiis admitted that
he had no business organization as such, that he operated out
of instinct. As an example, he said that he had been talking to
an author who had only written ten pages of a projected book;
he asked to see those ten pages and optioned the work for
$500,000, turning it later into a successful movie. If he'd had
a board of directors, they would have told him he was crazy to

put out $500,000 on the strength of ten pages, DeLaurentiis explained. It's that sort of gamble, inspired by genius and uninhibited by cost-counting committees, that so often pays off at the box office for magazines and books as well as movies. Since the Digest has been both blessed and baffled by this kind of leadership for all these years, can it really survive without it?

There are those who not only think it can't—but won't. Having dutifully reported what I could learn in interviews and surmise by logic about the Digest's probable future, I feel at the end obliged, because of the nature of the source, to relate an entirely different scenario which would prove to be the last and greatest of the Wallace surprises. Without apologies, here it is, stated as starkly as it was to me—when Wallace goes, the Digest goes with him.

Incredible as this may sound, it deserves a hearing by reason of the arguments put forward by my source. To begin with, why haven't the Wallaces at such an advanced age divested themselves of voting stock? Long estranged from the relatives who might logically have been inheritors, they have also shown themselves unwilling to put real power into the hands of two generations of subordinates. If they don't feel that other people can run the organization while they are still around to supervise, wouldn't they be even more skeptical of what could happen to the Digest when they're gone? According to my informant, Wallace has long been distressed over the way the wishes that Henry Luce personally expressed to him before his death have seemingly been frustrated by subsequent developments at Time, Inc.—perhaps including Time's editorial switch on the Vietnam war, leaving the Digest almost alone to wave the flag. In view of this and in view of the Wallaces' extreme devotion to the idea and ideals of the Digest, it almost defies intelligence to think that they would hold absolute control until the bitter end and then let go with an "out of sight, out of mind" attitude. Better by far to have the Digest end with a bang—to let it remain in history like a bright comet that lighted up the sky for a time and then was gone.

Precisely how the Wallace assets would be distributed to

achieve this result was beyond my informant's knowledge, but he was positive, as I would be, that ample provision would be made for present Digesters. Still, it would be a withering shock to them; they would be left like priests who have suddenly discovered that there is no heaven after all. But people in Pleasantville have been shocked before by the lightning bolts emanating from High Winds, and while this might be more blinding than all the rest, the possibility of its being hurled at them has to be considered. It fits with so many aspects of the Wallace character—the love of secrecy, surprises, practical jokes and, above all, the Digest as the pure voice of his own perceptions.

All these traits were dramatically displayed in the most recent glimpse of Wallace in action. Appearing with Mrs. Wallace, slowed a bit at eighty-seven by having to use a walker but still game, at an "old-timers" party for veteran employees, he dropped what Joseph Egelhof called in the *Chicago Tribune* a "Christmas bombshell." Wallace thanked the employees for the good job they'd been doing and then announced raises of 6 percent for everybody making less than $40,000, 3 percent for those making more and an across-the-board raise of 5 percent. While the audience cheered, Wallace's newly appointed high command, taken completely by surprise, got out their pencils and started figuring.

If nothing else, the incident made it clear to all hands that the Wallaces were still running the place their way. "They say they're retired, only we know better," one staffer told Egelhof. "If you're projecting for a year and all of a sudden the payroll is up by 11 percent, you have to admit he's involved," said another. Egelhof went on:

"Their 'retirement' seems to have had more credibility outside the magazine. Last February the *New York Times* made reference to 'the late DeWitt Wallace.' The *Times* later apologized for the slaying, which drew from Wallace the following staff memo:

" 'Here we are in the glorious Out Yonder, looking over your shoulders and applauding the work you are doing, just as we did in our previous incarnation. We are happy, too, to be able to confirm the findings of psychic research proving the reality of communication with those who have passed on to another world. Happy day to you. The late DW and LBW.' "

Naturally nobody in Pleasantville with whom I discussed this scenario gave it the slightest credence. They point to Wallace's own publicly expressed hope that the Digest be here 500 years from now. Nevertheless, I am more intrigued by it now, having written this book, than when I first heard it. I, too, find the Digest almost unthinkable without Wallace. Might he not share this feeling? Yes, he might. Wallace brought the Digest into being alone and in the face of ridicule from most of the reasonable people around him—friends, family, other publishers. He could as well usher it out in the same way since for the longest time he's really owed nothing to anybody except his readers. And this could be his last and most Quixotic service to them—leaving in their hands copies of the inimitable Reader's Digest to pass along as heirlooms from generation to generation.